MSP FOR DUMMIES®

A Wiley Brand

by Alan Ferguson

FOR DUMMIES®
A Wiley Brand

MSP For Dummies®

Published by: **John Wiley & Sons, Ltd.,** The Atrium, Southern Gate, Chichester, www.wiley.com

This edition first published 2014

Registered office

John Wiley & Sons Ltd, The Atrium, Southern Gate, Chichester, West Sussex, PO19 8SQ, United Kingdom

For details of our global editorial offices, for customer services and for information about how to apply for permission to reuse the copyright material in this book please see our website at www.wiley.com.

For general information on our other products and services, please contact our Customer Care Department within the U.S. at 877-762-2974, outside the U.S. at (001) 317-572-3993, or fax 317-572-4002.

For technical support, please visit www.wiley.com/techsupport.

A catalogue record for this book is available from the British Library.

ISBN 978-1-118-74640-0 (pbk), ISBN 978-1-118-74637-0 (ebk), ISBN 978-1-118-74638-7 (ebk)

Printed in Great Britain by TJ International Ltd, Padstow, Cornwall

10 9 8 7 6 5 4 3 2 1

FSC www.fsc.org MIX Paper from responsible sources FSC® C013056

Contents at a Glance

Table of Contents

Part II: Moving Forward with Managing Your Programme 67

Introduction

I wonder what you think of when you see the word 'programme': perhaps a TV show such as *New Tricks*, *The Simpsons* or *The Wire* (or *Rastamouse* if youngsters are in charge of the remote control in your home). Or do you immediately picture a concert programme detailing the evening's entertainment? Perhaps you even interpret the word in a chilling Orwellian way, in the sense of indoctrination requiring de-programming (don't worry, no brainwashing in this book – just masses of useful info!).

However you think of it, as far as this book is concerned a *programme* is a structure within an organization that aims to manage the delivery of benefits from change (I provide a much fuller explanation in Chapter 1). *Programme management* means many different things to different people, but I use the term to mean, quite simply, *managing big change*. By 'big' I mean larger than can be comfortably managed in a single project.

Some people like to arrange significant organizational change into multiple projects, and while I cover managing multiple projects in depth in *MSP For Dummies*, a growing body of experience shows that transformational change needs more than project management. You also need to deal with the outputs from projects in business as usual and to help people come to terms with the change they are undergoing. In other words, you need programme management, and in particular, MSP.

For me, programme management becomes really exciting when it combines managing multiple projects with achieving change in business as usual.

Managing Successful Programmes (MSP) has been describing how to do all this since the turn of the millennium. I've been fortunate enough to be involved in programme management and MSP for all that time. I've had some exciting and fulfilling experiences helping organizations around the world to change themselves fundamentally. Now I want to share the tips and tricks that I picked up over the years, many of which are included in MSP, to help you achieve transformational change in your business.

About This Book

Although *MSP For Dummies* builds on the MSP manual *Managing Successful Programmes*, which is owned by a UK government joint-venture called Axelos and published by TSO, it isn't intended to be a complete replacement for the manual. Instead this book is an abbreviated guide to MSP and, most importantly, a practical commentary. If you want the full detail of MSP, I recommend that you look in the manual.

My aim in *MSP For Dummies* is to bring MSP alive. I try to explain some of the exciting new ideas in MSP in engaging and amusing ways. I also give you lots of examples from my own experience to give you a real feel for programme management.

Many people go on to take exams in MSP, so I make sure that *MSP For Dummies* helps you if you want to sit these exams later. I cover most of the terms and items in the MSP syllabus for at least the first exam – the Foundation. If you come across an MSP term that's new to you, check it out in the index or the Glossary in Appendix B.

But as well as the official MSP line, I also give you my personal views on programme management in general and MSP in particular. I've trained thousands of people in MSP from around the world. I'm aware that MSP programme management contains some incredibly useful, but pretty large, ideas. Therefore, I lay out *MSP For Dummies* in a way that shares these new ideas with you and also shows you how to apply them in a practical way while running your programme.

People often understand these big ideas when I first share them, but they lose track of the message when they start applying them. If that happens to you, don't worry. Follow the book's cross-references to all these exotic new ideas and get them clear in your mind.

Foolish Assumptions

I'm very keen that this book is accessible to as wide an audience as possible, and so I make a few assumptions about you:

- You don't know about projects (but if you do, I promise not to talk down to you).
- You're familiar with what typically happens in business as usual (that is, the way the business normally achieves its objectives), even if you aren't working in the business-as-usual part of an organization.
- You are familiar with some reasonably large organizations, whether public, private or third-sector.
- You don't think a programme is the schedule at the heart of a project. Programme management involves more than working out when you can deliver something.

By the way, this book is aimed primarily at Programme Managers, the people who undertake the day-to-day management of programmes.

Icons Used in This Book

I sprinkle the chapters of this book liberally with icons that highlight some key points.

This icon shows a simple way of making a particular part of programme management more flexible in the real world.

Check out the text besides this icon to see the key points to bear in mind around a subject.

Pay attention when you see this icon, because here I describe a problem or trap to help you avoid difficulties.

Here you can get a precise definition of an MSP term: useful stuff for exams or when you want to agree a definition with colleagues in your programme.

This icon indicates an opportunity to consolidate your understanding by applying new ideas to your programme.

Beside this icon I relate examples of programme management in practice.

Beyond the Book

In addition to the material in the print or e-book you're reading right now, this product also comes with some access-anywhere goodies on the web.

Check out the free Cheat Sheet at `www.dummies.com/cheatsheet/msp` and head to `www.dummies.com/extras/msp` for free online bonus content about managing successful programmes.

Where to Go from Here

The simple answer is that the world is your oyster. Well *MSP For Dummies* is your oyster, anyway. You can go wherever your mood takes you in the book.

I suggest you begin with Part I and see how many of its ideas are familiar to you and how many are new. You then have a chance to reflect on new ideas as you look elsewhere in the book. Part I also describes the beginning of a programme, so it's a great place to look if you're just about to get started in a programme.

If you're logical and practical, you may want to look at the processes (flip to Chapters 3 and 7), as well as the chapters in Part V. If, on the other hand, you prefer to get your mind round the concepts first, look through the Table of Contents to find the chapters covering the theme you're after. If you want to get a feel for programme governance themes, Chapters 5 and 6 are good places to start.

If you're in a tearing hurry, because you're in the middle of a programme and managing it doesn't leave you much time for reading a book, start with Chapter 4, which covers the fundamental ideas behind programme management. If you apply these principles pragmatically to your change initiative, you really are doing programme management.

Good luck and have fun.

Part I
Getting Started with Managing Successful Programmes

For Dummies can help you get started with lots of subjects. Go to `www.dummies.com` to learn more and do more with *For Dummies*.

In this part. . .

- Discover how to tell the difference between a programme and a project.
- See how a programme delivers from projects and into business as usual.
- Decide with senior management if you're going to start a programme.
- Understand the principles behind programme management.

Chapter 1

Introducing Programme Management: Projects, Programmes and MSP

In This Chapter

- Thinking about the differences between projects and programmes
- Discovering the key programme management terms
- Uncovering the structure of MSP

The term *programme* can have lots of different meanings in business and within organizations. Perhaps you think of a programme as a schedule in the heart of a project. Be careful if that's what your colleagues think – they may consider Managing Successful Programmes (MSP) a scheduling tool! Or it can mean a set of projects, which is fine because you can use parts of MSP successfully to look after such a set. Let's call that *multi-project management.*

In this chapter, I explore the nature of programme management. I look at projects and programmes, building on the idea of a project to introduce the concept of a programme. I also share with you a few terms used frequently in programme management, to help you develop that all-important common vocabulary, and I have a quick look at the programme management structure as it's used in MSP.

TIP

If you already have a fair amount of programme experience and are reading *MSP For Dummies* to discover additional details of good practice in managing transformational change programmes, by all means skim rapidly through this chapter.

But more than likely you're newly arrived at the programme management station and want to orientate yourself. Well if any of the following applies to you, you're in the right place:

- Your project is getting a little complicated and someone at work mentions programme management (perhaps at the coffee machine while you're waiting for a so-called espresso that in fact looks more like washing-up water when it's dispensed).
- You're looking after a number of projects and really want to tie them together a little more tightly (as much as you really want a caffeine boost – right now).
- You know that your business has to change and your gut feeling is that putting a few people to one side to deliver a technical solution from a project isn't going to suffice (just like that machine-produced cup of joe won't do).

Understanding Projects and Programmes

Whatever your level of programme management experience, no doubt you already have some ideas on the following:

- What a project is
- What a programme is
- What the difference is between a project and a programme

As you read through this book, I share some new ideas with you, and so I want you to be clear in your own mind about genuinely new ideas or ones you have some previous experience of.

Start by folding a piece of paper in half. Label one half 'project' and the other half 'programme'. Then write down a characteristic of a project and the equivalent characteristic of a programme. Repeat this exercise until you've identified six to twelve sets of characteristics.

Take your time with this important exercise; perhaps leave the list on your bedside table.I bet you wake up in the middle of the night (especially if you read the list before trying to sleep) and think of another pair of characteristics.

Whatever you write on your comparison list is fine; this is your starting point, so there are no wrong answers.

Getting a group on the same programme page

If you're already working on a potential programme with a group of colleagues, run through this exercise with them. Get each person to write down their views on the characteristics of projects and programmes and then combine the lists. You then understand both the group's view of the differences between project and programmes as well as each person's opinion.

Don't send me your lists (please don't!). I've done this exercise with thousands of people all over the world, so I'm getting pretty good at guessing what gets written on these pieces of paper.

Checking on the characteristics of projects

Here's a fairly typical set of project characteristics:

- Projects are finite; they have a defined start and finish.
- Projects deliver a predetermined product, service or output.
- Projects have a clear development path.
- Project benefits accrue at the end of the project or afterwards.
- Projects have a shorter timescale than programmes.

You can have, and I frequently do, a debate about each of these characteristics; they aren't set in tablets of stone. This list serves my purpose for now by giving us a point of comparison for the characteristics of programmes (look at the later section 'Working out programmes' characteristics').

Definition of a project

Your programme contains one or more projects, and so you may as well have a definition of a project to hand.

MSP SPEAK

A *project* is a temporary organization created for delivering one or more business outputs according to a specified business case.

Note that the word 'business' appears twice in the definition: you only do projects because they make business sense.

Project constraints

When discussing project characteristics, people often mention that a project is time-constrained, temporary or has a start and end; perhaps even that a project is fundamentally defined by time. Let me put that another way: whenever someone mentions the scope for a project, do you tend to come up with an inevitable and reasonably fixed timescale?

This is the way many people see projects, but I like to think about them in a different way. I consider project constraints as performance targets.

I suggest that a number of different elements of a project exist that can be constrained and which the project manager may have to manage. I show the project constraints in Figure 1-1, and discuss them below:

- **Time.** The obvious one as just mentioned.
- **Scope.** The need to deliver a certain amount of functionality, for example, adding an online store to a company website.
- **Quality.** The fitness for purpose of deliverables or perhaps even the rigour with which fitness for purpose is demonstrated.
- **Benefits associated with the deliverables.** They may be defined quite rigorously so that you have to achieve a certain amount of saving, for example, or may be quite vague, for example, if you're putting in place a new marketing image.
- **Resources.** To put it narrowly, the costs available to carry out the project.
- **Risk.** You may have to reduce the risk and the project or taking some risks may be acceptable.

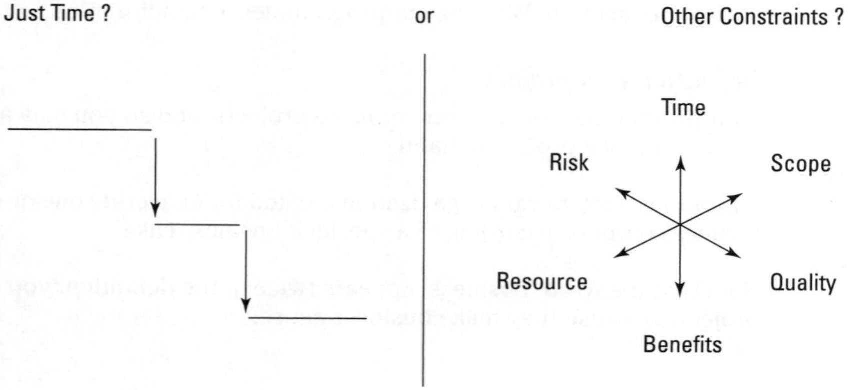

Figure 1-1: Project constraints.

You can put these constraints in some sort of order, because certain constraints are more constraining and others less so, which increases the amount of flexibility when a project is executed. (The question of how a programme constrains projects is discussed in Chapter 10.)

Working out a programme's characteristics

Here's a typical list of the characteristics of a programme:

- A programme is bigger than a project; people use terms like *strategic* when talking about programmes. Bigger change initiatives are more likely to affect the whole organization and its future direction. That's the sort of thing people mean when they talk about something being strategic.
- A programme has a vision of an end state.
- A programme's end state may be some distance in the future and therefore it involves uncertainty: no path is defined to that end state.
- A programme can involve changing culture, working practices, business operations and services as well as delivering outputs.
- A programme needs to co-ordinate the output delivery from a number of projects so that benefits can be realized during the programme and afterwards.
- A programme may give you an opportunity to include infrastructure projects that don't directly deliver benefits.
- A programme's timescale is longer, possibly much longer, than a project's.

Check out Chapter 2 for loads more info on what a programme is.

Definition of a programme

MSP SPEAK

A *programme* is a temporary, flexible organization structure created to co-ordinate, direct and oversee the implementation of a set of related projects and transformational activities. Its aim is to deliver outcomes and benefits related to the organization's strategic objectives.

Now that's a pretty long definition, so I break it down into chunks to understand what it's about:

- **A programme contains a set of projects and so is liable to be large.** Therefore, you're talking about something that relates to strategic objectives.

- **A programme is an implementation of a set of related projects and transformational activities to co-ordinate in business as usual.** Doing one or more projects may not be enough. Projects give businesses the outputs; the ammunition if you like. Business then has to fire the gun; it has to transform or, to put it simply, to change. You do all this to deliver outcomes and benefits (defined in the later section 'Being Clear about the Four Central Terms').
- **Despite being large, the programme is still a temporary organization.** It needs to evolve over time as its goals change and as the organization changes.
- **The programme has to manage.** In other words, it must co-ordinate, direct and oversee the work to deliver the projects and to do that transformation in business as usual.

Nature of a programme

You can start to see that a programme covers a much wider range of issues than a project.

REMEMBER: A programme isn't just a big project.

I discuss this wider range of issues throughout this book, but some of these aspects of programme management may already be occurring to you. If so, tick them off against this checklist:

- Focus on strategy
- Vision and Blueprint within a tranche boundary
- Timescales loosely defined
- Risk management focuses on risk aggregation
- Issue management being orientated towards inter-project and benefits-related issues
- Planning to deliver outcomes through tranches
- Benefits delivery
- Governance through strategies and standards
- Wide stakeholder engagement
- Quality management spreading out to look at processes
- Business Case focused on benefits

TIP: Don't spend too much time yet on the checklist, because it contains lots of terms and subjects that I explain later in the book. As you move on through the chapters, you may like to come back to this list to see whether you're building up a picture of what a transformational change programme can be.

Being Clear about the Four Central Terms

Four terms are crucial to understanding programme management:

- **Output.** An output is simply something that is made or produced. It's also sometimes called a *project deliverable* or just a *product*. This term will be familiar if you've worked in a project environment.
- **Capability.** A capability is a complete set of outputs. If outputs are a project view of what's made in a project, you can think of the capabilities as being the business-as-usual view of a collection of those outputs.
- **Outcome.** A new operational state (some people define it as the *effect of change*). Outcomes are vitally important within programme management. They're the result of change normally affecting real-world behaviour and/or circumstances. They're a manifestation of part or all of a new state conceived in a programme's Blueprint.
- **Benefit.** A measurable improvement resulting from an outcome perceived to be advantageous by some stakeholders and which contributes to organizational objectives.

Following the projects-to-benefits-delivery sequence

The delivery sequence, shown in Figure 1-2, adds gloss and context to the terms:

1. **You deliver outputs from projects.** Output is a term relevant in the world of the project. While it's still relevant in programmes, it isn't the be-all and end-all. After you've got the outputs from the projects, you're about halfway through the heavy lifting.
2. **You produce capabilities, which are one or more outputs from the point of view of your business as usual.**
3. **You exploit capabilities so that they become outcomes.** (Outcomes are significantly different from outputs).
4. **You measure the achievement of outcomes as something quite specific: benefits.**

The last two activities take place within business as usual and not within a project.

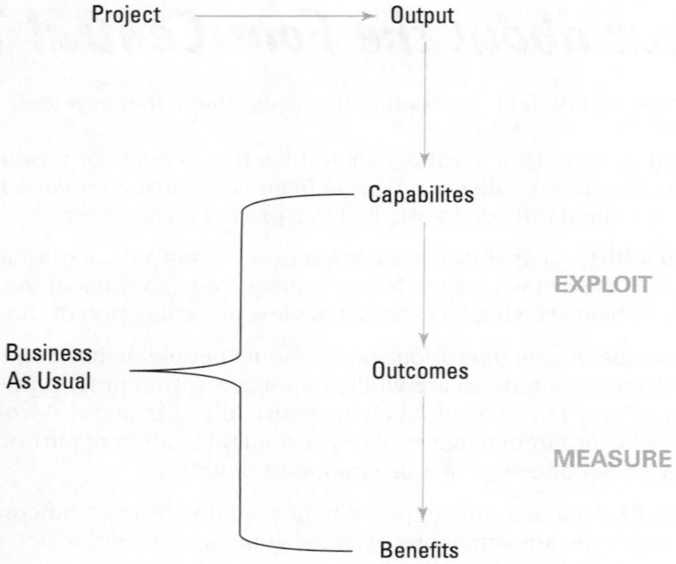

Figure 1-2: Project to benefits delivery.

Programme management is project delivery plus capability exploitation to achieve outcomes and benefits.

Comparing outputs, capabilities, outcomes and benefits

Take a good look at Table 1-1, which is really useful in enabling you to think about the differences between outputs, capabilities, outcomes and benefits.

Study the table and then try completing a similar one for your initiative, identifying the outputs, capabilities, outcomes and benefits for your programme.

Table 1-1 Comparing Outputs, Capabilities, Outcomes and Benefits

	Output	*Capability*	*Outcome*	*Benefit*
Description	The deliverable developed by a project from a planned activity.	The completed set of project outputs required to deliver an outcome; exists prior to transition.	A new operational state achieved after transition of the capability into live operations.	The measurable improvement resulting from an outcome perceived as an advantage by one or more stakeholders and which contributes towards one or more organizational objectives.
Rationale	Answers at least in part the fundamental question 'What do we need to create to enable the change?'	Answers the question 'What do we need to have in place to enable the new operating state?'	Answers the question 'What is the desired operational state of the organization using these new things?'	Answers the question 'Why is this justified?' (that is, it explains what a programme delivers).
Example	An individual component of an e-commerce system, application, hardware, new business processes training and so on.	An e-commerce system tested and ready to go into operation and with trained staff.	Transformed client service organization, faster processing, fulfilling and charging for web-based orders.	Increase in percentage sales revenues.

Based on AXELOS MSP® material. Material is reproduced under licence from AXELOS

Seeing the Structure of MSP

In this book I don't just talk about programme management in general; I look particularly at programme management as it's described in Managing Successful Programmes (MSP).

REMEMBER

The MSP framework – the method if you prefer – consists of three concepts or elements:

- **Principles.** The common, universal and high-level factors that underpin success. They guide the organization on what to aim for.
- **Governance themes.** Help an organization put in place the right aspects of programme management. They include aspects such as organization and planning and control.
- **Transformational flow.** Provides a route through the life-cycle of a programme, from conception to delivery and closure.

Discerning the factors for success: Principles

MSP covers some pretty big ideas, which are universal, self-validating and empowering. These *principles* emerged as people like you learnt from their experience of managing programmes.

I look in depth at the MSP principles in Chapter 4.

Creating the right aspects: Governance themes

Governance is the control framework through which programmes deliver change objectives and demonstrate to the corporate level of the organization that they're under control. You have to negotiate and manage resources and deliver outcomes and benefits in a changing environment. You do so by using the governance themes:

- **Business Case.** The vital test of the viability of the programme.
- **Benefits management.** Benefits of a measurable improvement resulting from an outcome at the heart of the programme.

- **Blueprint, design and delivery.** The Blueprint is a description of the future state and expansion of the Vision.

  Be careful that the Blueprint isn't a plan for reaching that future state.
- **Leadership and stakeholder engagement.** Stakeholders can affect or be affected by a programme. They even include people who simply *perceive* that the programme affects them. Engaging with stakeholders links to achieving the Vision, leading through transition, achieving benefits and using resources (see Chapter 14 for more on stakeholders and Chapter 17 for leading people through change).
- **Planning and control.** Key to the success of any programme, at the beginning and as it progresses (I discuss planning and control more in Chapter 10).
- **Programme organization.** Involves defined roles, clear accountabilities and responsibilities, management structures and reporting arrangements.
- **Quality and assurance management.** Ensures that the programme is working appropriately and stays on target to achieve its objectives.
- **Risk and issue management.** Uncertain events *(risks)* and unplanned events that have happened *(issues)* can affect the direction of the programme and you need to manage and resolve them.
- **Vision.** A picture of a better future; it's the basis of the outcomes and benefits of the programme.

Tracing a route through the programme life-cycle: Transformational flow

As illustrated in Figure 1-3, you can represent a programme as a set of processes:

- **Realizing the Benefits.** Where transformation or transition takes place.
- **Delivering the Capability.** From where projects are delivered.
- **Identifying a Programme.** Where the business decides to take a programme approach to an initiative.
- **Defining a Programme.** Where you set up the governance for the programme.
- **Closing a Programme.** Where you wind down that governance.
- **Managing the Tranches.** Where you look after each chunk of a programme. A tranche delivers a step change in capability.

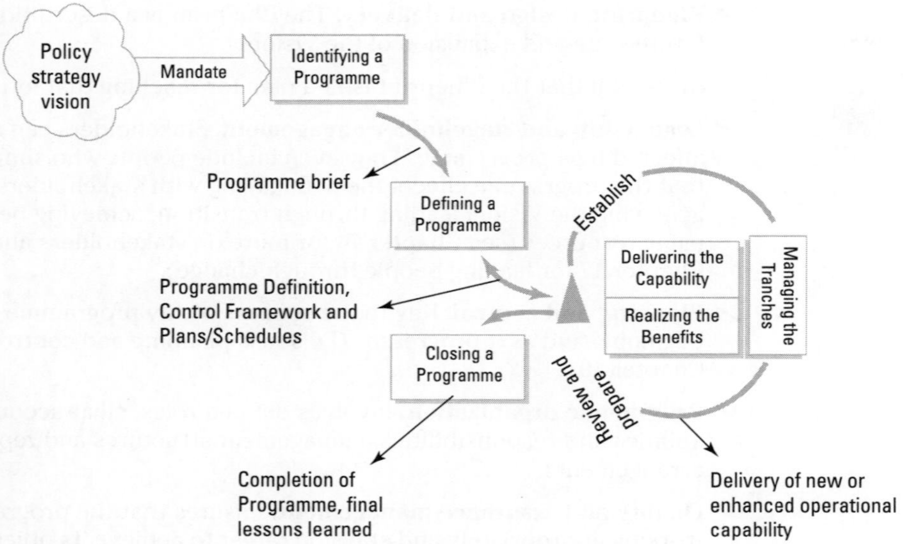

Figure 1-3: Transformational flow.

Chapter 2

Understanding What's Involved in a Programme

In This Chapter

- Recognizing the reasons for programme management
- Managing benefits within the programme
- Thinking about documenting your programme
- Describing the programme's end state
- Choosing the sort of programme that's right for you

Most likely you haven't come across programmes before (as I define them in Chapter 1). Or perhaps transformational change in your organization has been run using a series of projects, with the change in business as usual taking place in a less controlled way. Understanding the differences between programmes and projects is crucial to successfully understanding programmes, so if you are uncertain about these differences, I suggest taking a look at Chapter 1 before reading this chapter.

In the sections that follow I give you a simple picture of what a programme is like and introduce you to some of these new ideas. I provide a helpful model for picturing a programme and discuss the benefits, documentation and various types of programme available.

Using the Ferguson Factory Model: What a Programme Looks Like

I want to share with you a model that I draw up for my clients when they ask me: 'what's different in a programme?' or 'what do we have to do within the programme?'

Shifting your paradigms

Taking on a new idea is called a *paradigm shift.* Here's a simple example of a paradigm shift as an illustration.

Five hundred years ago you'd have probably believed that the Earth was flat. Looking around, you had no reason to think otherwise. Then some clever astronomer or explorer came along and explained that the world was round. After you understand that the world is round, you can never look at the Earth in the same way: that's a paradigm shift. You now have a new model in your head.

But the other important thing about a paradigm shift is that if you're now a round-Earth person, you can still understand how some people believe in a flat Earth; you've just moved your ideas to a higher level. But a flat-Earth person simply can't understand that the Earth is round.

So stand by in this chapter for some paradigm shifts!

Oh, by the way, as you read through this book you may find yourself losing some of the new ideas you're exploring. You slip back from believing in a round Earth to believing only in a flat Earth. Don't worry when this happens. This behaviour is perfectly normal as you get comfortable with any new paradigm. After a few months of working with these new ideas, they become natural to you. But when you revert to a flat-Earth frame of mind, this sidebar and section is a good place to come back to.

I've evolved this Ferguson factory model over 15 years to help people understand the nature of programmes. But a word of warning! This isn't a simple little diagram. It almost certainly contains a whole heap of new ideas for you. Even if you've considered some of these ideas previously, you're likely to be unfamiliar with them all.

Entering the Ferguson factory

Figure 2-1 illustrates the Ferguson factory model. Come on in! I explain what each of the symbols means in the next section.

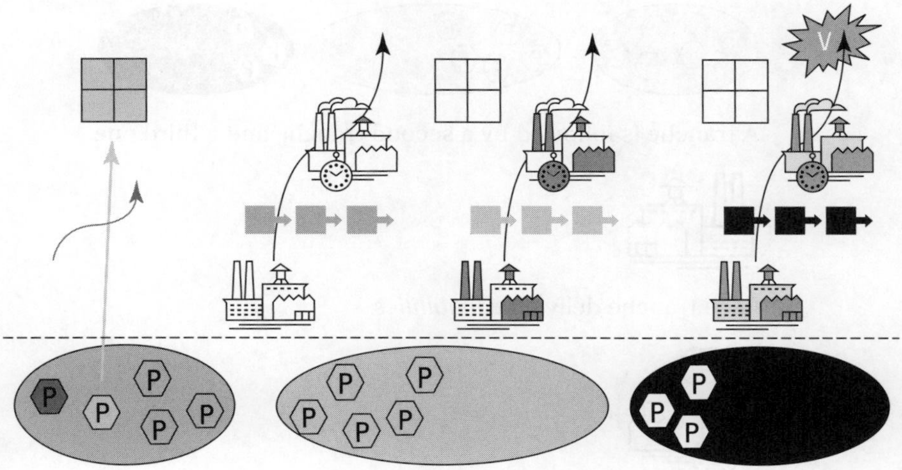

Figure 2-1: The Ferguson Factory.

Exploiting capability

A programme starts with the *Vision* – a high-level picture of the future.

The Vision is complemented by a *Blueprint*, which contains more detail.

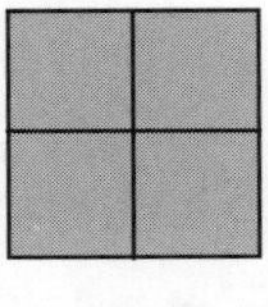

This detail means that the Blueprint has to be created over time, so you're going to have incremental versions of it.

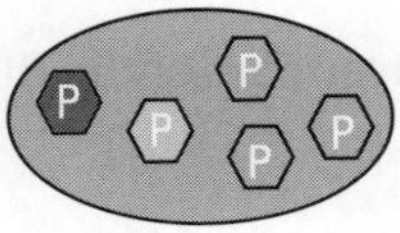

TIP

The dotted lines in Figure 2-1 mark the boundary between *project* world below the line (that is, the environment in which you're undertaking one or many projects) and *business as usual* above it (that is, the existing, everyday business environment).In project world you have a series of projects, which come together in something known as a *tranche*.

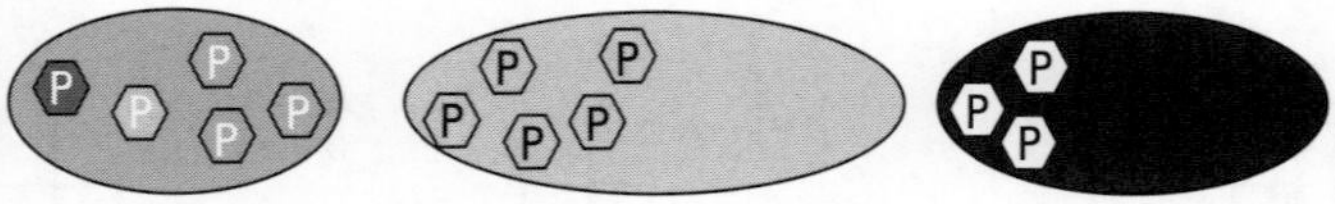

A tranche is followed by a second tranche and a third one.

Each tranche delivers *capabilities.*

Capabilities are exploited in business as usual to become *outcomes.*

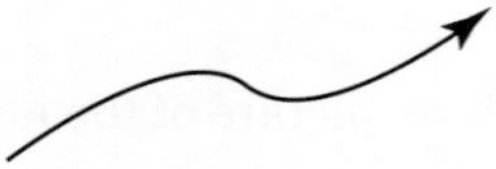

The achievement of outcomes is measured as a *benefit.*

In order to achieve those outcomes, you're going to need to carry out *transition* (the planned activities that you can undertake to help people change from an old to a new way of working) within business as usual.

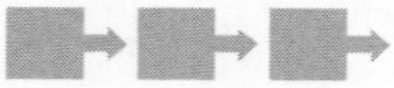

You then have another capability: more outcomes, more benefits management and more transition. All these elements are happening in business as usual.

Just a couple more elements. The Blueprint evolves over time and therefore you have early and intermediate Blueprints, the latter describing intermediate states as different outcomes are achieved.

Some projects don't deliver capability – they deliver part of the Blueprint: if you like, it's a design project.

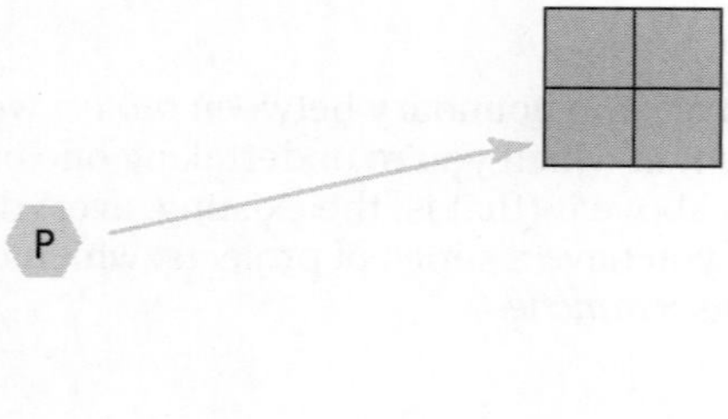

Only one more element to go.

Another little project or activity in business as usual delivers some early benefits perhaps even before you deliver capabilities.

This diagram may take a few hours to come to terms with, but if you understand even a little of what I'm discussing here, you're well on your way to grasping programme management.

Appreciating the Benefits

The trigger for any change initiative is that you want to create benefits – some value.

I use the term *change initiative* at the moment, because in the very early stages you may not know whether it's going to be managed as a project or a programme (flip to Chapter 1 for the distinctions between projects and programmes).

Understanding the central role of benefits

Benefits are a result of change; they don't occur in the case of the status quo, where nothing changes for years and everyone repeats the same process again and again, like the aptly named rock band. (In Chapter 15, I look at how you can make sure that your benefits are measuring change and not the status quo.) Therefore, benefits are the fundamental reason for a programme's existence.

Of course, benefits can be the trigger for any initiative, but the real test is whether the organization wants to manage benefits in a structured way, co-ordinated with structured management of the capability-delivering projects.

Take a second to read that short but rather involved paragraph again, because it contains some pretty important ideas. If the organization wants to manage benefits and projects within the same environment, you probably want to take a benefits- or outcome-driven approach to planning. In fact, you can say that the main focus needs to be on achieving change and that *only* a benefits- or outcome-related view can help you understand and manage change.

Now, of course, some organizations stick resolutely to a project view of the world. They think that a project's role is to build something and that exploitation of that something is someone else's responsibility. If that's the case, you aren't going to be able to deploy all of programme management. Sometimes an organization's culture is just too strong and rejects the idea that you can manage project delivery and achieve change in business as usual as part of the same initiative.

But I want to assume that the culture is going to accept co-ordination of the two sides of transformational change – projects delivering outputs on the one hand and those outputs being exploited in a managed way to result in benefits realization on the other – and have a look at what that means.

The key points are that:

- Change results in outcomes, because outcomes are defined as being a result of change.
- Benefits are how you count those outcomes.

For now all you need to do is to grasp these two ideas.

Programmes are about:

- Co-ordinating delivery from a set of projects.
- Integrating the outputs into a capability.
- Delivering the realization of a set of benefits.

Achieving benefits

You need to manage the achievement of the benefits, as opposed to simply waiting for them to happen.

To manage benefits, identify them fairly early in the programme, before change starts to happen. Then you may have to take a baseline measure of the benefits, using any new measurement methods you need to introduce. Consequently, as you go through the programme, you can measure the benefits in a consistent way, as follows:

- Change produces outcomes
- Measurable improvements are called benefits
- Programme needs active benefits management, which involves:
  - Identification of benefits
  - Baselining of benefits
  - Measurement of benefits

Avoiding the mistakes of others: Why change initiatives go wrong

HAVE A GO Try This

Ask yourself why some organizations fail to deliver change and so fail to achieve the desired benefits. After you've listed your own reasons, take a look at the following list of why organizations fail to deliver change:

- Culture not being changed
- Insufficient board-level support
- Insufficient focus on benefits
- No widely understood picture of future capability – no Blueprint
- Poor Vision
- Stakeholders aren't engaged
- Unrealistic expectations of organizational capacity and capability
- Weak leadership

TIP

Turn this list round: instead of seeing these problems as obstacles, view them as opportunities to fix problems and so achieve benefits. Programme management encourages you to focus on precisely these sorts of thing.

Documenting Your Programme

I can hear you stifle a yawn from here. Yes, I know that documentation sounds dull, but please don't skip hurriedly passed this section. Documentation isn't about bureaucracy: it's about sharing an explicit understanding of your programme with possibly a very wide readership.

TIP

Document only the things that you really need to record – information that you want to share with others. And don't record things twice. Record information once and, where necessary, link to that single source of information.

I'm not going to get hung up on the format of documentation (I talk much more about documenting your programme in Chapter 7). Very few people keep paper records these days, though it may be appropriate in certain circumstances. More likely, you carry out some form of information management from within a document or information management system. Just use an appropriate format given the size of your programme. (I cover information management in more detail in Chapter 13.)

I do, however, want to mention two useful documents to give you a feel for the type of documentation you create in a programme.

Planning for the upside: The Benefits Realization Plan

In a Benefits Realization Plan you record your plan for realizing benefits. Who said programme management was hard!

Figure 2-2 is a simple diagram representing a Benefits Realization Plan. A real plan is clearly more complex, but I hope that the figure illustrates how the benefits need to come together into a single co-ordinated plan that includes dates.

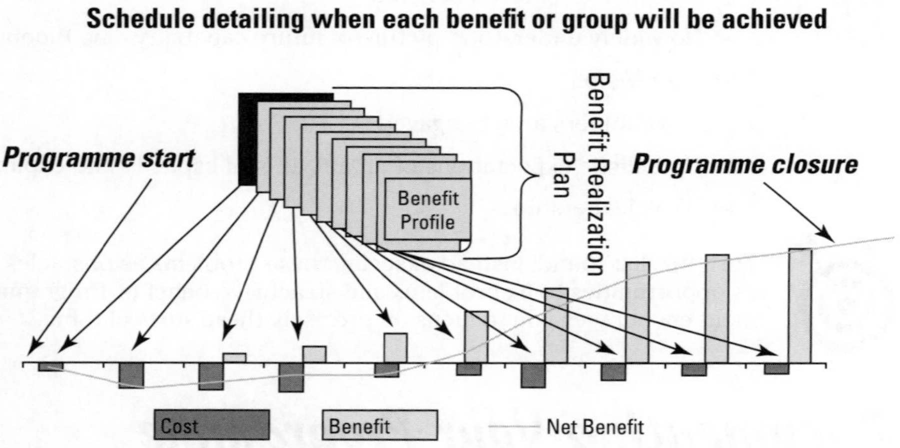

Figure 2-2: A Benefits Realization Plan.

You describe each significant benefit in a Benefit Profile. (I cover the detail that goes into a Benefit Profile in Chapter 15.) You take all the Benefit Profiles, integrate them, remove the anomalies and double counting, and plot the benefits on one or more schedules in the plan. So, for example, if one benefit profile said you need 4,000 staff and another benefit profile said you need 5,000, you have an anomaly. Or if two different benefits link to a five per cent increase in turnover, is that a total ten per cent increase or are they both claiming the same five per cent? As you assemble your Benefits Realization Plan you resolve these sorts of anomalies.

Figure 2-2 shows costs. Strictly speaking, that's moving towards an investment appraisal in a Business Case, so people debate whether costs should be shown on the Benefits Realization Plan. On the other hand, the Benefits Realization Plan may need to show net benefits and hence, by implication, costs. This argument is really a technical point. You may find that you simply have to conform to the accounting rules of your organization.

MSP SPEAK

Some experts say that the items marked below the line in Figure 2-2 are in fact *dis-benefits.* What's a dis-benefit? Well, usually benefits are how you measure an outcome that's perceived to be an advantage by a stakeholder. But other stakeholders may perceive some outcomes to be a disadvantage. For example, the Finance Director may be highly pleased with a benefit called *reduced staff costs,* whereas the staff would regard the resulting reduced pay as a dis-benefit.

Do you really want dis-benefits appearing so early in a programme? It depends on the programme. One thing's certain: if benefits and costs are being shown on a single graph (as in Figure 2-2), the vertical axis must be financial. Therefore, all these benefits are financial benefits.

Organizations often debate whether softer, intangible, indirect benefits can indeed be expressed financially, but the answer's usually decided by the culture of the organization in question. I can't give you hard and fast rules (sorry!).

TIP

You may want to note in your Benefits Realization Plan when programme closure happens. Benefits and dis-benefits continue to flow after the end of the programme.

Anticipating advantages: Benefits Management Strategy

The Benefits Management Strategy is one of the set of strategies you create during the Defining a Programme process (check out Chapter 7 for more on Defining a Programme). It documents your approach to realizing benefits and is the framework within which benefits are to be realized.

REMEMBER

In broad terms, you may want to cover the following:

- Do you want benefits as early as possible, no matter what sort of disruption that causes?
- Or do you want to minimise organizational disturbance, even though that delays the realization of benefits?
- Does an overriding necessity exist to maintain services while you're putting in place the new world?
- What's the situation regarding existing projects? If you're running an emergent programme, you may have to cover this aspect in the Benefits Management Strategy.
- What sort of approach are you going to take to early benefits possibly being delivered even before you have delivered any capabilities (which I describe in the earlier section 'Exploiting capability')? Check out Chapter 15 for discussions around this idea.

Reaching towards the Destination: Vision and Blueprint

Figure 2-3 describes the programme environment rather neatly. Take a look first at the external environment (at the top) where political, economic, sociological, technological, legal or environmental drivers are causing your organization to function in a particular way. Working down the figure, these external drivers cause your organization to adopt certain strategies and policies and, more importantly, to change the strategic direction of the organization. That strategic change gives rise to one or more programmes.

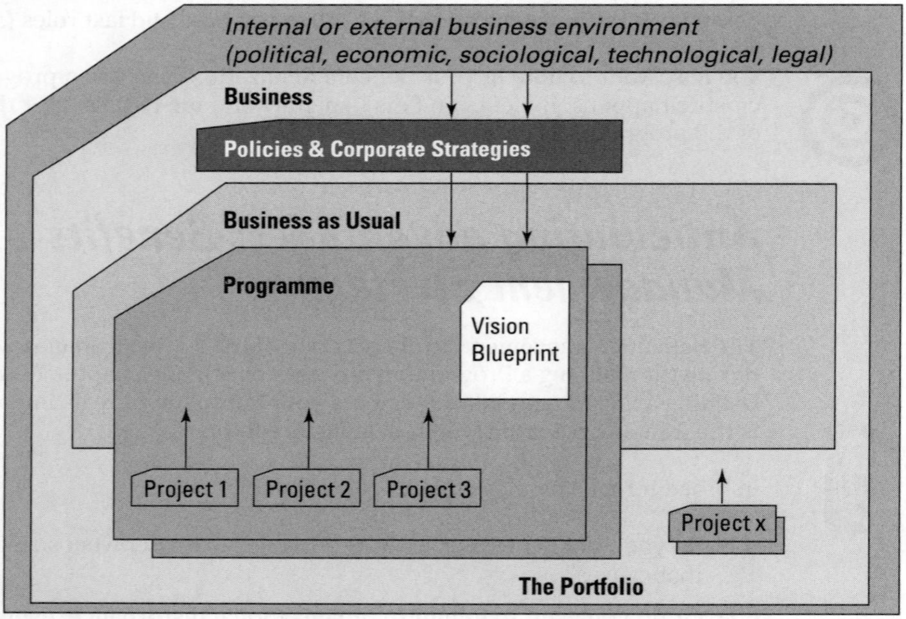

Figure 2-3: Programme management environment.

MSP SPEAK

The programmes, along with any standalone projects, are called the *portfolio.* A single programme has certain characteristics. It contains projects and has an effect on business operations. In addition, because the programme is long, you need to have a high-level Vision of the desired end state. That Vision may be supported by a more detailed description of the end state: a Blueprint.

I discuss the Vision in Chapter 5 and look in detail at the Blueprint in Chapter 6. You start to create the Vision right at the beginning of the programme when the most senior people in your organization decide to use programme management for a change initiative (check out Chapter 3 for more). You put the detail on the Blueprint when you're fleshing out the programme, which I cover in Chapter 7.

I give you a few more details on the Vision and Blueprint in the later sections 'Viewing the Vision Statement' and 'Considering the purpose of the Blueprint', but in the next section I want to examine briefly the context for a programme.

Aligning with organizational elements

Sometimes people talk about how a programme aligns with various organizational elements, which unfortunately is a pretty dry and abstract way of thinking about how the programme fits in with some of the critical aspects of the culture within the business.

REMEMBER

Programme management aligns with three critical organizational elements: corporate strategy; the mechanism used to deliver change; and the environment in business as usual.

Corporate strategy

All organizations have an approach they want to take to moving the business forward in the future; simply put, this may be growth or expansion. Most organizations also have a more detailed set of corporate strategies. Each programme needs to align with corporate strategy: after all, programmes are about strategic change.

Delivery mechanisms for change

Each organization achieves change in different ways. The most familiar way of doing so is project management, even though many argue that project management is not, in itself, a particularly good tool for achieving change.

A whole range of less structured mechanisms exist for achieving change. Well-known methods include quality circles, lean and kaizen (continuous improvement).

TIP

As a programme manager you want to be aware of the mechanisms that are used in business as usual to achieve change, and then choose to fit in with those approaches or deliberately select a different approach. Whatever you do, you don't want to be ignorant of the way that change happens in business as usual.

Business as usual environment

Business as usual is focused on exactly that – keeping day-to-day business going. Therefore, it looks at the efficiency and effectiveness of existing processes. The aim is to do the same thing again and again but increasingly well.

REMEMBER

The programme needs to fit in with this environment while aiming for transformational change.

Role of programme management

Programme management balances the tension between running the business and changing the business, as well as managing the transition of outputs delivered by projects into the organization. It does so by breaking effort into manageable chunks *(tranches).*

Programme management also provides a framework for reconciling competing demands for resources.

Viewing the Vision Statement

The Vision and the Vision Statement are similar things: the Vision Statement is the document in which the Vision is recorded.

Purpose

REMEMBER

The purpose of the Vision Statement is to communicate the end goal to all stakeholders. So it needs to be written in *customer-facing terms* – by which I mean it needs to be understandable to ordinary people. (If you want an example of something that isn't written in customer-facing terms, just look at the terms and conditions of a piece of software – they're usually incomprehensible!) Think of it as an artist's impression of the future state.

Here's an example of the challenge of writing a Vision in the right way. Imagine that you need to compose a Vision about reducing the number of staff in the company in a way that's acceptable to the firm's staff. The answer may be to include something in the Vision about having to achieve levels of productivity that match the best in the industry. If productivity in the organization is currently lower than the benchmark and no hope exists of increasing market share in a flat market, staff numbers have to reduce as productivity is improved.

Composition

The composition of the Vision is pretty straightforward, partly because it has to be very brief: it's a clear statement of the end goal of the programme – something short and memorable.

Perhaps you need to include any imposed constraints on the programme – the situation in which the programme is being undertaken. You can expand on this external view by setting the context for the programme and project teams. Maybe you also require relevant information to help set expectations. You're trying to put the context of the programme into the broader business context.

TIP

Consider including information to support the justification for change, for example, a clear description of the unsustainable current reality.

Considering the purpose of the Blueprint

Formally the purpose of the Blueprint is to maintain focus on delivering transformation and business change. It elaborates on the Vision of the programme and may also be known as the target-operating model. Figure 2-4 illustrates the Blueprint.

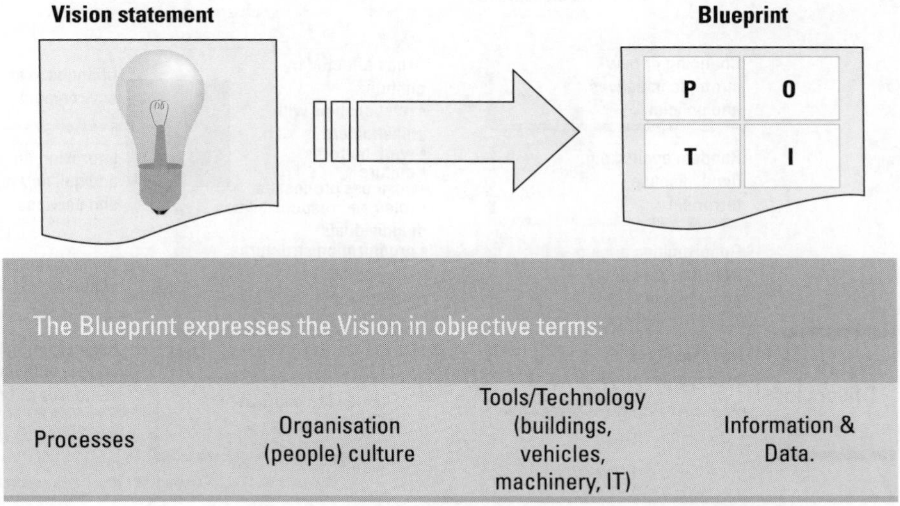
Vision statement
Blueprint
P
O
T
I
The Blueprint expresses the Vision in objective terms:
Processes
Organisation (people) culture
Tools/Technology (buildings, vehicles, machinery, IT)
Information & Data.

Figure 2-4: The Blueprint.

Here's the dilemma. If the Vision is going to engage stakeholders, it needs to be short and memorable. As a result, it also has the added advantage of being more likely to remain stable. The disadvantage of a short Vision is that it lacks detail.

Therefore, you create and hold the detail in the Blueprint. At the beginning of the programme, you have very little detail in the Blueprint: it's just a simple amplification of the Vision. But over time, as additional work is done to understand the future state, more and more detail goes into the Blueprint. By the end of the programme, the Blueprint is a comprehensive description of the future state.

Moving towards drivers for change

Drivers for change isn't a motorist action group, but is about identifying the external factors that are pushing your organization to do things differently. A change initiative rarely affects only a single part of a business – more likely you experience a string of knock-on effects. In Figure 2-5, I list the typical areas affected by a strategic transformational (in other words, big) change.

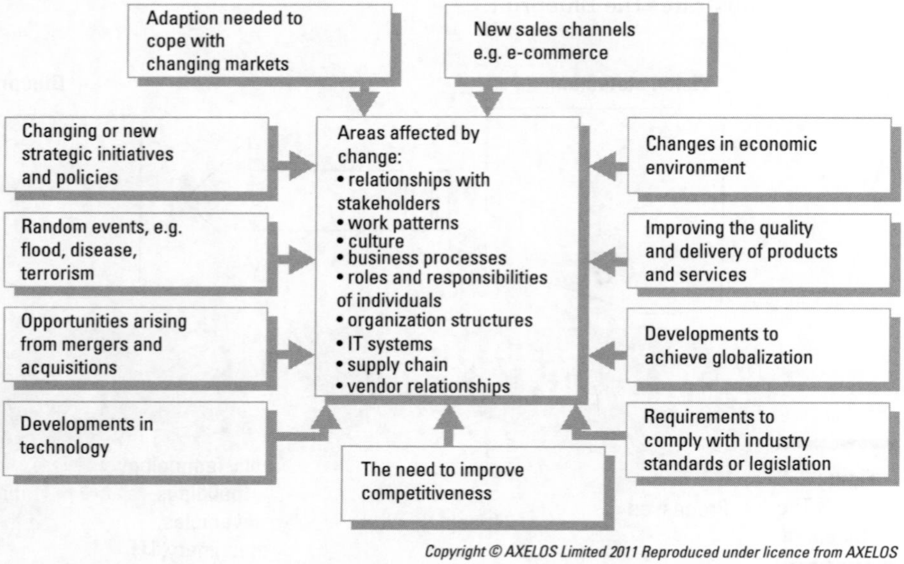

Figure 2-5: Drivers for change.

Identifying the drivers for change in your own organization is extremely useful and makes future changes less unexpected. Figure 2-5 contains a generic list of drivers for change, which you can use when you can't brainstorm your particular drivers.

Deciding on the Type of Programme

One of the difficult things to get your mind around is the sheer diversity of available programmes. Some are like projects (in that they mostly deliver outputs, but are so big that you break that output delivery into a number of projects and you need something sitting above the projects, which you call a programme). Others focus on changing society, with almost no project-like delivery of outputs. Some programmes are clearly defined at the beginning, whereas others only become clear partway through as the situation becomes better understood and pilot studies show what does and doesn't work.

Using the Programme Impact Matrix

When looking at the diversity of programmes, you may sometimes hear people talking about programme impact. Figure 2-6 show the range of impacts a programme can have.

Programme Impact Matrix

Predictability of outcome (columns) / Focus of the change (rows)

	High	Medium	Low
Specification-led	Major engineering programmes, e.g. Olympic park Complex products based on known design Large-scale technology replacements	Globalization of technology services Adoption of technology that is new to the organization, e.g. ERP Multi-organization delivery	Pioneering engineering techniques Unproven technology implementation Specification-led organizational change
Business transformation	Implementation of approaches used in similar organizations e.g. ISO adoption Process change affecting technology and structures	New products or services to existing market place Changing historical working practices, values and structures Supply chain change, e.g. outsourcing of services	Diversification of new products into new markets Internal external and customer behaviour Radical restructuring of supply chains
Political and societal change	Change to current legislation or policies Increases or decreases to investment programmes Predictable or clear stakeholder base	New legislation reacting to societal trends Legislative change to affect socio-economic behaviour Changes to public service delivery models, e.g. health provision	Changes to societal values and behaviour, e.g. criminality Incentive-driven change to lifestyles and economic behaviour Long-term societal effects, e.g. health

Figure 2-6: Programme Impact Matrix.

Impact is related to the focus of the change and the predictability of outcome:

- **Focus of change:** This focus may be narrow, such as implementation of a technological solution, through to wide, such as affecting part of society.
- **Predictability of outcome:** This may vary between low, where a proven approach is being taken, to high, where complex, innovative or unpredictable outcomes are sought:
  - **Specification led:** Where the change is based on making and delivering something, you have low levels of ambiguity about what's being delivered. Nevertheless, complexity and risk still exist in the delivery.

    You may then want to use a scaled-down version of programme management in this situation.
  - **Business transformation:** Where the change is focused on changing business functions, the programme is Vision-led. Some ambiguity exists around the impact of the changes – the greater the impact on customers, the greater the ambiguity and risk.

    MSP is designed for this type of programme.
  - **Political and societal changes:** Where the change is focused on improvements in society, predictability is reduced because of uncontrollable external factors. The scope may need to be adjusted as ambiguities are resolved.

    Programme management is extremely suitable for such high levels of complexity, ambiguity and risk.

Exploring programme types

Some programmes come about because you know what you want – you have a Vision. But other types of programmes exist; for example, a number of projects are bumping into each other, or several organizations have to work together. I explore these different types of programmes along with a few others here.

Vision-led programme

A *Vision-led programme* comes into existence when you have a clear Vision. Consequently, the programme is likely to be defined from the top of the organization and include the work of a number of different functional specializations; for example IT, HR and facilities management. In the private sector, it's linked to innovation, for example, new products and services. In the public sector, a Vision-led programme is probably triggered by political priorities necessitating the delivery of change to a population.

Emergent programme

MSP SPEAK

An *emergent programme* comes into being whenever you recognise that a group of existing projects would be better managed together. In other words, an emergent programme evolves from concurrent projects. For example, you may recognise that in order to achieve change and deliver benefits a co-ordinated programme approach is more useful. By its nature, an emergent programme is transitory. Initially it pulls together a group of projects, but when stable it becomes just another programme.

Compliance programme

MSP SPEAK

A *compliance programme* is often known as a must-do programme. It arises because the organization has no choice but to change as a result of an external factor such as new legislation. The benefits associated with a compliance programme are factors such as compliance with legislation or even the avoidance of an undesirable consequence, such as a fine.

Multi-organization partnerships

A *multi-organization partnership* isn't a separate category of programme, but programme management is often used when a number of organizations need to co-ordinate. These organizations share a Vision for the outcome of the programme, but each participating organization has its own business objectives to achieve. These objectives are complementary to the overall Vision, but may not encompass all that Vision.

Checking out the characteristics of a programme

This section describes briefly some of the key characteristics of a programme.

Consider having a look at the change initiatives that are going on around you and check how many of these characteristics each one has. I bet that many of the change initiatives that are called *projects* now feel much more like *programmes*.

A programme has the following characteristics (I expand on each of these items throughout this book):

- Focus on strategy
- Vision and Blueprint within a boundary
- Governance through strategies and standards
- Business case focused on benefits
- Timescales loosely defined
- Risk management focused on risk aggregation
- Issue management focused on inter-project issues and benefits
- Planning to deliver outcomes through tranches
- Quality focused on processes
- Stakeholder engagement is wide
- Benefits delivery

Linking programmes, projects and business as usual

Figure 2-7 shows another view of a programme, to help you understand how the elements in your programme fit together. Changes at the corporate level trigger a programme. Within the programme you have a variety of projects going on. Those projects deliver products, outputs or deliverables.

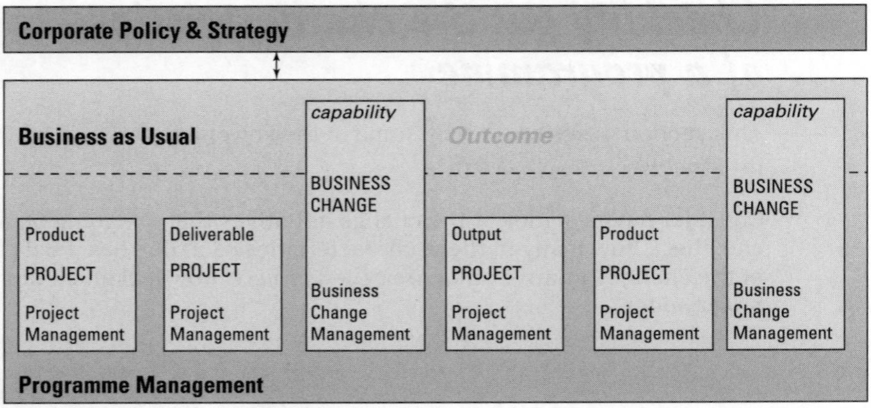

Figure 2-7: Programmes, projects and business as usual.

But you know (from the earlier section 'Exploiting capability') that you want to achieve outcomes, and outcomes appear not in project world but in the real-world operational environment. In more detail, you need to achieve outcomes, but those outcomes come into place when you exploit capabilities. That exploitation of capabilities happens in business as usual. But the exploitation of capabilities also happens within the programme.

Business Change Managers carry out the business change and exploit the capability in order to achieve the outcome. Therefore, the Business Change Managers need to work in project world *and* in business as usual, and consequently the programme management happens in project world and in business as usual.

Now try it for yourself:

1. **Describe the context of your programme.** You can do a PESTLE (political, economic, social and technological, legislative and environmental) analysis or a SWOT (strengths, weaknesses, opportunities and threats) analysis if you're familiar with these.
2. **Identify the drivers for change for your programme.**
3. **Identify the areas of the business that are going to be affected.**
4. **Decide what type of programme it's likely to be and its impact.**

Chapter 3

Identifying a Programme

In This Chapter

- Deciding when to use programme management
- Working out whether a change initiative is a programme
- Getting the right people involved in decisions
- Understanding the roles, responsibilities and requirements of the Sponsoring Group

Identifying a Programme is the first step in the MSP transformational flow, to which I introduce you in Chapter 1. The transformational flow (in effect, the programme's life-cycle) is part of the top-level structure of MSP, and although it's a process model, the authors helpfully use the word *flow* in order to emphasise that the processes aren't discrete, rigid or formal. Figure 3-1 shows where Identifying a Programme falls within the transformational flow.

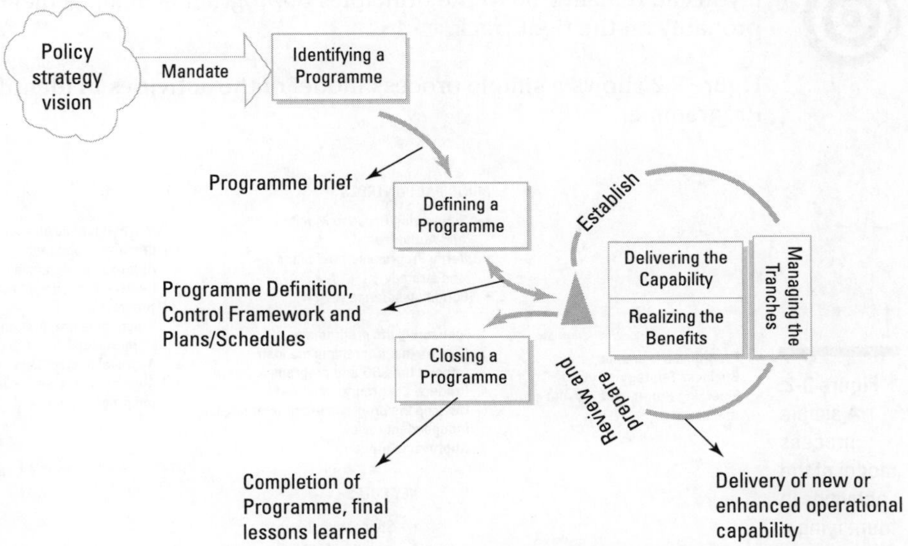

Figure 3-1: Identifying a Programme in the transformational flow.

In this chapter I describe the steps that the Sponsoring Group – that is, the most senior decision-makers in an organization – takes when it decides to treat the *change initiative* as a programme. A change initiative is simply a convenient term you can use if you haven't decided if something is a project or a programme. Or you can refer to your change initiatives when you want to cover all your programmes and stand-alone projects. I lead you through answering the vital questions of when to use MSP, what's involved and who's best placed to do the work.

Recognising When to Use MSP

Within the transformational flow, you're often working with very senior managers who don't react well if you tell them that they have to do this or that 'because it says so in the process model'.

REMEMBER

Consequently, the process model (that is, the transformational flow) in MSP places emphasis on how the individual processes merge together and need to be adjusted to suit the environment. Remember also that the scale and impact of programmes can vary enormously (take a look at Chapter 2 for more details).

Another way of thinking about how you can tailor processes in the transformational flow is to look at the principles of programme management (which I cover in Chapter 4). Modify the processes as much as you want.

TIP

If you can remain true to the principles of programme management, you're probably on the right track.

Figure 3-2 shows a simple process model of the activities in Identifying a Programme.

PRINCIPAL CONTROLS
• Sponsoring Group to Monitor and Authorize
• Verify Programme brief maps and strategy
• Formal Assurance review
IN
• Programme Mandate
• Business Strategy
• Emerging Programme current status and plans
1. Sponsoring the programme
2. Confirm the programme mandate
3. Appoint the SRO and programme board
4. Produce the programme brief
5. Develop the programme preparation plan
6. Independent review
7. Approval to proceed
• Independent assurance report
• Confirmed mandate
• Approved programme brief
• Decisions on current activities for emerging programmes
• Programme preparation plan for 'Denfining a Programme'
• Approval to start 'Denfining a Programme'
• Appointment of senior responsible owner and programme board
OUT
KEY ROLES
• Sponsoring Group
• Senior Responsible Owner
• Programme Board
• Small Team (optional)

Figure 3-2: A simple process model of the activities in Identifying a Programme.

As you can see, the inputs are pretty sparse at the beginning of a programme, the people involved are pretty senior and the only really interesting control is an assurance review.

REMEMBER

At the beginning of a change initiative, when you're considering whether or not using programme management is sensible, you'll find the three project or programme questions I supply in Chapter 1 helpful. In the following list, I give you a few additional typical circumstances in which considering programme management is a good idea:

- Co-ordinating complex activities
- Coping with scarce resources
- Designing interfaces between projects
- Dealing with economies of scale between projects (doing something once at programme level rather than many times in different projects)
- Needing a framework in an uncertain environment
- Handling high risk across multiple projects

Of course, using programme management for a change initiative isn't always necessary or sensible. For an example, read the nearby sidebar 'When MSP isn't appropriate'.

When any change initiative starts, it rubs up against (to a greater or lesser extent) other change initiatives that are also going on or are planned. That's when you may need to consider using programme management.

TRUE STORY

When MSP isn't appropriate

Back at the turn of the century, in the dot-com boom, I was setting up lots of ordinary projects in a rapidly expanding business environment. The organization I was working in was within an ever-broadening universe. Everyone working for the firm was so ambitious that each new initiative took place in a dramatically different part of the business environment. Consequently, almost no links existed between any two change initiatives. If we wanted resources, we just bought them and our risk appetite was huge.

As a result, I concluded that the business wasn't meeting any of the circumstances I mention in this section, so we simply didn't use programme management. We just had a very large number of projects all taking place in different areas of our business, with very little overlap between them. No overlap between projects meant that programme management didn't offer any added value, so we were right not to use it. But that situation is rare. Most organizations are in a much more constrained business environment.

Understanding What's Involved in Identifying a Programme

In this section, I discuss the nature, purpose and (rather authoritative-sounding) Mandate of the Identifying a Programme process.

Discerning the nature of Identifying a Programme

The best way to understand what's involved in Identifying a Programme is to think about *where* it happens. Imagine that you're working in a fairly large business: now picture the headquarters. Not just the head-office building, but the row of offices where the most senior managers lurk threateningly (sorry, I mean reign majestically!). This area is often called the C-suite, because the CEO, CFO, CIO and so on sit together in close proximity, and the decision to treat a change initiative as a programme is made here. The decision is made in this C-suite, because programmes are about achieving strategic objectives.

The C-suite doesn't take long to decide. The managers recognise that they have to make a decision, so they do some preparation, gather the facts, meet and decide. That's the nature of Identifying a Programme.

Here are some characteristics of this process:

- Lasts only a few weeks
- Displays a cautious commitment to a new programme
- Involves the necessary preparation before committing to the Defining a Programme process (which is more intensive; check out Chapter 7 for more)
- Turns a concept into a tangible business proposition

Clarifying the purpose of Identifying a Programme

The formal purpose of the Identifying a Programme process (refer to the earlier Figure 3-1 to see where it lies in the wider scheme) is to take the Programme Mandate and formalise it in a Programme Brief, which describes what the programme is designed to achieve and its benefits (check out the next section and the later 'Moving from Mandate to Programme Brief' for more). The Brief then forms the basis for deciding whether the programme is justified and whether the organization can proceed to the Defining a Programme process.

Considering the Programme Mandate

One vital idea is important to grasp about the Programme Mandate: the programme doesn't exist at this point, so the programme or MSP can't dictate the form of the Programme Mandate.

Indeed if someone is dictating the form of a Programme Mandate, things are probably getting off to a less-than-great start. Ideally a *Programme Mandate* is some sort of external trigger that comes in at the strategic level and makes the organization think that it needs to respond (read the nearby sidebar 'Locating the origins of Programme Mandates' for an example).

Of course, you hope that it describes the outcomes from the programme based on strategic policy objectives, but a Programme Mandate is more likely to be a consultant's report than a document labelled 'Programme Mandate'. Strategic policy and objectives aren't terms most of us use every day, but the strategic planners in your organization may well use them. They just describe where the organization wants to be in the medium to long term.

Here's what you hope to see in a Programme Mandate (though you may not always be that lucky):

- Boundaries of the programme
- Constraints
- Context
- Critical success factors
- Current initiatives
- External drivers
- How assurance is to be carried out initially
- How the Mandate's going to fit into the corporate arena
- Initial budget
- Intended organizational improvements
- Nature of the organization improvement
- Related strategic objectives
- Relevant strategies and approaches
- Something about the 'as is' state (I explain about 'as is' and 'to be' states in Chapter 6)

As I say, you're unlikely to have all these pieces of information available when you receive an initial Programme Mandate.

Locating the origins of Programme Mandates

I just picked up today's newspaper and within a few pages read a report of a Parliamentary Select Committee interrogating the chief executives of three large companies about certain actions the companies had or hadn't taken. In each case the parliamentarians were unhappy with the responses.

I think I've found not one Programme Mandate but three here! Tomorrow the companies' chief executives are going to return to the C-suites and say 'we have to do something about this'.

Meeting the People Who Identify an Initiative as a Programme

MSP SPEAK

In the earlier section 'Discerning the nature of Identifying a Programme', I talk about senior management in your organization being called the C-suite. Well, in MSP the term is the *Sponsoring Group* (which I look at in more detail in Chapter 9).

In this section, I describe who makes up the Sponsoring Group and what the members do in the context of Identifying a Programme.

TIP

The first thing to say is that you don't find committees calling themselves Sponsoring Groups. Therefore, when I'm with clients, the first thing I do is I ask them the name of their top-level management team. Usually, they come up with phrases such as the Corporate Board or the Executive Management Team. I replace Sponsoring Group with this local term and that's what I suggest you do as you read through this chapter and, more importantly, while you're implementing programme management.

Making up the Sponsoring Group

The Sponsoring Group contains the people who have the strategic overview of your organization and decide on strategic direction. Of course, lots of non-strategic initiatives are going on in all organizations and various other governance bodies approve this type of change initiative. But some initiatives are so significant that they're sure to come to the attention of the Sponsoring Group. They may be projects and so outside the scope of this book, but some are potentially going to be programmes.

The Sponsoring Group considers an appropriate initiative, thinks about how important it is and whether to invest in it. The members are unlikely to manage (or perhaps a better term is 'direct') the programme as a committee.

The best approach that the group can take is to choose a member of the Sponsoring Group to own the programme.

MSP calls this person the Senior Responsible Owner (SRO).

Here are three things to be wary of when choosing the SRO:

- If the organization feels that it has to appoint several SROs for one programme, it suggests that the managers aren't comfortable delegating a major strategic change to just one member of the Sponsoring Group. This situation may indicate that problems lie ahead in making decisions quickly enough to achieve the necessary transformational change.
- Be careful if a slightly more junior manager (though still at a very senior level within the organization) is appointed as SRO. The person may not have the authority to make the decisions that are needed when directing the programme.
- If the SRO is accountable for delivering the programme, that person ideally needs to remain with the programme for its whole life, which may mean being in the same position for an uncomfortably long time – perhaps three to five years.

The ideal solution to this last point is when an organization is bold and says to an SRO, 'we want you to remain with this programme for a long period and we'll reward you suitably if the programme is successful'. I've come across organizations that have done so. The situation to worry about, however, is when the SRO changes every six months or every year in a programme that's running for four or five years: inevitably, the individual's interests are short term whereas the programme's interests are longer term. I know of many programmes that failed badly because the SRO changed too frequently.

Sponsoring the programme

The Sponsoring Group is made up of senior executives on whom the programme impacts and who are required to bring about change. They need to have:

- Strategic interest
- Responsibility for the investment

All the members need to clarify their perspectives and interests, confirm their levels of engagement and commitment, and understand other change initiatives and any overlaps, conflicts and gaps that may apply.

Taking these considerations into account, appoint as SRO the most appropriate individual from the Sponsoring Group to lead and direct the programme.

Moving from Mandate to Programme Brief

Some work behind the scenes is necessary when moving from Mandate to Programme Brief. The SRO gets this work done by the newly appointed Programme Manager or by some consultants, so draft documents such as a Programme Brief and Programme Preparation Plan can be presented to the Sponsoring Group.

Bringing on the Programme Brief

As I say in the earlier section 'Considering the Programme Mandate', the Mandate may be incomplete. Therefore, the Programme Brief is simply the result of refining and filling out that Programme Mandate.

MSP SPEAK

The key purpose of a *Programme Brief* is to allow the Sponsoring Group to assess whether the programme is viable and achievable.

TIP

The initiative is likely to be Vision-based, so understanding the Vision right from the very beginning and including an outline Vision in the Programme Brief is worthwhile. Make sure to outline the benefits, plus familiar items such as expected costs, timescales and effort, risks, constraints and assumptions, and perhaps options. Table 3-1 shows the contents of a Programme Brief.

Table 3-1 Contents of a Programme Brief

Contents	*Description*
Vision Statement	Describes the goal and is developed further during the next process.
Benefits	Outlines descriptions of the types of benefits to be expected. Provides estimates of when they're likely to be achieved. Considers the sharing of benefits across multiple organizations.
Risks and issues	Identifies those you know now as well as known constraints, conflicts and assumptions.
Estimates	Covers costs, timescales, effort. Provide a best guess for now. Includes as much detail as justifies the programme. Forms the basis for the later programme Business Case. Outlines the plan, covering projects known at this point, but only at a high level; that is, with very rough or approximate estimates.

You may already have some idea of the candidate projects, particularly for an emergent programme. But don't focus too much on these projects, otherwise the result is a project-focused initiative not a benefits-focused initiative. Also, remember to include something about the current state of the part of the organization that will eventually be changed by the programme.

Outlining the Vision Statement

The Programme Brief includes an outline Vision. Here I give only a very brief summary of the purpose of a Vision. Check out Chapter 5 for more details, where I also give you tips on what makes a good Vision.

The Vision:

- Paints a simple picture of the required outcome
- Describes what's going to be different for the organization(s) because of the programme
- Expresses benefits such as:
  - Capability
  - Capacity
  - Effectiveness
  - Efficiency
  - Performance
  - Resilience
  - Risk levels
  - Services
- Expresses how stakeholders (anyone affected by or who can affect the programme) will see the benefit(s) and how these improvements are to be measured.

Here are the characteristics of a great Vision Statement:

- Written in future state
- Understandable by all stakeholders, with the broadest group being the target audience
- Describes a compelling future, not just dry facts
- May well include targets and constraints
- Memorable

Considering the Characteristics of Your Programme

I look at different types and aspects of programmes in Chapter 2, but certain other ideas are relevant when Identifying a Programme with the Sponsoring Group: how much control needs to be exerted; creating a plan for the Defining a Programme process; and gaining that all-important approval to go ahead.

Staying loose or tightening up your programme

As you study MSP, you may come to believe that programmes have to be centrally and tightly controlled. But in fact some of the most successful programmes I've been involved with were very loosely controlled by a very small central team.

Organizational culture plays an important role in helping the Sponsoring Group decide whether the programme needs to be loose or tight. As Table 3-2 reveals, loose and tight programmes have their own advantages.

Table 3-2 Loose and Tight Programme Advantages

Loose Programme	*Tight Programme*
Buy-in from stakeholders	Speed
Avoids alienation	Control
Encourages individuality	Structure

TIP: As regards control, *right not tight* is the way to go.

Preparing for the programme

I describe what you need to do when Defining a Programme in Chapter 7, but for now just note that it may require a substantial amount of work. Therefore, you need to have a plan for Defining a Programme. This document is called the *Programme Preparation Plan* and it details how to undertake Defining a Programme.

A Programme Preparation Plan is a pretty conventional plan that covers the following:

- Assurance
- Boundaries
- Deliverables
- Estimates of effort and cost
- Governance and controls
- Resources
- Schedule
- Role of the Programme Board (which I discuss more in Chapter 9)

Gaining approval to proceed

The Programme Brief and the Programme Preparation Plan from the preceding section set the context for the programme and its initial direction. The formal approval that the Sponsoring Group gives means that the SRO confirms the following aspects (see the earlier section 'Making up the Sponsoring Group' if you've still to select this person):

- The programme meets some set of business requirements
- The Programme Board commits to supporting delivery of the programme
- The Sponsoring Group authorises the programme and commits to support and resource the Defining a Programme stage.

The authorisation is relatively short term, because it's only up to the end of Defining a Programme; although you hope to go ahead with the programme, it may be a distinctly different shape by the end of Defining a Programme.

Chapter 4

Focusing on the Principles of Programme Management

In This Chapter

- Defining programme principles
- Encouraging the necessary principles
- Making sure that your programme improves

This chapter covers the *principles* of programme management – those universal, proved-through-experience, empowering concepts that underpin the whole of programme management. I describe what you can do to ensure that the crucial programme principles exist: aligning with corporate strategy, leading effectively, seeing and conveying a better future, achieving – and protecting – benefits, creating value and delivering a coherent capability. In addition, I point out that the programme needs to develop, adjust and improve throughout its life.

I cover powerful ideas in this chapter, some of which may seem a little daunting to achieve. But I hope that the discussions and examples in this chapter help you to see that living by these programme principles is entirely practical, thus encouraging you to apply the principles of programme management to your own programme.

REMEMBER: No hard and fast rules apply to the principles. You just need to reflect on how you're going to utilise them in your programme.

Considering the Characteristics of Principles

When you come to set up a programme, you need to ask yourself a central question: what does a successful programme look like? Fortunately, the answer is fairly straightforward. You consider the *principles* that reflect the characteristics of a successful programme: the common factors that underpin the success of any programme of transformational change.

I worked with the authors of MSP to identify the principles that underpin programme management. We asked ourselves what differentiated principles from any other aspect of programme management. We came up with three conclusions that are in themselves useful if you're setting up and running a programme:

- **Universal.** Principles apply to every programme you come across, no matter how big or small, no matter what its impact. Principles have to be genuinely universal. They aren't aspirations to strive for, which some programmes may achieve but not others: they're the basics.
- **Self-validating.** Principles are proved in practice. They're not bits of theory picked up from a quick Internet search. Experts have observed these aspects of programme management in the real world and found that they really do work.
- **Empowering.** Principles give practitioners added ability or power to influence and shape transformational change. In other words, they aren't constraining. They don't tell you what you must do and limit your flexibility. Instead, they open up an area for you to think about and encourage you to be innovative in the way you align with the principles in your programme.

Ensuring that Your Programme is Principled

You need to make sure that your programme contains, provides and encourages a set of essential principles. In this section, I discuss six important features of all successful programmes. They:

- Tie up with your organization's overall strategy
- Display effective leadership
- Supply solid, lasting transformational change
- Bring benefits
- Deliver value
- Maintain a coherent direction

Keeping aligned with corporate strategy

Programmes can deliver outcomes and benefits of strategic significance for your organization. As a result, most programmes (though not all) are large and involve significant investment by the organization. Consequently, you're going to (and indeed should) face constant pressure to justify the programme. After all, if it's going to cost a lot of money, senior management may want to consider stopping it.

TIP

The best way to safeguard your programme is to demonstrate not only that the programme is aligned with corporate strategy, but also that it's essential if the organization is going to achieve its strategy.

Staying focused

Aligning a programme with corporate strategy isn't as simple as when you're running a project. Projects are relatively short and consequently relatively inflexible. In a project, you start out with an idea or perhaps even a design or a specification. You may identify options towards the beginning of the project, but then you build what you have designed so that it meets the specification or fulfils the idea.

I don't want to make project management seem easy – I know from experience that often it's not – but the nature of project management is that (unlike with most programmes) you're trying to build something that you already have reasonable understanding of. Even with a high-level programme Vision, some uncertainty is likely to exist about how you achieve that Vision. You'll probably require a considerable amount of time before you successfully complete the Vision. (I cover creating the Vision in more detail in Chapter 5.)

REMEMBER

You hope that the Vision is fairly static, but the journey to achieve it may have many twists and turns. Furthermore, your organization's strategy may well change over the course of the programme. Consequently, you may have to confirm regularly and frequently that the programme, as it's currently understood, is indeed aligned with the organization's ever-changing strategic objectives. This confirmation of alignment is an on-going task.

Making a strategic contribution

If your programme remains aligned with corporate strategy, you can contribute to that strategy in several ways:

- **Make a contribution towards achieving corporate performance targets.** Different organizations operate performance management in different ways. Typically an organization has some high-level, strategic performance indicators – perhaps known as key performance indicators (KPIs). You may then have a hierarchy of lower-level performance indicators.

A reasonably sized programme can't justify itself by making minor contributions to a series of low-level performance indicators. A substantial programme needs to make a difference to one or more strategic performance indicators.

Therefore, you and the programme management team need to engage with the performance management function within your organization as follows:

- **Endeavour to understand the nature of the current strategic performance indicators.**
- **Enter into a dialogue with the performance management team to agree the contribution your programme can make and how to measure it.**
- **Consider talking with others who see their primary job as being to achieve the identified performance indicators.** If a senior line manager's role is to contribute to a particular performance indicator, that person may not be willing to share achievement of that performance with a new programme.

  Additionally, even though discussions may have taken place in the Sponsoring Group when your programme was identified, at a working level you may need to be diplomatic. Don't try to tell senior line managers, who have an established position in the organization, that the programme is now in charge. Negotiate with them to understand their views and persuade them of the value of the programme.
- **Remember that this exercise isn't a one-off: you may need to maintain these links over a prolonged period.**
- **Prove or disprove strategic ideas.**

For example, put in place a pilot of new ways of working. If it works, great! Roll out the new way of working across the organization. But if the pilot's unsuccessful, the programme has still made a valuable strategic contribution, because it's prevented the organization reorganizing into a structure that wouldn't have worked.

Plus, the organization is sure to have certain *strategic drivers*, the things the business wants and needs to do with the highest level; for example, generating more business from the web. You can make sure that these drivers are extended to and understood in projects and business change activities.

REMEMBER

An organization's strategy changes over time and therefore the programme must create a robust but flexible working environment. You need to establish what I think of as a porous programme boundary. The boundary is the limit of the effect of a programme; it needs to be porous so that ideas and scope can move in and out of the programme as the strategic environment changes (check out the later section 'Seeing a different picture of benefits' for more details).

Leading change

For an organization to undergo strategic change, it needs more than just management. Leaders in the programme need to lead that change actively. Here are just a few examples of the sort of leadership that your programme requires:

- **Leaders need to give clear direction on where the programme is going.** In other words, they must champion the agreed Vision.
- **Leaders need to make sure that they're trusted.** They do so in the dynamic and fast-moving world of the programme by behaving consistently and encouraging transparency. Discussing issues freely and evaluating risks openly requires courage, but such behaviour reinforces trust and demonstrates strong leadership.
- **Leaders need to engage honestly with stakeholders.** Which means talking to them and listening to them. People used to talk about *stakeholder management,* but today the preferred term is *stakeholder engagement.* From a leadership point of view you have to engage actively with stakeholders, listening to and valuing their perceptions of what's going on. A programme often focuses more on people than is the case if you're just running a project.
- **Leaders need to accept that the programme is going to change significantly over time.** They must appoint the right people to the team at the beginning of the programme. Programmes often need a rare mix of skills and abilities. You need to get that team in place while you're Defining the Programme, but you also have to adjust the composition of that team as the programme evolves.
- **Leaders need to be comfortable with uncertainty.** You can't run a programme using a Gantt chart (one of those diagrams showing when activities will occur that you often see around projects). Fundamental uncertainties exist within any major programme.

  If you're trying to transform your organization profoundly, you can't follow a predefined life-cycle based on a series of templates. The leaders need to be comfortable with the complexity and ambiguity in the early parts of a programme and make others in the programme team equally comfortable with uncertainty.
- **Leaders need to understand that they can't know everything.** Problems come thick and fast in a typical programme, appearing from all sorts of different directions within the programme – internal, external, from projects, from business as usual and from the design area. Leaders need the mental agility and sheer resilience to cope with and resolve an endless stream of problems.

REMEMBER

- **Leaders need to appreciate that business as usual has to undergo the painful activity of transition to new ways of working.** They must understand the pain of this transition and support it.

  Never neglect or underestimate the amount of work that needs to be done to take the outputs from projects and embed them in business as usual.

I look in more detail at leadership within a programme in Chapter 17.

Envisioning and communicating a better future

Here's a useful way of looking at your programme's goal: if the new world isn't better than the old world, why are you going there?

Leaders need to envision and communicate a better future. So they need to describe a clear Vision of that future – what the world will be like when you arrive in the future state. But here I ask you to consider why you need to focus so much on the Vision – the better future.

Purpose of programme management

You can use much of MSP if you're managing a large specification-led change initiative. In that case, the emphasis is much more on a network of projects and subprojects. Programme management can do much more than that, however. Over the years the team of people who came together to create MSP have created a tool to allow you to achieve genuine transformational change.

REMEMBER

Transformational change isn't about doing the same thing slightly better. It is, fundamentally, about doing something different. And I don't mean a couple of people in an organization taking on a new role; I mean hundreds or thousands of people doing different roles, in different places for different purposes. Programme management really does change the business. (I don't want to come across as a zealot – but then again I'm not sorry if I'm showing a real enthusiasm for the subject!)

Programme management is the best tool for achieving transformational change. No amount of project management or even portfolio management can help your organization become radically different. Only programme management contains, assembled from a wide range of sources, the tricks and techniques you need to change fundamentally your organization.

A better way of delivering change

In the preceding section I want to communicate how programme management can give you a better future, if you're involved in change delivery. I hope my passion and enthusiasm goes some way towards doing that.

In your programme, the leaders of the programme need to show similar passion and enthusiasm for the new future that you're all working so hard to achieve.

Doing so involves more than simply describing the future verbally. The leaders of the programme need to:

1. **Record the better future.**
2. **Distribute it.**
3. **Listen carefully to the concerns of the wide range of stakeholders in the programme about that future.**
4. **Respond to those concerns by working with individual stakeholders and stakeholder groups, if necessary by altering the boundary of the programme to accommodate those concerns.**
5. **Ensure that the Vision is communicated clearly and consistently within all levels of the programme.**
6. **Keep the Vision current.** Hopefully that means just making minor changes to the Vision to keep it fresh. If the Vision changes fundamentally, you need to reconsider whether the programme can still continue in its current form.

Communicating a better future is a challenge when you're trying to deal with stakeholders who may be nervous about the new future, but ultimately they'll see that the new future is indeed in their own interests. An even greater challenge, however, is communicating a new future with stakeholders who may be disadvantaged in the new world, or indeed may not even be part of it. Not everyone can be a winner in a transformational change programme.

Real leadership involves supporting such people as they come to terms with no longer being part of an organization's new world or must accept that the power they held in the old world is going to be diminished.

Programme leaders have to take the time to help people on the road to their new world.

Focusing on the benefits and threats to them

Programmes are about creating benefits. Therefore your programme needs to maintain a focus on the benefits and an awareness of what threatens them.

Seeing a different picture of benefits

Before I go on to talk about those threats (in the later section 'Focusing on threats to the benefits'), I want to ask you to look at benefits in a different way. Benefits are one of the new ideas in programme management, and they're extremely important. You may not have dealt with benefits realization before or have a great deal of experience of managing change in a structured way, as happens when you do benefits management.

I cover benefits a little in Chapter 2 and a lot in Chapters 15 and 16. In Chapter 2, I show you the full version of the Ferguson Factory, but Figure 4-1 features a simple version of the model focusing on benefits that many of my clients find helpful.

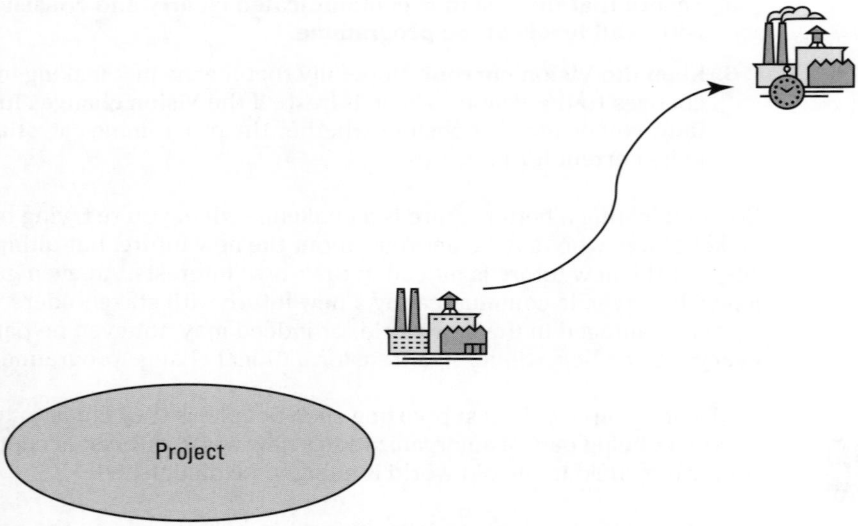

Figure 4-1: Exploiting project capability.

The model shows a single project that delivers a capability. Capability is exploited in business as usual in order to achieve an outcome – the effect of change. You measure the effect of the change (that is, the outcome) via benefits.

In other words, a programme isn't about a predefined dossier of projects, the capabilities identified in the Blueprint or even a set of outcomes. A programme is about achieving a set of benefits.

As I describe in the earlier section 'Making a strategic contribution', the programme has a boundary. Within the boundary are the outcomes, capabilities, outputs and activities you have to deal with in order to achieve the benefits. The programme boundary is porous and may well change, in order to ensure optimum realization of benefits.

Areas of work move in and out of the programme as certain areas display opportunities for significant benefit realization. Remember that the ultimate success of the programme is determined by the ability of the programme to realize the benefits. Furthermore, those benefits need to continue to be relevant to the organization and align strategically.

Focusing on threats to the benefits

The programme needs to focus on benefits and threats to them such as late delivery of outputs, difficulty in implementing capabilities in business as usual or changing strategic priorities.

One way of doing so is to put benefits as an early agenda item for each Programme Board (whose role I describe in Chapter 9). If you do that you probably need to have benefits on the agenda of lower-level bodies in the programme and business as usual. In this way you can feed progress on benefits up through the programme to the highest level.

Adding value

If a programme doesn't add value over and above the individual projects, it doesn't justify its existence. Indeed at programme reviews, if you can't demonstrate additional value, people can see a reason for closing the programme.

But when your programme offers benefits over and above those from projects, you have *programme benefits:* ones that can't be claimed by individual projects but only by the programme.

Therefore, your programme has to manage the complete set of benefits being delivered, which also helps the programme to prevent double counting of benefits by projects.

I expand on this concept a little more here, by considering a number of standalone, but related, projects. Each of those projects has a project business case (which is different from the programme Business Case that I describe in

Chapter 8; what difference a couple of capital letters make!) where the benefits associated with the project are described. (The benefits are expressed sufficiently rigorously so that they're not only claimed in the business case, but also demonstrated in business as usual after the project delivers its outputs.)

If you now group the projects into a programme you can add up the benefits from each of the projects and claim them as the benefits of the programme. At least, that's one approach.

But costs are associated with running programme management over and above project management. The programme needs to demonstrate that it can deliver additional benefits that more than outweigh these additional costs.

Here are some examples of the ways in which programme management can add value:

- The programme can make projects more efficient by:
  - Rapidly sharing lessons between similar projects
  - Centrally managing resources shared across the projects
  - Building once products that several projects can use
- The programme can make projects more effective by managing their scope more tightly. It can ensure that the projects only build capabilities that are essential for achieving the Blueprint.
- The programme can simplify the management of issues and risks that inevitably arise between closely related projects. I discuss these subjects in Chapters 11 and 12.
- The programme can centralise and streamline the planning of projects and also provide an effective route for reporting across multiple, related projects. I look at these subjects in more detail in Chapter 10.
- The programme can ensure that quality is achieved appropriately and consistently across the projects. This prevents some projects paying insufficient attention to quality management, perhaps because staff in the project aren't familiar with the concepts. The programme can also ensure that other projects don't gold plate their outputs by over-engineering outputs or putting too much emphasis on quality. I cover quality in Chapter 13.
- The programme can speed benefits realization by providing a focal point for managing benefits. In the Programme Office you may want to appoint a benefits co-ordinator. This person builds up experience of techniques associated with benefits management such as benefits modelling and reporting, which helps the Benefits Owners spread through business as usual to accelerate achievement of the benefits. Flip to Chapter 9 for more on programme roles.

- The programme can ease handover between projects and business as usual by putting in place a structure: the Programme Board where the Programme Manager and Project Executives can meet regularly with Business Change Managers to sort out the details of the handover from projects to business as usual and to build trust between those two communities.
- The programme can provide more effective engagement with stakeholders, particularly where they have an interest in more than one project, by providing centralised or co-ordinated stakeholder engagement. I provide more on this subject in Chapter 14.

REMEMBER

You may be daunted by the prospect of having to demonstrate objectively the value that programme management brings over and above the value of project management. But I hope that this list helps you to feel more comfortable about identifying value from programme management.

Designing and delivering a coherent capability

With everything that's going on in a programme you can all too easily find different elements of the programme pointing in different directions. Therefore, the programme must design and deliver a coherent capability. You define that capability in the Blueprint, from where you can work out the scope of projects and the outputs to be produced.

REMEMBER

The programme doesn't operate solely at the level of the individual projects; it needs to focus on the bigger picture. Nevertheless, it must also give clear direction to projects.

The Blueprint evolves over time and the programme must ensure that it delivers the current version of the Blueprint. If strategy changes to the extent that the capability described in the Blueprint is no longer coherent, or even no longer relevant, the programme may need to be stopped.

I cover the mechanics of designing and delivering a Blueprint in Chapter 6. But the principles apply across the full breadth of programme management, not to one particular theme. Therefore, in this section I explore some of the softer aspects of maintaining coherence.

A coherent Vision

At the risk of stating the obvious, everyone needs to be working towards the same Vision. But I take the risk because achieving this aim in practice is often a lot more difficult than it seems. I regularly come across programmes that lack a Vision, feature a poorly communicated Vision or even have several different Visions.

For many people a programme Vision is an alien concept. Business as usual may recognise the mission of the organization, but that may be significantly different from the Vision of one particular programme. Plus, projects often have nothing as inspirational as a Vision.

The programme management team needs to get across to the people working in and around the programme that the Vision is important and is something they need to think about and understand if the programme is going to create that coherent capability.

Coherent stakeholder engagement

Organizations are becoming more familiar with stakeholder engagement, from the point of view of business as usual and from within projects. Sometimes, the different groups within a programme can feel (wrongly) that they're engaging effectively with their stakeholders by communicating a local message. They communicate their understanding of the programme from the perspective of their project or business unit.

The problem is that this local message may be distinctly different from the overall coherent messages that the programme wants to communicate. I pass on two anecdotes, one good and one bad, which help you appreciate the significance of stakeholder engagement when establishing a coherent capability.

The first example concerns a programme that was operating on two sites a few hundred miles apart. One site contained the Programme Office and the other site had a small public relations (PR) team carrying out stakeholder engagement. The latter team was dedicated to the programme, but when I visited a beautifully designed and professionally executed road show that it was delivering, I was astonished to see that the PR team simply didn't understand the broader messages the Programme Office was trying to push out from the programme centre.

Two breakdowns in coherence were at work:

- The people at the centre assumed that the PR team understood what the Programme Office was about. The latter failed to recognise that it needed to treat PR staff as stakeholders and engage with them if they were to understand the breadth and detail of the programme.
- The PR team was communicating the wrong messages to all the stakeholders they came into contact with. The more enthusiastically the staff members worked to engage with stakeholders, the less coherent the messages became!

My second example involves a programme with many external stakeholders. Other organizations were interested in the programme, as well as local, national and international regulators looking at different specialist aspects of the programme.

The programme had put in place a system whereby one person was nominated as the point of contact for each stakeholder group. The programme made sure that each point of contact understood what the programme was about and consequently that person was able to maintain a link with the external stakeholders. As a result, the programme maintained coherence.

Learning from Experience

In this section I look at a programme principle that's slightly different to the six I lay out in the earlier section 'Ensuring that Your Programme is Principled', but is no less important. Instead of being a corporate aim that the programme needs to achieve – alignment, leadership, a better future, benefits, value or coherence – this principle is something less tangible that the programme has to do. Your programme (and indeed you) must learn from experience to produce a learning organization.

TIP

You need to adjust the programme's approach to each individual theme based on previous experience, building into its review mechanisms opportunities to reflect on experience.

Demonstrating maturity

The ability to learn from experience often reflects the maturity of programme management. *Programme and project management maturity* considers the way in which the organization is structured to do the right things repeatedly and reliably.

You may already be familiar with the idea of maturity from some of the processes that take place around you. When you go to the supermarket you expect to find the same products to the same quality standard being stocked in the same place in the supermarket whether you visit on a Monday morning, Friday afternoon or in the middle of the night.

Process maturity is fundamental to business as usual. But in the modern world of delivering change, people often put much less emphasis on process maturity. One person may argue that her programme may be so fundamentally different from another programme running in the same organization that very little good practice can be transferred from one programme to the other. Thinking about common ideas for running both programmes is known as *programme management maturity*.

But within a programme, undertaking a series of similar or related projects is fairly common. Therefore, your aim is to run those projects in similar, more mature ways. You want to change your culture from one that's populated by individual projects doing their own thing, to a culture where you have a project factory slickly and efficiently turning out project outputs for the good of the programme.

In this context, the programme needs to discover what works and what doesn't in order to increase the maturity of what you're doing within the programme.

Logging and reviewing

Put in place opportunities at all levels for people to record their experiences within the programme.

In projects, this requirement may mean setting up *lessons logs* (sometimes called *lessons learned logs*). Because simply recording something in a log doesn't necessarily mean that the lesson has been disseminated to people and learnt by them, I also like to set up discrete opportunities for actually learning the lessons.

If you're carrying out transition within business as usual on a number of different occasions, and at a number of different locations during the programme, you may also want to put in place opportunities to capture the lessons that you want to learn from each little transition event.

Of course, logs aren't the only way in which you can capture lessons. Sometimes a better approach is to get groups of people together to have a meeting to review and capture what they've learnt. The lessons that have been captured can then be put into an end-of-project, or end-of-transition, report.

You have to consolidate the acquired learning in some way, and a great opportunity to do so is through the formal reviews that are carried out at various points through the programme. The programme needs to define the different types of internal and independent review that occur before, during and after structured initiatives (such as projects) and less structured work (transition).

This subject is substantial and hugely important. I cover governance and assurance of quality in Chapters 13 and 14.

Training and educating

When you gather together all the learned lessons, you have to communicate them to people working in the programme and those about to join it.

For a large programme, you may need to set up induction training and regular retraining for people working within the programme.

I recall one programme where I was proudly told about a pack of PowerPoint slides, which explained the programme to new arrivals. Sadly when I talked to new arrivals, none of them had seen the slides! Make sure that people have the opportunity to look at the lessons recorded and apply them to behaviour in the programme in future.

Part II

Moving Forward with Managing Your Programme

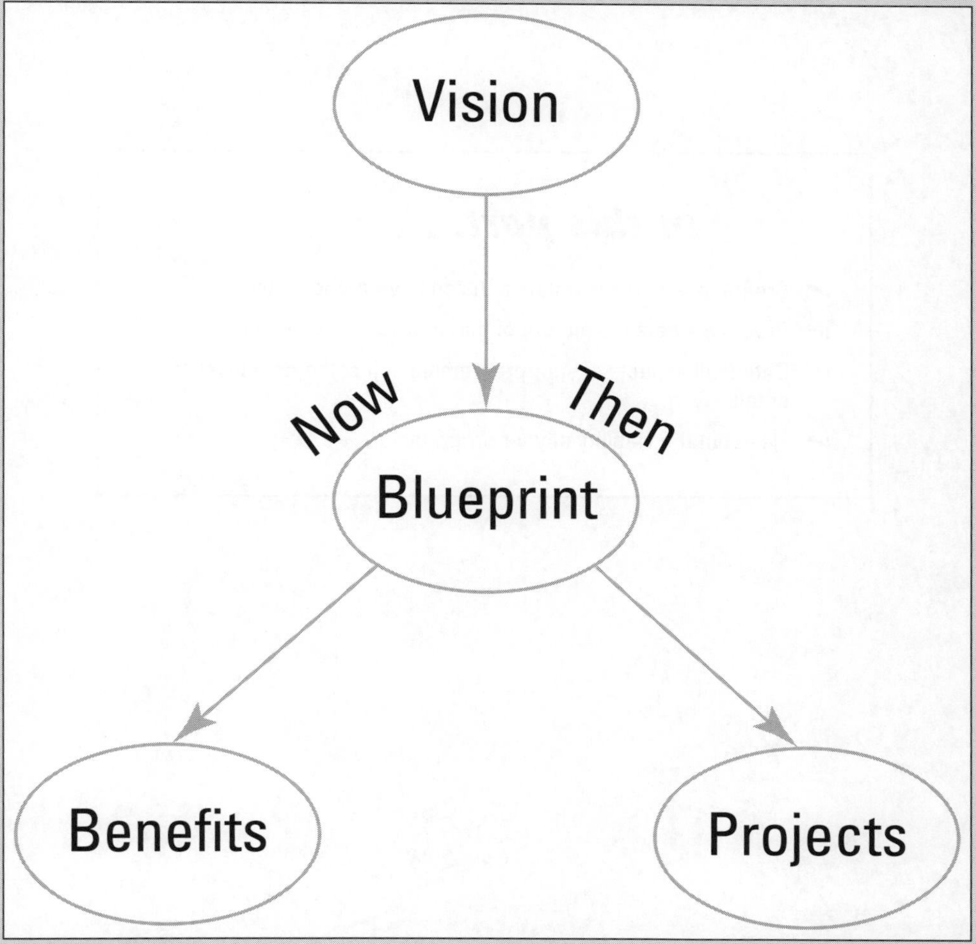

Go to www.dummies.com/extras/msp for free online bonus content about managing successful programmes.

In this part. . .

- Create, share and maintain a Vision of your end state.
- Produce a detailed picture of that end state – a Blueprint.
- Define all aspects of your programme at just the right level of detail.
- Flesh out the viability of your programme.

Chapter 5

Creating Your Programme's Vision

In This Chapter

- Understanding why a Vision is vital for your programme
- Incorporating all the key elements in a Vision
- Striking the appropriate tone in a Vision
- Getting the right people involved in your Vision

Most programmes are long – three to five years is typical. Some may be substantially longer; I've worked on one that's planned to last for a century! Their length or the fact that they're being carried out in an uncertain environment means that most programmes can't be planned from start to finish. Therefore, all you can say about a conventional plan for a programme – in other words, a schedule showing activities and timescales – is that it won't happen. The difficulty is working out what will happen.

You and the other stakeholders in your programme can't know the nature of the entire journey. You know only a portion of it: perhaps what's going to happen in the next year. So in order to keep on track, you need to have a clear picture of the destination. In MSP, this picture is called the *Vision.*

REMEMBER

The Vision is the destination, not the journey.

As well as describing the characteristics of a good Vision in this chapter, I talk about developing and maintaining a Vision Statement and where the Vision sits within the life-cycle of your programme – what MSP calls the *transformational flow.* (You can find out more about the transformational flow in Chapter 1.) You can refer to the 'Vision' or the 'Vision Statement', they're the same thing.

Picturing your Vision

The Vision is a picture of a better future; its focus is on outcomes and benefits. If the future isn't going to be better than today, you don't need to do the programme.

The Vision isn't the same as a plan – it doesn't describe the route to a destination, it describes the destination itself. When you first try to write a Vision, you may well get that aspect wrong. Perhaps you talk about building a new hospital instead of a hospital that will serve the community. Don't worry: everyone takes a little while to adjust to the language of a Vision.

Defining a Vision

Instead of being a plan, the purpose of the Vision is to be a way of encouraging and maintaining the commitment and enthusiasm of all those involved and ensuring everyone is on the same page. The Vision is a summarised expression of the desired future state.

If you need to sacrifice detail in your Vision in order to achieve impact, that's absolutely fine. You can include the necessary detail in the Blueprint (which I describe in Chapter 6). Many things in a programme are going to be unstable and volatile, but your aim is to keep the Vision itself as stable as possible to help maintain stakeholder credibility and to signal strategic alignment. Indeed, some people go further and say that if the Vision has to change, you have to question whether the programme has remained the same.

The Vision needs to be compelling, so it can simply be one side of a piece of paper with a lot of white space on it, or a couple of slides from a presentation. Don't make it a dense 400-page technical report.

If the Vision is a compelling, high-level description of the future state, it can act as an effective focal point for the programme.

Understanding why your programme needs a Vision

A programme without a Vision is like a country singer without a sob story. Your programme needs a Vision for two reasons:

- The detailed description of the future state, the Blueprint, is based on the Vision. Just as important aspects of the programme such as the Benefits Model and the Project Dossier evolve from the Blueprint, so everything hangs off the Vision.
- The Vision is the rallying point for your team. In the same way that team members in sport gather around a flag or mascot, and military units have an emblem, when things get complex and confusing with the programme – when you and other members of the programme team can't understand what's happening – you can rally to the Vision.

The Vision is one of the key concepts within programme management, as well as one of the governance themes in MSP.

Dreaming Up Your Vision

The composition of the Vision is pretty straightforward and very brief. It's a clear statement of the end goal of the programme, something short and memorable. It may well need to include any imposed constraints on the programme – the situation in which the programme is being undertaken.

You can expand on this external view by setting the context for the programme, perhaps including relevant information to help set expectations. Your aim is to put the context of the programme into the broader business context.

TIP

Consider including information to support the justification for change, for example, a clear description of the current reality. I often use the phrase *a burning platform*: if you describe the current reality as unsustainable, people are prepared to move on to a future state.

REMEMBER

Here are three vital aspects to include in your Vision:

- **End goal:** Describe briefly what the world will be like when the programme has finished.
- **Constraints:** Summarise the constraints on achieving that end goal.
- **Context to set expectations:** Explain a little about the current wider situation so that stakeholders realise why changing is a good idea.

Creating a great Vision

Here are a few pointers on making your Vision effective:

- Write the Vision as if you're already in the future state: say 'The world is like this,' rather than 'In the future the world will be like this'.
- Think carefully about the stakeholders and write the Vision in a language that they can understand. Some stakeholders may think that it's too simple and doesn't contain enough technical language. That's a good thing. The Vision needs to be written for the broadest possible target audience, because you're trying to build a consensus around the programme.

- Describe a compelling future. The future must be one that's necessary, in contrast to a current reality that's less than compelling. Don't say that the future must be a good future (that's a bit simplistic).
- If possible, paint a picture of a desirable future and not just of a compelling future.
- Match the nature of the Vision to the nature of the transformation: modest if the transformation is modest, but bold if the change is bold. If possible, try to avoid future dates. If you say that your Vision is going to be the 2050 Vision, the year 2050 will arrive just after New Year's Eve in 2049. But that may not mean you've achieved your Vision.
- Make sure to say how people will know whether the Vision has been achieved. You want the Vision to be verifiable, but without putting in detailed performance targets. The Vision has to be sufficiently flexible so that it can remain unchanged over the course of the programme. For example: if you're going to move to 12 new office blocks, don't say 12. Just say 'a set of new office blocks'. In that case, if you end up in 11 blocks, the Vision is still stable.
- Remember that the Vision complements the Blueprint, which contains the detail. Therefore the Vision has only to give sufficient context for the Blueprint to make sense. Make your Vision short, memorable and relevant.

REMEMBER

As always, the proof of the pudding is in the eating (ahhh, pudding!). Ultimately a Vision is good if the key stakeholders think that it's good.

Communicating your programme's goal

The purpose of the Vision Statement is to communicate the end goal to all stakeholders, so write it in language and terms that customers can understand.

Don't get lost in the language of customers, however. Imagine a person in each of your stakeholder groups. Think of them as someone you're providing a service to – a customer. The Vision needs to describe the service you'll eventually be providing to them.

As an example, think about how you'd write a Vision about reducing the number of staff in the company in a way that's acceptable to those staff. That's the type of challenge you face. The answer's probably something like 'achieving industry standards of productivity'.

TIP

The Vision needs to communicate the programme's end goal effectively: see it as an artist's impression of a future state.

Now it's your turn. Write a Vision for your own programme or for a programme that's in the public eye that you're familiar with. Then check it using the tests I give of what makes a good Vision.

Don't worry if you find that you write something more like a plan than a Vision and with too much detail. That's quite normal, and practice makes perfect.

Watching Your Vision Evolve

To start, the Vision is drafted during the Identifying a Programme process by the Senior Responsible Owner (see the later section 'Taking overall responsibility: Senior Responsible Owner') and key stakeholders. You can refine it in the Defining a Programme process, but after that it is kept as stable as possible. If it's changed you run the risk of confusing stakeholders or even undermining the credibility of the programme, as well as of indicating that the current programme is no longer strategically aligned (in other words, it isn't helping achieve the longer term direction of the organization) and so a different programme is required.

In this section I also convey what it feels like when you get the right people contributing in the right way. I use the formal terms for the different roles in programmes, which I describe in Chapter 9.

Identifying that you have a programme

In the Identifying a Programme process, you want to have a brief session with the Sponsoring Group to flesh out the Programme Brief. The Brief contains an outline Business Case and outline Vision. All you need to do at this point is get them describing the future – the destination – not the plan for getting there.

Defining the programme in more detail

In Defining the Programme, one of your first actions is to carry out stakeholder analysis. (I talk more about this subject in Chapter 14.) In an ideal world you want to have someone from each of the main stakeholder groups present while you do more work on the Vision. At the beginning of a programme, people are usually nervous about engaging with stakeholders.

I was recently in the IT department of a very large bank. The programme manager said to me that he didn't want to do stakeholder analysis because he wouldn't be able to influence all his stakeholders.

I talk more about how to deal with this attitude in Chapter 14, but as far as the Vision is concerned, your aim is to get as many stakeholder groups as possible present when working on the Vision. If a stakeholder group is so sensitive that you feel you can't invite them, ask someone who you're more comfortable with and who knows this tricky stakeholder group to represent the views of that group.

TIP

Get together a small team of probably very senior people who'll do some work on the Vision. When they understand that the Vision is, in terms of process, the document from which the rest of the plans are created and the cultural rallying point for the programme, you usually find that they get pretty interested in the Vision. No, they get *very* interested in the Vision. No, strike that: they get absolutely obsessive about the Vision.

Don't worry if your little working group spends hours trying to get the wording of the Vision absolutely right: that's a great thing. It means that they're engaged and that your stakeholder engagement with them is working! The one thing you have to guard against is the Vision becoming a camel: in other words, a clumsy compromise. A camel is a horse designed by a committee, remember?

The Vision needs an inner voice and passion about it to make it compelling. If the Senior Responsible Owner takes hold of the Vision and expresses it in his own words, that's great. It means that when he stands up to champion the programme, he can read the Vision and speak from the heart.

As you go through Defining a Programme and more detail is put onto the programme, expect to have to go back to your Vision working group several times. However, by the end of Defining a Programme, you should have a very stable Vision.

TIP

All you need now is to give the Vision to the PR people and get them to put together the mugs, mouse mats, T-shirts and biscuits. No, I'm not joking (well, only partly). The Vision is a marketing tool, and you want to see it on as much merchandise as possible.

Managing the tranches

REMEMBER

Throughout the rest of the programme, look back at the Vision at each tranche boundary to check that it hasn't altered. If it has changed, you have a big problem and should think seriously about terminating the programme. The Vision is that important.

I look at tranche boundaries in Chapters 10 and 18.

Allocating Responsibilities to Your Vision

In this section I describe what each of the members of the programme management team may do to contribute to the Vision or how they may use it. To discover more about each of these roles, have a look in Chapter 9.

Taking overall responsibility: Senior Responsible Owner

The Senior Responsible Owner is the senior individual who's accountable for the success of the programme: the head honcho, the big Kahuna. This person is responsible for the following:

- Engaging the Sponsoring Group in the development of the Vision.
- Producing the Vision Statement.
- Gaining the endorsement of the Sponsoring Group and senior support and commitment for the Vision.
- Ensuring that the organization is capable of achieving the transformation described.
- Maintaining focus on the Vision Statement.
- Authorising any changes of formal interpretations to the Vision Statement.

Running day-to-day: Programme Manager

The Programme Manager operates the programme on a daily basis and is responsible for:

- Developing programme documentation aligned to the Vision Statement.
- Ensuring that the Vision Statement underpins the Programme Communications Plan.
- Co-ordinating the development of the Blueprint based on the Vision Statement.
- Designing the delivery of capability to align with the Vision Statement commitments.
- Processing any changes or updates to the Vision Statement.

Implementing in the business: Business Change Manager

Business Change Managers bed down the changes in their particular part of the business. They're responsible for:

- Supporting the Senior Responsible Owner in the development of the content relating to the business areas to be changed and contributing to the content of the Vision Statement.
- Interpreting the Vision Statement in the context of their business operations.
- Assessing the impact of the Vision Statement on business operations.
- Communicating the Vision Statement to their particular areas of the business.
- Delivering the operational changes needed to achieve the desired end goal.

Administering: Programme Office

The Programme Office looks after the administration of the programme and is responsible for the *configuration management* of the Vision Statement. (I explain configuration management in Chapter 12. For now, think of it as being good version control.)

Chapter 6

Building Up a Blueprint

In This Chapter

- Linking your Blueprint to your Vision
- Establishing your Blueprint
- Evolving your Blueprint
- Getting the right people involved in your Blueprint

Like all *For Dummies* books, I design this one for you to dip into and out of at your leisure. Having said that, however, people tend to create programmes in a particular order: when you come to produce your Blueprint you're likely to have received the sign-off from the Sponsoring Group at the end of the Identifying a Programme stage. You also have an outline Vision, which is a pivotal document within your programme as I discuss in Chapter 5.

In this chapter I consider the relationship between the Blueprint and the Vision. The Vision is a high-level picture and therefore needs to be complemented with a more detailed model of the programme's desired future state. This *Blueprint* is a comprehensive document, or set of information, covering the processes, organization, tools (and technologies) and information that exist in the desired future state.

I also talk your through creating your Blueprint, how it needs to develop and the best people to help you with it.

Tying Up Blueprint and Vision

Take a look at Figure 6-1, which is a simple but powerful diagram depicting the relationship between the Blueprint and some of the other key elements within a programme.

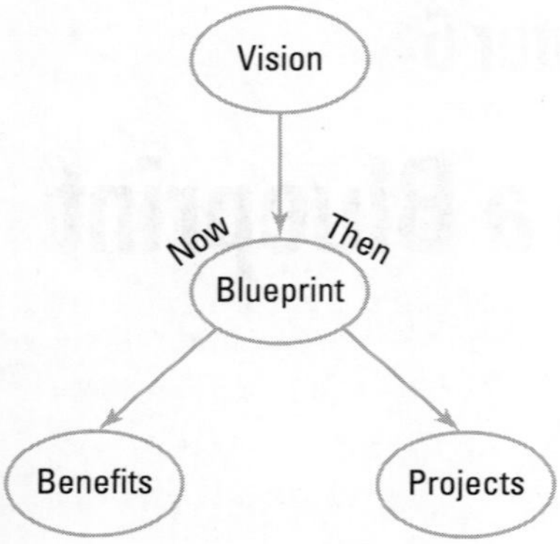

Figure 6-1: Blueprint relationships.

You start with the Vision, which I like to see as your postcard from the future ('the weather's great – glad you're not here, ha ha!'). Using the same analogy, you can consider the Blueprint as a detailed report from the future.

In fact, the Blueprint contains even more than that. It features a 'now' model of the present and a 'then' model of the future. A properly developed Blueprint makes understanding the outcomes easier, which consequently helps you to identify the benefits; the benefits are how you'll measure, or assess the achievement of, those outcomes.

In addition, when the Blueprint contains those outcomes, you can identify which projects you need. The projects lead to the outputs and then the capabilities, and when the capabilities are exploited they become the outcomes.

Spend some time becoming familiar with these links between the key elements in MSP. Getting them clear in your mind is important, as is becoming comfortable with them.

Situating the Blueprint within the programme

The Vision is an early customer-focused description of outcomes, which is at a summary level so that you can retain the interest of all the stakeholders. In contrast, the Blueprint is a detailed description of the changed organization, often called the *to-be* or *future state.*

Formally, the purpose of the Blueprint is to maintain focus on delivering transformation and business change. It elaborates on the Vision of the programme and can also be known as the *target operating model.*

Therefore, the Blueprint is the destination. The Project Dossier and the Programme Plan describe your journey – how to get to that future state.

Entering the programme environment

In Chapter 2, I include a model of what I call the Ferguson Factory. Well, Figure 6-2 shows an expansion of that factory. Before reading on, work through the diagram and see how many symbols you recognise.

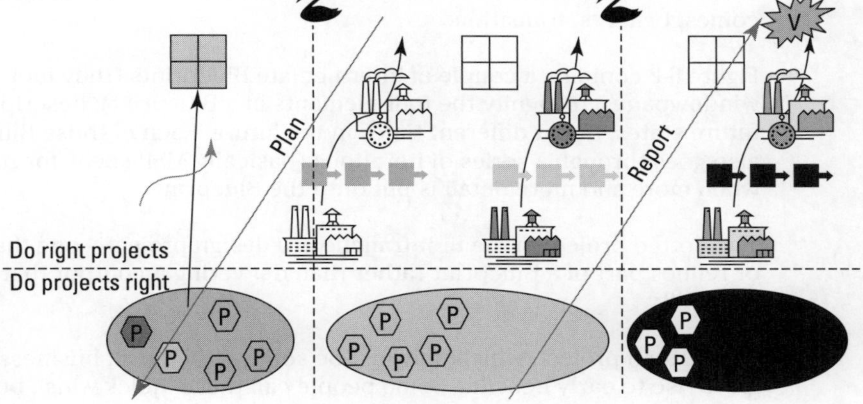

Figure 6-2: Programme environment.

My intention in this section is to describe a more complex, volatile and unpredictable programme environment, which is the reality in most, if not all, the programmes on which I've worked. In such circumstances, you need a Blueprint even more to allow you to focus on the destination.

REMEMBER

As the programme changes course at tranche boundaries, you may well require intermediate Blueprints that describe the point where your programme can consolidate and draw breath, before continuing on its long and winding road.

Vision becomes Blueprint

A transformational change programme needs a Vision that can be expanded into a Blueprint. Both of those items describe business as usual – the area above the horizontal dashed line in Figure 6-2. The area below the line is the project environment.

Tranches and transition

Each oval indicates a *tranche* (a set of projects that provides a change in capability) with, not surprisingly, a number of projects in it. I show three tranches. The left hand tranche in Figure 6-2 delivers some outputs that are seen in business as usual to be a capability. When the capability has been exploited it becomes an outcome – the effect of change. You use benefits management to monitor achievement of those outcomes.

The three linked horizontal arrows represent the transition activities (pre-transition, transition and post-transition) that need to take place in business as usual in order to exploit capabilities properly. Transition occurs in each tranche. So the sequence in subsequent tranches is again: capabilities, outcomes, benefits, transition.

Figure 6-2 contains a couple of intermediate Blueprints (they look a bit like windowpanes, to signify the four elements in a Blueprint): descriptions of future states, but at different times in the future. Each of those Blueprints also goes through a series of iterations (basically MSP-speak for revisions), when more and more detail is put onto the Blueprint.

The dotted project in the first tranche is a design project – one that creates or refines part of a Blueprint rather than delivering an output that is part of a capability.

The striped project, which may just be some activities in business as usual, gives rise to early benefits. Some people call these 'quick wins', but often this term is misused. Early benefits excite stakeholders and early outputs on their own are insufficient. I like the term quick wins, but you have to be careful to stop people claiming quick wins when they haven't actually delivered any benefits.

MSP SPEAK

The straight vertical lines in Figure 6-2 are the tranche boundaries. The black swans at the top of each boundary symbolise unforeseen consequences. A *black swan* is something out of the ordinary, an event with the following attributes:

- An outlier (meaning it's outside the expected range)
- A rarity outside your regular expectations, because nothing in the past has suggested to you that it would happen
- An extreme impact

Yet in spite of its outlier status, when you think about the black swan after the event, it's explainable and has retrospective predictability.

(The term *black swan* comes from the excellent book of the same name by Nassim Nicholas Taleb, *The Black Swan*. It refers to the fact that before Europeans went to Australia, they thought that all swans were white. In Australia they discovered that some swans were black.)

Black swans are relevant in a programme, because you may think of a tranche boundary as being a planned, predictable event in the future. Sometimes a tranche boundary is just that, but quite often in a programme a tranche boundary is triggered by a black swan – an extreme and unpredictable event that was inevitable with hindsight.

I expand on planning tranches in Chapter 10 and managing planned and unplanned tranches boundaries in Chapter 18.

The relevance of tranches, when looking at the Blueprint, is that you may well need an intermediate Blueprint for the end of each tranche.

Right projects (done) right

As you move down the diagonal plan line, you want to do the right projects as well as do projects right. Doing projects right is project management, while doing the right projects is part of planning within the programme environment. So when you do your planning you want to make sure that you place sufficient emphasis on doing the right projects, and then some emphasis on doing projects right.

The same balance is relevant when reporting on the programme (see the upwards diagonal line). Of course you need to report that you're doing projects right (you need project reporting), but you must also have programme reporting to continue to confirm that you're doing the right projects. This means linking your achievement of outputs from projects back to benefits, outcomes and ultimately to the Blueprint.

Take look at Chapter 10 for loads more on planning and control.

Connecting the Blueprint and other themes

Figure 6-3 shows the broader set of relationships between the Blueprint and the other themes in MSP. The diagram is self-explanatory, but just to illustrate how it works, you can see that the Blueprint informs the Business Case and the Business Case justifies the Blueprint.

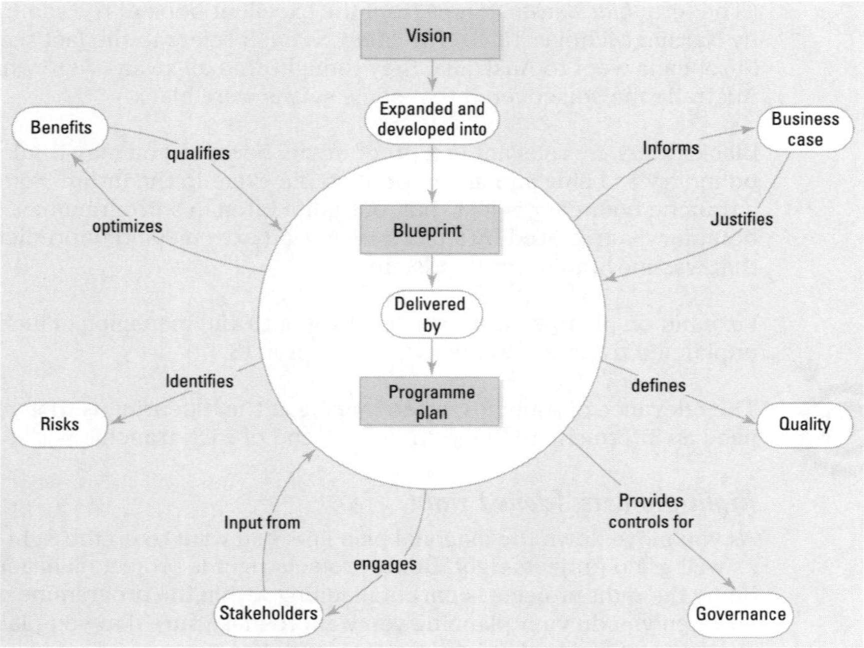

Figure 6-3: Blueprint and other themes.

Building a Blueprint

In this section, I describe the steps you need to take as you and your team build a Blueprint. I begin with a basic description of a Blueprint, which I illustrate in Figure 6-4, so you can see what you're aiming to create.

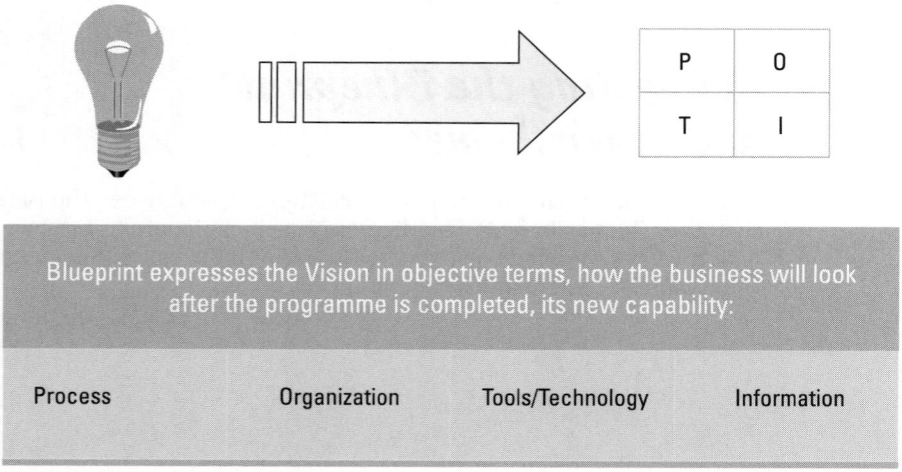

Figure 6-4: Basic Blueprint.

Defining a Blueprint

In essence, a Blueprint is a model of an organization. MSP recommends breaking a Blueprint into four parts – processes, organization, tools (and techniques) and information (or POTI, which is best not pronounced 'potty'!). If the relevant experts in your programme want to break the Blueprint down in a different way, however, that's absolutely fine too – whatever works for you.

A Blueprint is quantitative not qualitative – it contains numbers. You need to quantify the Blueprint by adding performance metrics to each of the sections. So, for example, in the organization section say exactly how many staff are at each grade, or in the tools section say how many giant dumper trucks the mine needs. Initially, these values are indicative, but with each refinement (each *iteration*) they need to become more precise.

For example, in the first iteration of the Blueprint you may decide that you need about 4,000 staff. In iteration 2, you refine that figure to 4,215. In iteration 3, you work out that 1,484 are Grade 1, 233 are Grade 2 and so on.

When you look at the Tranche 1 Blueprint, you decide to put in place 742 Grade 1 and 195 Grade 2 staff in that tranche. Tranche 2 may be 355 Grade 1 and 46 Grade 2 staff. When you review the final figures during Tranche 2, the total may change to 3,958 staff.

Don't check my figures too closely! I just want to illustrate that the numbers become more detailed as time goes on, but also vary as you learn more about the future state.

You iterate around all the different versions of the Blueprint to bring them into line.

Minding the gap: Current and future states

As you put more detail on your Blueprint, you'll find a whole series of gaps between what you have in the current state and what you need in the future state. Identifying how to practically fill each of those gaps gives you a really good indication of what each of your tranches should be. These gaps are illustrated in Figure 6-5.

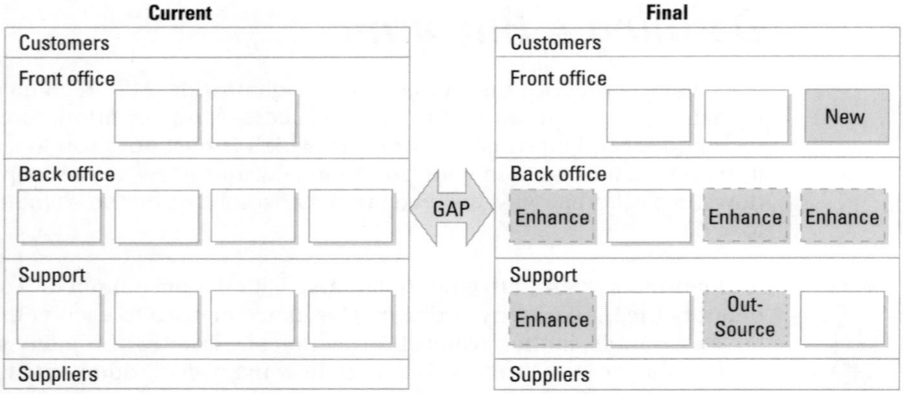

Figure 6-5: Initial analysis of the gap.

1. **Carry out sufficient analysis so that you understand the current (or 'as is') state.**
2. **Model the future or ('to be') state.**
3. **Perform a gap analysis, comparing the current and future states in order to understand that gap.**
4. **Plan and manage the journey from one state to the next.**

Wherever you discover a gap in outcomes, fill it with capabilities. Aiming to provide those capabilities triggers you to plan the projects that deliver outputs to fill the capability gaps.

TIP

You only need to understand the current state in enough detail to inform the journey. Don't fall into the trap of becoming paralysed, analysing an illogical and ever-changing current state. Also remember that the more radical the transformation, the less the current state can inform the nature of the future state.

Defining tranches

After you carry out the gap analysis in the preceding section and start to put together a Project Dossier, you can start to define your tranches. I give a brief description here but discuss tranches in more detail in Chapter 10.

MSP SPEAK

A *tranche* is:

- A step change in organizational capability. In other words, it's a major change in what the organization looks like, not something trivial.
- A distinct set of benefits

If tranche boundaries run across the full programme, you can carry out a strategic review to:

- Assess achievements to date
- Confirm necessary realignment of the programme

Therefore, projects are likely to run across tranche boundaries.

Creating the Blueprint for an Emergent Programme

The situation is slightly different for an Emergent Programme (which I introduce in Chapter 2). An *Emergent Programme* comes into being when the organization recognises that a number of existing projects are interrelated and would be better run as a programme.

In these circumstances the steps for creating the initial Blueprint are as follows:

1. **Analyse existing projects:**
    - Identify products and dependencies.
    - Step back to the underlying concept.
    - Create the inherent design.
2. **Merge project designs into the Blueprint.**
3. **Check whether the future state remains cohesive.**

These steps sound logical, if quite brief. In reality, however, you're likely to face a lot of politics and power plays as the sponsors of the individual projects become aligned with the reality of the Emergent Programme. You may need to use a great deal of tact as you pull together an Emergent Programme. Creating a Blueprint is one of the tools you can use to demonstrate how well, or how badly, the candidate projects fit together.

Helping Your Blueprint to Evolve

The initial Blueprint you create isn't the first version. You go through several iterations of the Blueprint during the Defining a Programme process (which I cover in Chapter 7).

In this section, I provide some checklists concerning what to consider as you create the later versions of the Blueprint in the Defining a Programme process or when updating the Blueprint later on in the programme.

Analysing your options

Each time you put more detail in the Blueprint, you may need to look at the options, perhaps adjusting the scheduling and scope to cater for the following:

- Balance in the Business Case
- Benefits
- Capability to manage work
- Need for funding
- Project and programme management capability
- Risks

Adopting existing projects

Even if your programme isn't classified officially as being an Emergent Programme (see the earlier section 'Creating the Blueprint for an Emergent Programme'), from time to time you may want to consider adopting existing projects. Here are some factors to consider:

- Proximity to delivery?
    - Perhaps adopt a project near to completion.
- Strategic fit?
    - Perhaps adopt projects that align with the Blueprint.
- Re-usability of delivered outputs?
    - Perhaps adopt parts of projects that can deliver outputs you want to re-use.

Setting up pilots

With this heading, I don't mean framing aviators for a crime they didn't commit (groan at the poor pun!). I mean that when you're running a large programme, you're unlikely to be able to go from the current 'as is' state straight to a final design for the 'to be' state. You may have to set up some pilot schemes to test which new business models are feasible:

- Pilot different delivery options
  - As early as possible
  - As cheaply as possible
- Have a plan for closing pilots when their feasibility is demonstrated

Refining your Blueprint

You revisit the Blueprint frequently and are certain to carry out fairly formal updating of the Blueprint at each tranche boundary (Chapter 18 describes this process). But you also need to update the Blueprint regularly and frequently in the middle of tranches. Here are a few items to consider:

- Revisit:
  - Definition
  - Scope
  - Delivery status
  - Expected benefits
- Carry out:
  - At tranche boundary
  - When a major change is proposed
- Before transition:
  - Check capability is ready for delivery
- After transition, test whether the capability:
  - Led to improvements
  - Resulted in benefits

Figure 6-6 shows you how you may end up with two intermediate Blueprints and the final Blueprint. The diagram shows how different pieces of work contribute to capabilities that can be exploited into outputs.

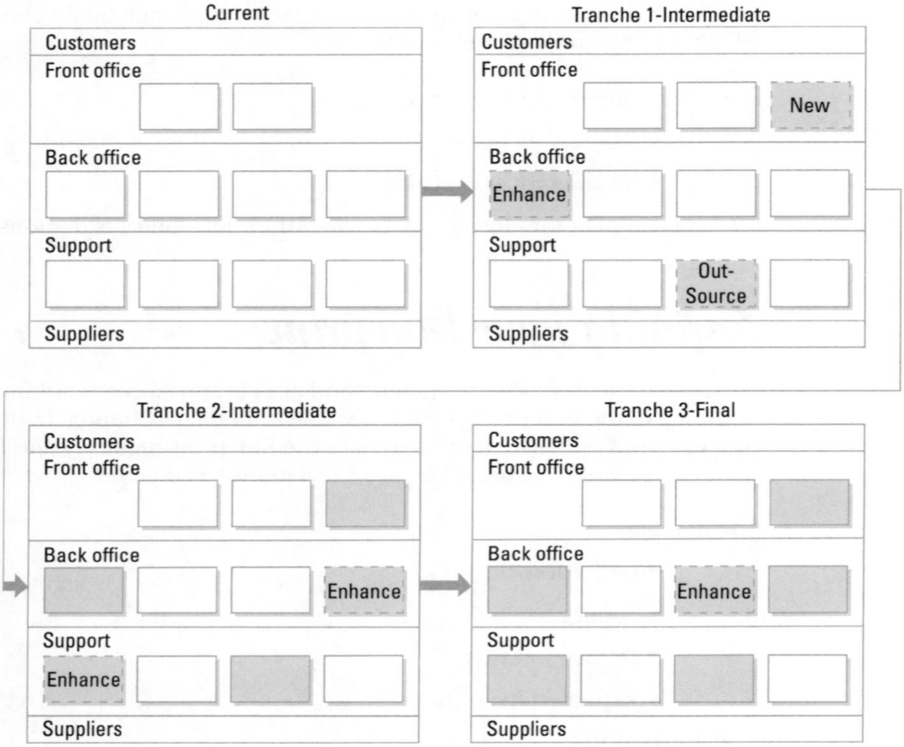

Figure 6-6: Multi-tranche Blueprints.

Knowing Who's Involved in the Blueprint: The Design Authority

Although the Programme Manager may do most of the work in designing the Blueprint in a very small programme, in a programme of any size you form a group to design the Blueprint initially.

A good name for this group is the *Design Authority.* Typically it includes subject-matter experts from each of the relevant functional specializations such as IT, HR and finance. You also want people with expertise in designing things like organizational structures, IT systems or process modelling.

Initially this group may create a strategic architecture covering each of the areas of the Blueprint and add sufficient detail to define performance levels. As the programme proceeds that role can change. The group may become the Business Design Authority, which provides assurance that the integrity of the Blueprint is being maintained as projects come up with local designs for outputs. Figure 6-7 illustrates maintaining Blueprint integrity. I talk about this more in Chapter 13.

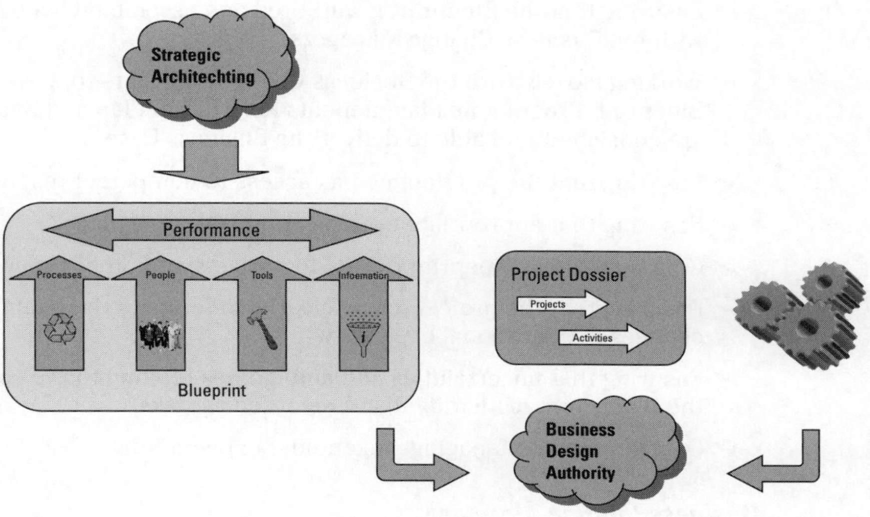

Figure 6-7: Blueprint integrity: making sure that the projects you're producing fit the Blueprint.

Reeling off the Blueprint responsibilities

Here's a list of how each member of the programme management team may contribute to or use the Blueprint. You can find more on roles in Chapter 9.

Senior Responsible Owner

The SRO is that very senior individual who's accountable for the success of the programme and is responsible for:

- Providing strategic direction for the Blueprint design.
- Ensuring Sponsoring Group authorization and commitment to the 'to-be' state, demonstrated through active co-operation; for example, making appropriate resource available to assist with design.
- Ensuring that the Blueprint remains aligned with the strategic direction of the organization and promotes a coherent capability.
- Providing the link to the Sponsoring Group and other key stakeholders, maintaining their commitment.
- Providing advice and direction to the Programme Manager and Business Change Managers.
- Ensuring that the Programme Board assesses and understands the implications of the Blueprint and its delivery.

Programme Manager

The Programme Manager runs the programme day-to-day and is responsible for:

- Ensuring that the Blueprint is authored and assembled in collaboration with the Business Change Managers.
- Working closely with the Business Change Managers to ensure that the Blueprint, Programme Plan, Benefits Realization Plan and Benefit Profiles are consistent and able to deliver the Business Case.
- Ensuring that the programme has access to competent resources.
- Ensuring that appropriate options appraisals take place.
- Communicating Blueprint details to projects and other programmes.
- Ensuring that the project teams clearly understand the planned step changes in operational capability.
- Ensuring that uncertainties and ambiguities relating to the content of the Blueprint are identified and recorded as risks.
- Contributing to managing stakeholder expectations.

Business Change Manager

Each Business Change Manager beds down the changes in her part of the business and is responsible for:

- Leading the development of the content and taking responsibility for the delivery of the design into business operations.
- Consulting with and gaining support from senior business managers for the 'to-be' state.
- Ensuring that the planned step changes in operational capability are clearly understood by the operational areas.
- Providing and co-ordinating essential input to the Blueprint with the assistance of experienced operational staff and specialists, and (where appropriate) authoring parts of the Blueprint.
- Ensuring that 'as-is' and 'to-be' information from the Blueprint is used to construct the Benefits Profiles.
- Aligning the creation of the capability within the Blueprint with benefits realization through approval of project outputs.
- Ensuring that operational changes during the life of the programme are being reflected in the evolving 'as-is' state in the Blueprint.

TRUE STORY

Grinding out a Blueprint

I'm involved in a programme with a value of less than £150,000, involving a disused windmill near where I live. A few years ago I became a trustee of the charity hoping to refurbish the mill. On that occasion we were overly ambitious and unable to secure funding.

When the committee reformed to have another go, I decided to be more assertive this time. At the first committee meeting I listened with growing impatience to colleagues discussing everything from the detail of window hinges to running a fully functional windmill. A windmill is more than a building (it's a piece of society), and I felt we were talking about a small transformational change programme. It was more than just a project to restore an old building; we were going to set up a facility that would be used by our village community.

The problem was that we didn't have a Vision. As I steered the conversation towards creating one, we realized that we had a diverse range of Visions. Our secretary was wonderful. She encapsulated the essence of the discussion, summarised the Visions and recorded our agreement that we were initially going for a more modest Vision.

I volunteered to help write a new funding bid and set to work with a few colleagues. Some were experienced project managers, but although we were able to describe the project, we hadn't fleshed out the detail of how we'd operate after the end of the project.

In other words, we had no Blueprint. But I'm not one for 'milling' around expecting a Blueprint to just blow in on the wind, and instead I set about grinding one out (any more groan-worthy windmill puns gratefully received).

At a fairly noisy sub-committee, I got agreement to put the Blueprint on the next full committee meeting agenda. Frankly my colleagues didn't really get what I was aiming for and I was given just 20 minutes to forge a Blueprint. So at the next committee meeting I again pushed my colleagues to get their help in creating this alien document. We agreed a Blueprint and it was enormously useful in helping us draft a coherent funding bid.

I was really pleased to read in a local paper an interview with our chairman. He was describing a better future: our Vision and Blueprint. I thought it read well – realistic but compelling. He even made a point of emphasising that we weren't going for some of the more ambitions Visions that had been bandied about at that first committee meeting.

We received the funding and the windmill has been rebuilt. But more than that, it's now open three days a week with a regular series of events, and people from the local community are coming along to visit.

Programme Office

The Programme Office looks after the administration of the programme and is responsible for:

- Providing or locating information and resources that can assist with the design of the Blueprint.
- Facilitating impact assessments of changes on the Blueprint.

- Maintaining configuration control of the Blueprint. That means keeping track of the versions and how they fit together.

Considering Blueprint responsibilities: A real-life example

Here's an anecdote from my own experience that shows the importance of a Design Authority in connection with Blueprints. I hope that it helps you to see how you can use the Blueprint to bring together the different players in the programme.

I was auditing a programme that had just started and was advising on how to set up the Programme Office. I'd already found evidence of a lack of co-ordination between different parts of the business (*silos*) when maintaining the Blueprint. This problem was caused by:

- Lack of explicit recognition of the need for Blueprint design and delivery
- Silo-based groups of projects
- Incompatible planning horizons for the different functions – some people were planning for the short-term; others were planning three years ahead.

As a result, the technology partner had very long lead times for ordering niche technology equipment while the creative business units were focused only on artistic output for the next season.

I was unsuccessful in making the intellectual argument for Blueprint management with the Programme Director who came from the creative, front-line part of the business. She saw it as a bureaucratic overhead. However, I did uncover a bottom-up eagerness to resolve Blueprint alignment issues.

So I asked a colleague to chair a series of informal meetings across silos. Over time these meetings became the Blueprint Design Authority. This person also looked after information management and as a result he was able to put in place a Blueprint, which had several interesting characteristics:

Testing your Blueprint knowledge

Try creating a Blueprint for your programme or a programme you know. To help, here are some tips on how to go about it:

- Break the Blueprint into four areas: process, organization, tools (and technologies), and information.
- Quantify each of these elements – put in some numbers.
- Don't try and describe everything in great detail all at once. Instead, create a hierarchical Blueprint. Each level you go down ideally contains about three times as much detail as the level above. Start at the top level of the Blueprint because that's the simplest and quickest approach.

  Above that top level create a single integrated model of outcomes (what you want to exist in the future state).
- Describe current *and* future states if you want, but you may find that just describing the future states is simpler.
- Don't create a plan – you're describing the destination, not the journey.

Good luck on creating your Blueprint in as much or as little detail as you want.

- The Blueprint was strictly hierarchical. Some silos were producing information at a lower level of detail than others. Adopting a hierarchical structure allowed us to make sense of these different levels of detail.
- The programme wasn't tightly controlled and we didn't have the power or the resources to take design functions from silos into the Programme Office. Therefore the Blueprint simply contained hyperlinks (links to where the information was really stored, like you find on a webpage, rather than a copy of the information) to the relevant information still being maintained within the silo-based work streams. The role of the Design Authority was to co-ordinate. This arrangement proved very successful.

For another illustrative example, read the nearby sidebar 'Grinding out a Blueprint'.

Chapter 7

Details, Details: Honing Your Programme

In This Chapter

- Understanding the aims of Defining a Programme
- Following the process
- Linking benefits and projects
- Planning your programme

This chapter covers the second process within the MSP transformational flow, Defining a Programme, which follows on from Chapter 3's Identifying a Programme. The Defining a Programme process is, broadly speaking, where you carry out the detailed work to plan the programme. I lead you step-by-step through deciding the programme's aims, understanding its various processes and planning it.

More is involved than simply planning an initiative. After all, the programme is going to involve a transformational change in the way your organization runs, so the programme itself may well need altered governance structures, a subject I also discuss in this chapter.

Figure 7-1 shows a process model. At first sight the diagram is a bit daunting. Don't worry about the activities or roles; I cover them all as you work through this chapter. The inputs are straightforward as well: they're just what comes out of Identifying a Programme. The controls are simply about getting approval for your programme. Finally I explain the outputs later in the chapter when I look at programme information.

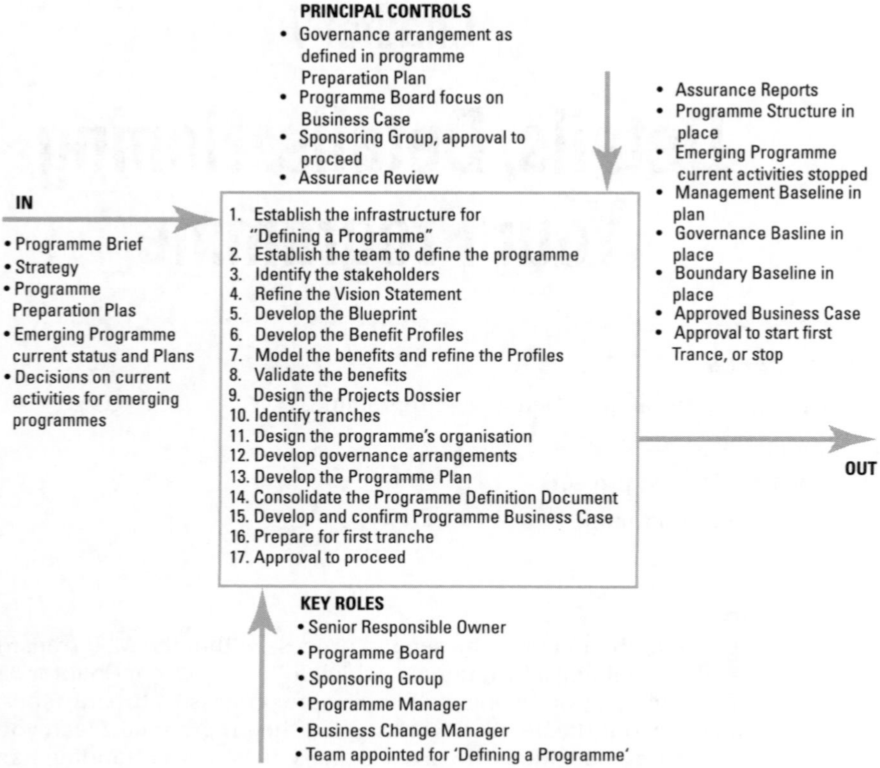
PRINCIPAL CONTROLS
• Governance arrangement as defined in programme Preparation Plan
• Programme Board focus on Business Case
• Sponsoring Group, approval to proceed
• Assurance Review
IN
• Programme Brief
• Strategy
• Programme Preparation Plas
• Emerging Programme current status and Plans
• Decisions on current activities for emerging programmes
1. Establish the infrastructure for "Defining a Programme"
2. Establish the team to define the programme
3. Identify the stakeholders
4. Refine the Vision Statement
5. Develop the Blueprint
6. Develop the Benefit Profiles
7. Model the benefits and refine the Profiles
8. Validate the benefits
9. Design the Projects Dossier
10. Identify tranches
11. Design the programme's organisation
12. Develop governance arrangements
13. Develop the Programme Plan
14. Consolidate the Programme Definition Document
15. Develop and confirm Programme Business Case
16. Prepare for first tranche
17. Approval to proceed
• Assurance Reports
• Programme Structure in place
• Emerging Programme current activities stopped
• Management Baseline in plan
• Governance Basline in place
• Boundary Baseline in place
• Approved Business Case
• Approval to start first Trance, or stop
OUT
KEY ROLES
• Senior Responsible Owner
• Programme Board
• Sponsoring Group
• Programme Manager
• Business Change Manager
• Team appointed for 'Defining a Programme'

Figure 7-1: Defining a Programme

Understanding Your Goals when Defining a Programme

At the end of the Identifying a Programme process, the Sponsoring Group has approved the Programme Brief and the Programme Preparation Plan (I explain that process in Chapter 3). The next step in the transformational flow is Defining the Programme.

Considering the purpose of Defining a Programme

The *Defining a Programme* process aims to:

- Provide the basis for deciding whether to proceed or not
- Explain the following:
    - What the programme is going to do
    - How it's going to do it
    - Who's involved
    - How it's going to be controlled
    - Why going ahead is justified

Using the Programme Definition Document

In order to justify the programme, you're going to consider the inevitable trade-off between resources, costs, quality, timings and benefits. Look at Figure 7-2 for a representation. You then present that balance to the Sponsoring Group and it represents the Group's contract with the Senior Responsible Owner (SRO; I cover these roles and others in Chapter 9).

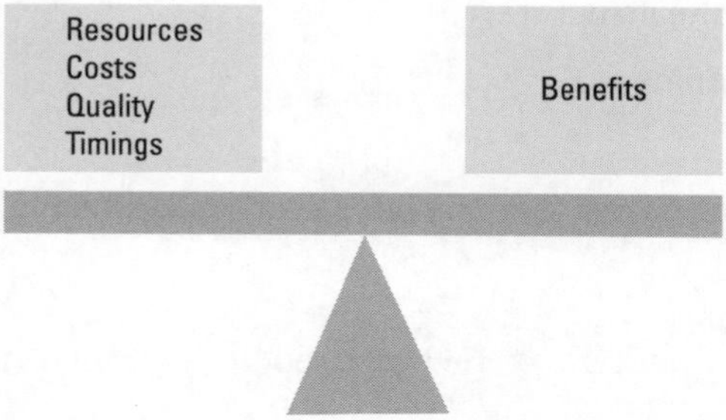

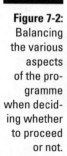

Figure 7-2: Balancing the various aspects of the programme when deciding whether to proceed or not.

The document that summarises the programme so that the Sponsoring Group can give a formal go-ahead is called the *Programme Definition Document*. This document involves more than a Business Case, which only shows that the programme is justified. The Programme Definition Document is more comprehensive, but still summarised, and also explains how the programme is to be executed.

Some organizations require a great deal of information to be presented to senior managers whereas others are happy with a summary. While some organizations put this information out for independent review and analysis, in others the senior managers want to look at it themselves.

MSP SPEAK

If your organization's culture does want to see such a summary document, MSP defines it for you. The Programme Definition Document consolidates or summarises the information used to define a programme. The sequence of information shown below usually goes down pretty well with the Sponsoring Group, but it's not set in stone; feel free to alter this composition or sequence depending on how the definition of your programme goes:

- Objectives for the programme
- Executive summary
- Justification and context for the programme
- Criteria against which it can be measured
- Vision Statement
- Blueprint summary
- Programme roles and responsibilities
- Governance principles that have been applied
- Summary of the current state
- Explanation of tranche structure
- Description of outcomes
- Summary of risks
- Summary of Project Dossier (see the later section 'Designing the Project Dossier')
- Stakeholder summary
- Benefits Map
- Timescales, milestones and tranches
- Information baselines, status and content

Phew, that's quite a list! All these items seem relevant, but with so many topics to cover I'm often asked: 'How on earth do we pull all this information together in a logical and structured way?'

The answer is that others and I have done this process before, and we've worked out a sequence that works pretty well: it's the activities in Defining a Programme. Of course you need to move backwards and forwards in sequence as you gather more information, but you can take my word that this sequence works.

I'm in preparation for running a couple of workshops for the senior management team of a company that's being spun off from a larger parent. The managers recognise that setting up their new company is a programme. I'm going to work through the activities in Defining a Programme with them.

When I briefed them on what I was going to do, and the sequence, they could see the underlying logic and were pretty impressed that I managed to come up with such a brilliant agenda. I didn't tell them that I'd worked it out by writing *MSP For Dummies*!

When you're defining your programme, use the sequence in the process model: it's a great starter for ten, but feel free to repeat the process, or *iterate* in MSP speak, if you feel you've learnt something new and need to modify some of your earlier models.

Gathering together programme documents and information

In this section, I lay out the full range of documents and information that you may gather as you run a programme. Understanding these documents and their interrelationships is useful *before* you embark on the sequence of steps or activities in Defining a Programme.

Take a look at Figure 7-3, which shows how all the documents that you use to manage the programme fit together. It's a complex but powerful illustration of your documentation and is worth becoming familiar with.

You can see that I split the diagram between Identifying a Programme (at the top) and Defining a Programme.

In the identification process, you look at the business strategy that leads to the Programme Mandate. You evolve the Mandate into a Brief in Identifying a Programme (as I cover in Chapter 3).

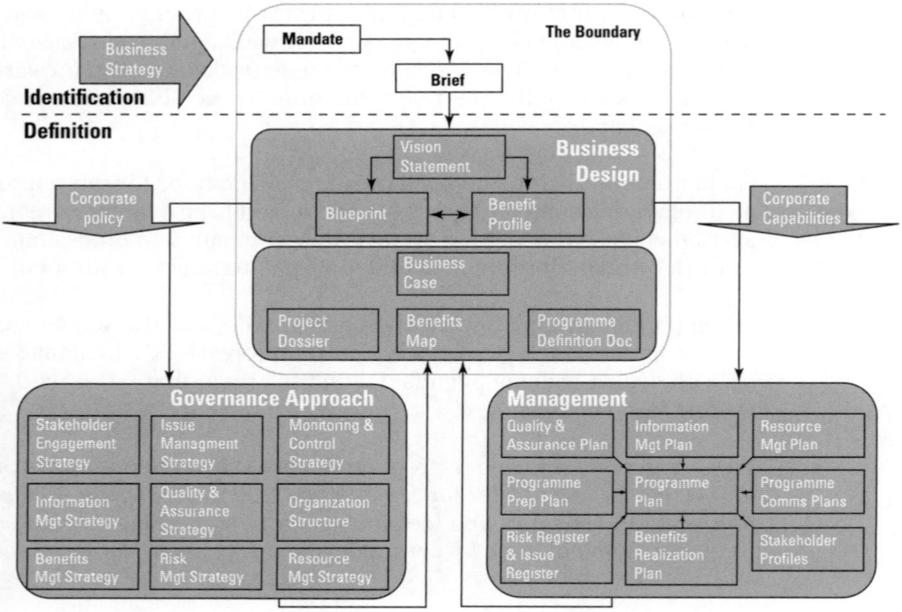

Figure 7-3: Information grouping: Documents used to manage the programme.

The programme is executed against a backdrop of corporate policies and corporate capabilities. In Defining a Programme, I break the documentation into three areas:

- **Business design:** What the business will look like in the future. The documents in this section include the:
  - Vision Statement.
  - Blueprint.
  - Benefit Profiles. These are key documents. The rest of the detail about the programme may be very fluid, but the Benefit Profiles – the benefits you'll achieve over time – need to be pretty static.

  The MSP boundary (the extent of the programme) goes a little further than just the business design to include:
  - The Mandate and the Brief.
  - A few composite documents such as the Business Case, Project Dossier, Benefits Map (a summary of the benefits) and Programme Definition Document.

- **Governance area:** Where you keep the strategies. Looking at the issue simplistically, you have one strategy for each governance theme. Although things aren't quite as straightforward as that, it's a good way of approaching this topic. The strategies are:
  - Stakeholder Engagement Strategy
  - Issue Management Strategy
  - Monitoring and Control Strategy
  - Information Management Strategy
  - Quality and Assurance Strategy
  - Organization Structure (for the programme, not the 'to be' state)
  - Benefits Management Strategy
  - Risk Management Strategy
  - Resource Management Strategy

  Just remember that sometimes one theme has two strategies, such as a risk strategy and an issue strategy, and sometimes a theme doesn't have a strategy: the vision theme for example.
- **Management area**: Every strategy has a plan. So you have:
  - Quality and Assurance Plan
  - Information Management Plan
  - Resource Management Plan
  - Programme Preparation Plan
  - Programme Communications Plan
  - Risk Register (in this case you've moved from a plan to a register). A Register is just the document where you record some information and keep it up-to-date. Your Risk Register is probably a spread sheet telling you a little bit about each of your current risks and what you're doing about them.
  - Issue Register (another register)
  - Benefits Realization Plan
  - Stakeholder Profiles (okay, these aren't called plans, but they're still details about stakeholders)

  All these items come together and feed into the Programme Plan.

Investigating the infrastructure for Defining a Programme

I cover the step-by-step activities to create the initial versions of these documents during Defining a Programme in the later section 'Carrying Out the Defining a Programme Sequence'. Here I look at setting up the process (to discover wrapping it up, check out the later section 'Getting approval to proceed').

Generally, Defining a (major) Programme may take half a dozen people six months. You'll find that you can survive hand-to-mouth during this period, begging, borrowing and stealing resources in order to complete programme definition.

But the most efficient approach is to seek agreement when drafting the Programme Definition Plan to get resources such as:

- Computers and other office equipment
- Configuration management
- Definition team
- Offices
- Software

The importance of infrastructure

I set up a reasonably small programme to put in place a document management system for a newly formed organization. I was successful in getting my team, but I had huge problems with the IT infrastructure.

Nine different organizations had come together, and as a result we had no core IT infrastructure. Consequently, new members of the team came with access rights to their existing IT infrastructure. We had extraordinary difficulty putting in place a common area for storing documents, and therefore had problems establishing the rules for configuration management. As we were aiming to put in place a document management system for the whole organization, you can understand how important this was.

We wanted to demonstrate the feasibility of the 'to be' state in our own working practices (I discuss the 'to be' state in Chapter 6). We wanted to demonstrate to people what the new world would look like.

If I'd taken the trouble early on of discussing the importance of a common filing area with the IT people, I would have saved us a lot of trouble and been able to show a better example to business as usual of how good document management can work.

The next time I set up programme, I got my Information Management Strategy agreed early on. That's what I recommend you do. I discuss information management in Chapter 13.

For an insight into the importance of getting a programme's infrastructure sorted, read the nearby sidebar 'The importance of infrastructure'.

Knowing who does what

When describing each of the activities in Defining a Programme, I refer frequently to 'you', the reader. But when you start to form a small team, you need to know who does which activities and takes which responsibilities. Here's a brief introduction (I describe these roles in more detail in Chapter 9):

- The SRO is accountable for everything.
- The Programme Manager is responsible for everything (with a few exceptions).
- The Business Change Managers are responsible for the benefits-related activities.
- When the Programme Manager is responsible, the Business Change Managers are consulted and vice versa.
- The Programme Office mostly supplies support.

Carrying Out the Defining a Programme Sequence

The heart of Defining a Programme is to amplify the Vision into the Blueprint and then identify the projects needed to provide the capabilities that are missing from the 'to be' state the Blueprint describes. In parallel, you can also work out the benefits associated with the 'to be' state.

You can then balance the programme costs, the majority of which come from the projects, and the benefits in the Business Case.

Identifying the stakeholders

The first step is to do a little more to identify and analyse the programme stakeholders (following on from your initial work with stakeholders when Identifying the Programme in Chapter 3). You need to build on that initial stakeholder engagement work with the programme team to carry out a more rigorous stakeholder analysis. You can find more on stakeholders in Chapter 14.

TIP

This is an *iterative* process. Iteration means that you jump right in and have a quick go at getting an answer that's good enough. After you've done that you'll know more. You may have to do a bit more detailed work – another iteration. Or your initial attempt may be good enough. Do your initial stakeholder analysis with the core programme team. If you identify stakeholder groups with high interest in and influence on the programme, invite them along to carry out further stakeholder analysis with you. Doing so reinforces your communication links with them and shows that you respect their importance.

Refining the Vision Statement

As you go through the Defining a Programme steps, you can expect the Vision to change – not in overall concept, but in the detail.

Therefore, look out for opportunities to:

- Refine the outline Vision Statement contained in the Programme Brief
- Focus on the beneficial future state

Developing the Blueprint

I look at Blueprint design and delivery in detail in Chapter 6. Here, I concentrate on the sequence of actions you may want to take, because my focus in this chapter is the process.

TIP

I recommend building on your Stakeholder information (see the earlier section 'Identifying the stakeholders') to put together a Blueprint workshop. The initial workshop can be quite short. Sometimes a few hours is enough for you to brainstorm the top-level future state Blueprint: processes, organization, tools (technologies if you prefer) and information. You can even simplify things further and produce just an outcomes model at the top level.

If this workshop is a success, attendees are going to be willing to come along to subsequent workshops to put more detail on the Blueprint in parallel with the work you'll be doing on benefits and projects. In this way you develop increasing levels of detail – you iterate.

Modelling the benefits and Benefits Profiles

I tend to find that more senior stakeholders are willing to participate in the Blueprint workshops I describe in the preceding section. On the other hand, slightly more junior stakeholders are likely to come along to the parallel series of workshops on benefits.

In Chapter 15 I look at the modelling techniques you use, but here I'm looking at the sequence. This process involves another series of iterative workshops that put on increasing levels of detail.

TIP

I prefer to plan half-day workshops. Anything longer and attendees have to work too hard.

Here's the sequence:

1. **Create a benefits breakdown structure at the top-level benefits workshop and turn its top level into a Benefits Map.**
2. **Your benefits expert, which may just be you at the moment, needs to review the logic in the benefits model before the next workshop and circulate it to the workshop attendees for approval.**
3. **Conduct a series of benefits modelling workshops going down into increasing levels of detail.**

The benefits breakdown structure helps you to be clear on what these levels of detail are. At each level, you can create a Benefits Map. In a simple programme, you may be able to get away with a single Benefits Map, but in my experience more complex programmes need a series of maps: some at a high level for sharing with more senior stakeholders, others in more detail to get to grips seriously with what's going on.

TIP

During the mapping workshops, take note of who's expressing most interest in each benefit. They're potentially the benefit owners. Your next step is to set up a series of workshops with the owners of each of the high-level benefits to create one Benefit Profile for each benefit at each workshop.

REMEMBER

When validating the benefits:

- Ensure that each benefit represents an aspect of a desired outcome.
- Bear in mind that non-strategic benefits may divert the programme.
- Assess the trade-off between the cost of realizing and measuring the benefit versus the value of having the benefit.

Designing the Project Dossier

The Project Dossier is where you go to find an authoritative list of the current projects in your programme so that, for example, you know what you intend to kick off in the immediate future. The Project Dossier is the next item to create, after modelling the benefits (in the preceding section).

From the Blueprint you can identify capabilities, required in the future state but not present in the current state. You can cross-check that these capabilities are essential if you're to realize particular benefits, identified by stakeholders as being in the Benefits Model.

Capabilities go into a big pot (a metaphorical one of course, otherwise it may get knocked over – think of the mess!). Then you break them down into outputs and put those outputs together again into candidate projects. Next you can run a little gentle scheduling to see whether:

- The timings of the projects are achievable from the project perspective within the constraints of budget, resource risk and so on.
- The capabilities are available in business as usual in time to allow the benefits to be realized quickly enough and also to fit in with any business constraints.

I look at how you plan the Project Dossier in Chapter 10. To round off this activity, however, I run through its purpose and composition.

Purpose of the Project Dossier

The purpose of the Project Dossier is really pretty straightforward: it's a list of projects required to deliver the Blueprint with high-level information and estimates.

Composition of the Project Dossier

Experience shows that recording slightly more than a list of projects in the Project Dossier is useful. Therefore, the composition is as follows:

- List of projects.
- Outputs and resources (at least an outline).
- Timescales and dependencies. Again I'm talking here about critical timescales and dependencies when viewed from the programme level.
- Initial requirements for each project, from the Blueprint.
- High-level budgets.

- Contribution that the projects make to outcomes and benefits – usually some sort of matrix that maps project outputs onto outcomes and then onto benefits.
- Issues and risks, but again high-level programme level issues and risks.

Identifying tranches

Carrying on along the same lines as when grouping outputs into projects (see the preceding section), you next need to group projects into tranches. I cover tranches in much more detail in Chapter 10. The capabilities delivered from early tranches can usefully be pilots that help explore, prove or disprove particular approaches to achieving the Vision.

REMEMBER

A tranche delivers a step change in capability into business as usual.

Deciding on the Programme Organization and Governance

Your programme definition is progressing well when you reach the point where you're:

- Fleshing out the Vision of the end state in the Blueprint.
- Expanding the benefits model into Benefit Profiles
- Putting together the Project Dossier and seeing the tranches emerge

In this section I cover the next few steps of compiling the programme organization and how you plan to run the programme, which means producing the governance strategies that relate to each of the themes.

Designing the programme organization

Figure 7-4 shows an extremely simple model of a programme's organization.

REMEMBER

This highly simplified diagram hides a wide variety of sins. Although I have seen a simple programme for a charity being run by a few part-timers, I've also been involved in programmes with many hundreds of people working in the central programme structure. Take a look at Chapter 9 for more details on the additional posts you may need to start defining.

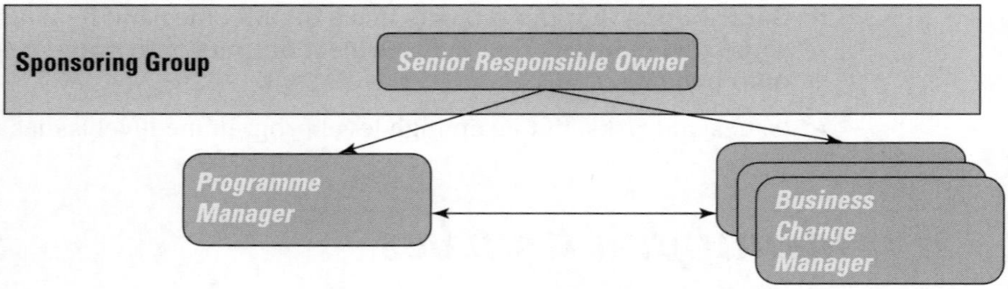

Figure 7-4: The organizational structure of a simple programme.

Developing the Programme Governance

You have to decide how your programme's going to be run in practice – and, indeed, how you're going to explain to people how the programme is to be run.

To do so you document your approach, your strategy, for each of the different aspects of the programme. In order to maintain alignment with existing corporate strategies, you may simply be saying how those strategies are to be applied in the particular circumstances of the programme. But if you're programme is more radical, you need to explain how the approach in the programme differs from the familiar approach in the 'as is' state.

You need to create strategies – that is, explain how you plan to manage each of these aspects of the programme:

- Benefits management
- Information management
- Monitoring and control
- Quality and assurance management
- Resource management
- Risk and issue management
- Stakeholder engagement

REMEMBER

Strategies aren't abstract theoretical documents – though I was once given an assignment to write a set of theoretical strategies for a programme that, not surprisingly, was rapidly abandoned. In a successful programme, you need to document the results of your negotiations with experts in each field on the approach you're adopting; these are your strategies.

I discuss each strategy further in the chapter on the related theme, but as I don't cover the Resource Management Strategy elsewhere, I look at it briefly here.

MSP SPEAK

The *Resource Management Strategy* covers how the programme is to acquire resources. The more you can agree in this document, the less tactical scavenging for resources you'll do later in the programme:

- Assets required
- Cost and expenditure profile
- Dispute resolution
- Funding requirements
- How resourcing is to be achieved
- Human resource management
- Internal/external mix
- Procurement approach
- Resource profile
- Skills and knowledge transfer
- Subject matter experts required
- Technology and services required

Planning, Planning, Planning!

As you near the end of the Defining a Programme process, you need to pull together the various plans for moving on.

Developing the Programme Plan

The Programme Plan is the detailed, central plan that you probably expect to see in a programme.

MSP SPEAK

Here's the purpose and composition of the Programme Plan:

- **Purpose:** Controls and tracks progress and delivery of the programme and the outcomes.
- **Composition:**
  - Programme schedule
  - Dependency network
  - Cross reference to the Risk Register
  - An explanation of project grouping
  - Transition plan

- Monitoring and control activities
- Programme tranches
- Effort and cost
- How the plan is to be deployed

Notice the *transition plan,* which describes how transition is to be carried out in business as usual. Consequently, the Programme Plan covers both the project area and business as usual.

Confirming the Business Case

This section focuses on pulling together the Business Case, which I discuss in more detail in Chapter 8.

You may well find that, on the first pass, the Business Case doesn't quite work and you have to return to the activities I discuss throughout this chapter. Figure 7-5 shows what you may need to do.

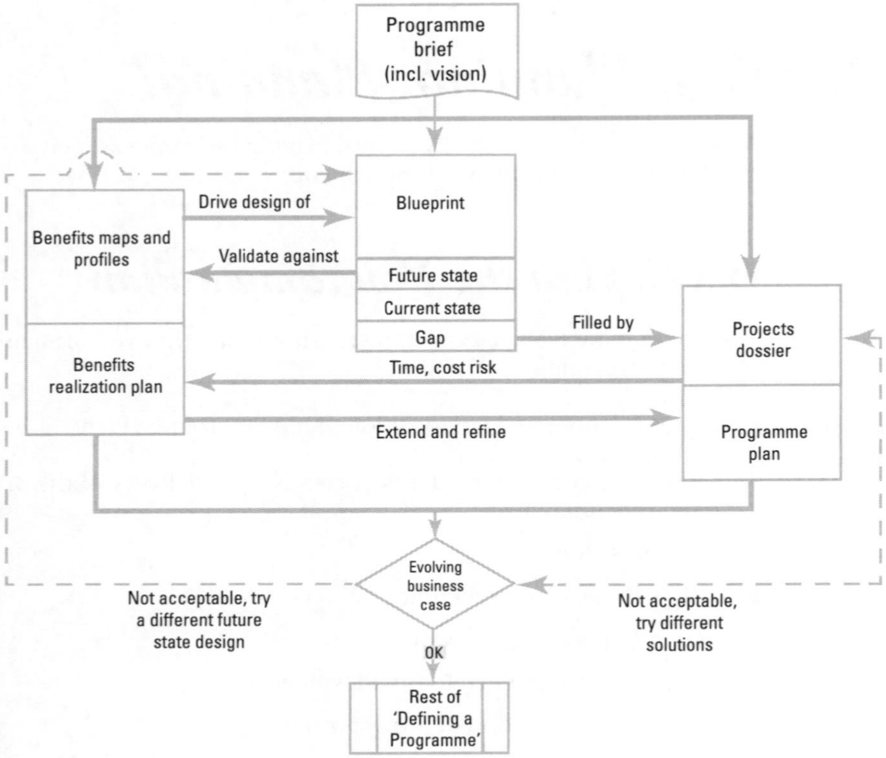

Figure 7-5: Developing the basis of an acceptable Business Case.

You start with the Vision, which is amplified into the Blueprint. From the picture of the future state, you can create Benefits Maps and Profiles and iterate them back into the Blueprint. Then you can put the Maps and Profiles together into the Benefits Realization Plan.

From the gaps identified within the Blueprint you can create a Project Dossier, which is integrated with the Programme Plan. You can now iterate between the Benefits Realization Plan and the Programme Plan to see whether you have a viable Business Case.

TIP

If you aren't getting a viable Business Case, you have a few options:

- Be less ambitious and design a Blueprint with smaller gaps between 'as is' and 'to be' states.
- Find a different approach that meets the constraints: more quickly, less cost, fewer threats, more innovation and you hope greater benefits.
- Iterate round, going back on the benefits and projects sides in the diagram back into the Blueprint until you achieve a viable Business Case or if necessary you can close the programme. This repeating loop is a useful one to bear in mind.

Preparing for the first tranche

Just before you leave the Defining a Programme stage, you need to prepare for the first tranche, which involves:

- Preparing to establish the programme governance and organization
- Acquiring the infrastructure for the next tranche
- Developing plans for:
  - Communications
  - Benefits realization
  - Overall programme
  - Resources
  - Quality

Getting approval to proceed

The final step in Defining a Programme is to get approval to proceed. In this section I propose a possible four-step process.

You may expect me to say that you need to get approval in accordance with your culture. Instead I'm going to say something different: you need to get approval to proceed in accordance with the governance strategies you create during the Defining a Programme process (see the earlier section 'Developing the Programme Governance').

Every organization gives approval to proceed in its own way, but experience shows that the following four-step approach is useful:

1. **SRO and Programme Board (which comprises key managers within the programme) approve**
2. **Sponsoring Group endorses**
3. **Independent review**
4. **Sponsoring Group authorises**

The first approval from the SRO and Programme Board is simply agreeing that the Programme Definition can be put to the Sponsoring Group for them to endorse it.

Endorsement doesn't mean approval – merely the Sponsoring Group saying that it's comfortable that the Programme Definition can go forward for an independent review to make whatever recommendations are appropriate. These recommendations are considered when the Sponsoring Group finally authorises further work on the programme.

You can see that the suggestion is for the documentation to go twice to the Sponsoring Group. You may find this approach useful, or you may discover that it doesn't fit with your organization's culture. But including independent review at such an early stage is a good idea.

At this stage, it really feels as though you've got your programme up and running!

See whether you can arrange the information about your programme into the documents I discuss in this chapter. If you spot any gaps, consider what activities you'd want to plan.

Chapter 8

Documenting the Business Case for Your Programme

In This Chapter

- Understanding the role of the programme Business Case
- Knowing what goes into a Business Case
- Tracing the life-cycle of your Business Case

If this chapter was an Agatha Christie story, perhaps detective Hercule Poirot would start by saying: 'Mesdames and messieurs, I 'ave gazzered you 'ear to uncover ze mystery of ze Business Case.'

Zis – sorry, that's enough of that – this chapter covers the Business Case for a programme, including its composition and how you use it as a communication tool and update it throughout the life of the programme.

REMEMBER

The purpose of a Business Case reaches beyond simply justifying the programme, as you'll discover in this chapter. If you're familiar with Business Cases, say from project management, you're sure to find the ideas in this chapter pretty straightforward.

Introducing the Case of the Business Case

The purpose of a *Business Case* is to:

- Validate initiation of the programme
- Demonstrate the on-going viability of the programme

In plain English, that means you can use the Business Case to check that you're starting the right programme and show that the programme has a good chance of being successful.

What's more, the Business Case links to the following principles:

- Focusing on benefits and threats to them
- Adding value

A prime reason behind creating a Business Case is that it allows you to answer questions such as:

- Is the investment in the programme (still) worthwhile?
- Do you have the best mix of information to decide whether the programme is desirable, viable and achievable?
- Have you identified the following:
  - Added value of the programme over and above that of the project (for the distinction between *programme* and *project,* see Chapter 1)?
  - Programme costs above projects' costs?
- Have you described the value to the organization of the outcomes?

TIP

I think of any Business Case as comprising costs, benefits, risks and timescales, and a little more as well. The order of the sections isn't fixed, but you're trying to tell a story. You might start with the options and then describe the chosen option in detail, or describe the selected option from big picture down to detail, ending up with the options to be rejected. The aim is to make the Business Case compelling and rigorous. The following sequence usually works for me:

- Strategic programme objectives
- Expected benefits or outcomes
- Confirmation that you have the capability to achieve transformation
- Overall risk profile
- Assumptions that can affect costs and benefits. For example, if you're moving into new premises you assume you can sell the old offices for a certain price.
- Costs and timescales
- Investment appraisal (check out the very next section)
- Forecasted cash flow
- Options that have been considered. Usually you include a 'do nothing' option along with a few options on what you could do. After you've selected what you want to do, you can then look at options on how to achieve that Vision.

Including an investment appraisal

The finance director, or equivalent, probably has a standard spread sheet template for how to show costs against financial benefits over time. Including the dry financial facts about your programme is pretty normal. This is known as an *investment appraisal.*

An investment appraisal enables you to objectively summarize the financial facts about your programme. If those facts are presented in this same style for your programme and other investment opportunities in the business, members of the Sponsoring Group find it easier to compare investment choices. So including a nice clear investment appraisal in your Business Case is in your own best interests.

An investment appraisal enables you to calculate the *cumulative net benefit* of the programme; in other words, the costs and the benefits over time. (For example, if I spend £10 in year 1 and get a benefit of £6 in year 1 and £6 in year 2, at the end of year 1 the cumulative net benefit is –£4, but at the end of year 2 the cumulative net benefit is +£2.)

Figure 8-1 shows costs against financial benefits over time. You can add up those figures to calculate the cumulative net benefit.

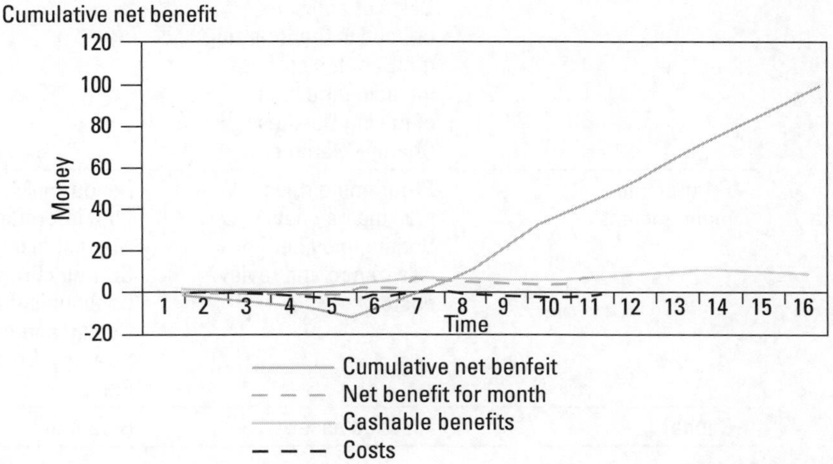

Month	1	2	3	4	5	6	7	8	9	10	11	12	13	14	15	16
Benefits	0	1	2	2	3	6	7	8	9	9	10	12	13	12	11	11
Costs	-1	-4	-5	-3	-6	-7	-3	-3	-1	-1						
Net Benefit	-1	-3	-3	-1	-3	-1	4	5	8	8	10	11	12	13	11	11

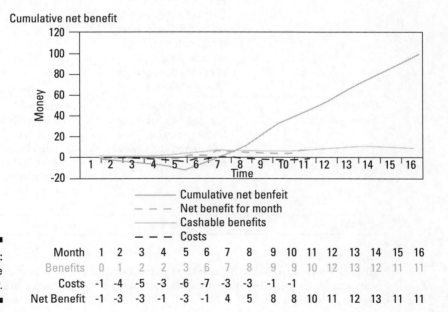

Figure 8-1: Cumulative net benefit.

Looking at different types of cost can be helpful when showing others where costs arise and so where the programme focuses its efforts. You can find these costs in the different documents you create during the Defining a Programme stage. Table 8-1 summarises the type of costs and which documents you use to find them.

Table 8-1 Types of Cost

Type	*Description*	*Documents Where You can Find these Costs*
Project	Cost of acquiring and delivering outputs. Contingency and change budget.	Project Dossier Programme Plan Project Business Case
Benefit realization	Implementing, measuring, monitoring and reporting benefits realization.Cost of realizing benefits.	Benefits Management Strategy Benefits Profiles Benefits Realization Plan
Business change and transition	Supporting operational units until new practices are embedded. Costs of activities defined in the Realizing the Benefits process, including the cost of having Business Change Managers.	Programme Plan Resource Management Plan Benefits Profiles
Programme management	Programme roles plus the on costs. Contingency budget. Assurance and review costs.	Resource Management Plan Information Management Strategy Programme Communications Plan Quality and Assurance Strategy. Programme Plan
Capital	For fixed assets.	Blueprint

Note that *on costs* in Table 8-1 are the costs over and above a person's salary. For example, they include accommodation costs and the cost of providing employees with IT.

Examining the net benefit line and stakeholder engagement

When you plot the cost information from the preceding section onto the graph in Figure 8-1, the net benefit line becomes a powerful tool for engaging stakeholders. For example, it can give evidence of early financial benefit realization, it can communicate the breakeven point and it can show benefits that still need to be realized after the programme closes.

TIP

By the way, if you're running a compliance programme (which I define in Chapter 2), you may need to express financial benefits as 'avoided costs'.

WARNING!

Be careful: by producing an investment appraisal you've reduced the benefits to a monetary equivalent. Sometimes, doing so is entirely valid and certainly makes comparing options more straightforward. But as you convert intangible or indirect benefits to an equivalent monetary value, you run the risk of severing the link with stakeholders who are interested in those benefits (check out the nearby sidebar 'The bottom line isn't the be-all and end-all' for an example).

TIP

If creating an investment appraisal is a little difficult, ask for financial advice and try to get a finance person seconded to the programme management team.

Following the flow of the Business Case

Figure 8-2 contains an elegant diagram that illustrates the relationship between various documents that feed into the Business Case.

TRUE STORY

The bottom line isn't the be-all and end-all

A politician was asked why school buses didn't have seatbelts. He gave the narrow financial answer and said that they'd cost too much. Parents, who are interested in the safety of their children and not cost, were horrified and the result was a huge uproar. The politician lost his job.

He should have said that the safety of children is paramount and that transporting children in school buses is safer than having children travelling alone to school or having numerous private vehicles dropping children off near the school and causing congestion and presenting a traffic hazard to other children. School buses travel only short distances and because they stop and start frequently, they also travel slowly. Seat belts don't significantly improve safety, but do reduce the number of children that each bus is able to carry.

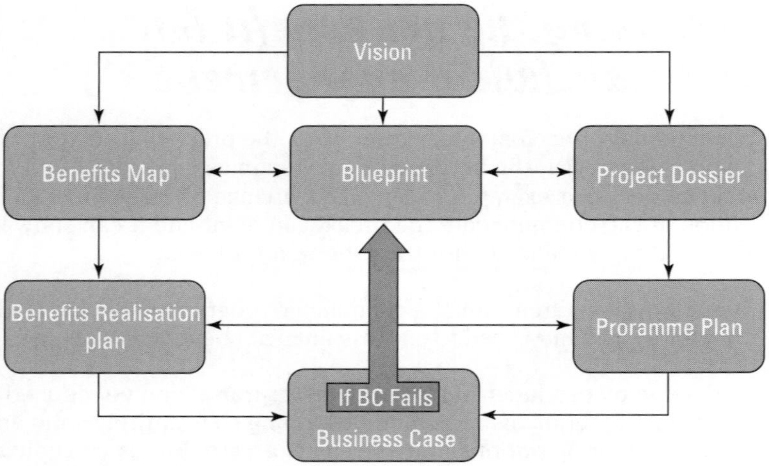

Figure 8-2: Related flow of the Business Case.

You start with Vision which leads to the Blueprint. You then have two loops that you go around again and again:

- **Benefits Map**: Describes, surprisingly, the benefits! It's fleshed out in the Benefits Realization Plan.
- **Project Dossier**: Shows projects at high-level. It's expanded upon in the Programme Plan (I discuss both in Chapter 7).

TIP

Carry out regular cross-checks to make sure that all these documents are in alignment. The two loops – costs from the Programme Plan and benefits from the Benefits Realization Plan – come together in the Business Case.

If the Business Case isn't viable, you have to go round those two loops again. You need to revisit benefits, revisit the costs and, if doing so isn't radical enough, you may have to revisit the Blueprint in order to envisage a different future state, which has a different set of benefits and a different set of costs. Figure 8-2 is a useful little model for getting your mind round the Business Case.

Reviewing and Communicating the Business Case

In this section, I lead you through reviewing your Business Case and describe the people involved in managing it.

Assessing the Business Case

When you're reviewing the Business Case (around the Defining a Programme process or subsequently, perhaps, at a tranche boundary; check out Chapters 7 and 18, respectively), here are the sort of questions you're trying to answer. Some are at a very high level and some are pretty detailed:

- Is the programme still affordable?
  - Does sufficient funding exist?
- Are the outcomes still achievable?
  - Can the organization cope with the change that it has to deal with?
- Is the programme still value for money?
  - Are the costs and benefits in balance?
- Have you considered and updated the options?
  - Is the Project Dossier still optimal?
- Is the programme still justified?
  - Will it still meet strategic objectives?
- Do you have contingency plans and the money to pay for them?
  - Do they cover a wide enough range of risks and uncertainties?

Meeting the key players

Here are the areas of focus of the various roles in the programme management team for creating and communication the Business Case. I cover roles in more detail in Chapter 9.

Taking overall responsibility: Senior Responsible Owner

The *Senior Responsible Owner* (SRO) is the senior individual accountable for the Business Case. This person approves it and must ensure that it's monitored, reviewed and updated. Here are the SRO's main responsibilities:

- Answering to the Sponsoring Group for the successful delivery of the programme and achievement of the Business Case.
- Securing investment for the programme.
- Ensuring that the Business Case is controlled and audit trails are in place to account for changes as the programme develops.

- Scanning the business horizons surrounding the programme for issues that lead to realignment of the programme in some way.
- Ensuring that the progress of the programme remains aligned with the Business Case.
- Consulting with the Sponsoring Group to identify any early-warning indicators of change that may undermine the Business Case or cause it to lose strategic alignment.
- Initiating independent assurance reviews of whether the Business Case is still viable.

Running day-to-day: Programme Manager

The *Programme Manager* operates the programme on a daily basis and may have a Financial Controller or Programme Accountant who helps with the following tasks:

- Preparing the Business Case.
- Supporting the SRO in the on-going validation and review of the Business Case.
- Managing the programme's expenditure against the overall investment defined in the Business Case.
- Identifying opportunities to optimize the Business Case.

Implementing in the business: Business Change Managers

Business Change Managers achieve change as their part of the business. Their primary focus in terms of the Business Case is management of benefits, but in addition their job is:

- Profiling the benefits and dis-benefits and their associated costs.
- Ensuring that benefits continue to be valid through regular Business Case reviews.
- Ensuring that the full cost of change is being captured in the Business Case.
- Identifying operational risks to the Business Case and ensuring that they're controlled.
- Measuring benefits at the start of the programme and tracking throughout, to feed into the net benefit line (see the earlier section 'Examining the net benefit line and stakeholder engagement').
- Managing business change costs.
- Managing benefits realization costs.
- Realizing the profiled benefits.

MSP SPEAK

Administering: Programme Office

The *Programme Office* looks after the administration of the programme and is responsible for:

- Supporting the SRO and the Programme Manager in compiling and updating the Business Case.
- Collecting and maintaining Business Case information.
- Facilitating Business Case reviews.

Observing the Business Case across the Life of the Programme

This section is sort of like a David Attenborough programme, where you get to see the details of the life-cycle of a Business Case. Take a look at Figure 8-3 and don't worry, it's not too icky!

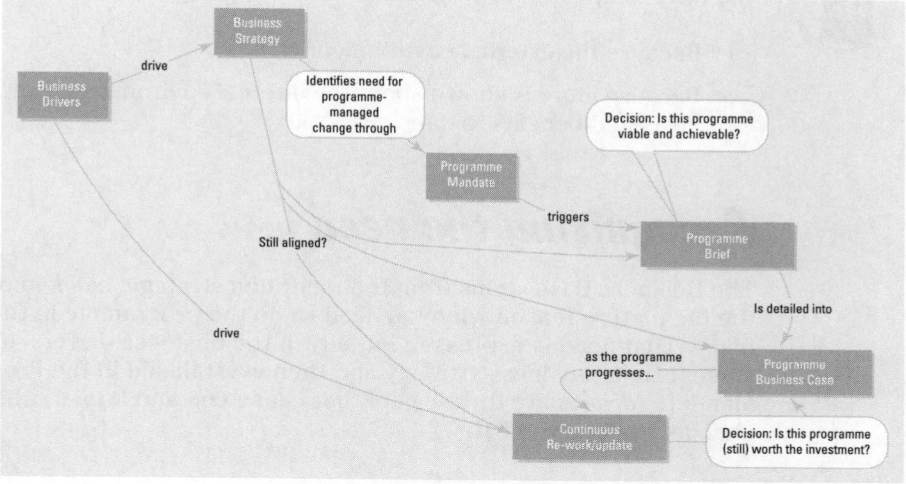

Figure 8-3: Life-cycle of a programme Business Case.

REMEMBER

You don't just write a Business Case at the beginning of the programme and then leave it in a filing cabinet gathering dust.

Defining the Business Case

After the Sponsoring Group agrees to meet the Mandate by starting the programme, the SRO creates the Programme Brief, which includes an outline Business Case (I provide more on that subject in Chapter 3).

The Sponsoring Group's approval of the Programme Brief triggers the Defining a Programme process within the transformational flow, which I discuss in Chapter 7. During Defining the Programme you identify outcomes and projects, which allow you to describe the benefits in detail. From those programme projects and from your benefits, you can extract cost and benefit information to put into the Business Case.

Revisiting the Business Case

You update and review the Business Case at each tranche boundary, but it may happen at other times during the programme. (I describe the end of one tranche and the beginning of the next in Chapter 18.)

You have to update the programme Business Case for two broad reasons:

- Because the external environment changes
- Because more is known about the internal environment: that is, the costs and benefits to date

Recognising the need

The Business Case stems from the identified strategic *need:* in other words, the big picture reason why you need to do the programme in the first place. That need is expressed initially in the business drivers, clarified in some form of business strategy and then crystallised in the Programme Mandate (*drivers* are the triggers that cause you and lots of other people to change; see Chapter 3).

Validating the Business Case

Take a look Figure 8-4, which shows how the Business Case evolves and what it's used for during each of the processes in the transformational flow.

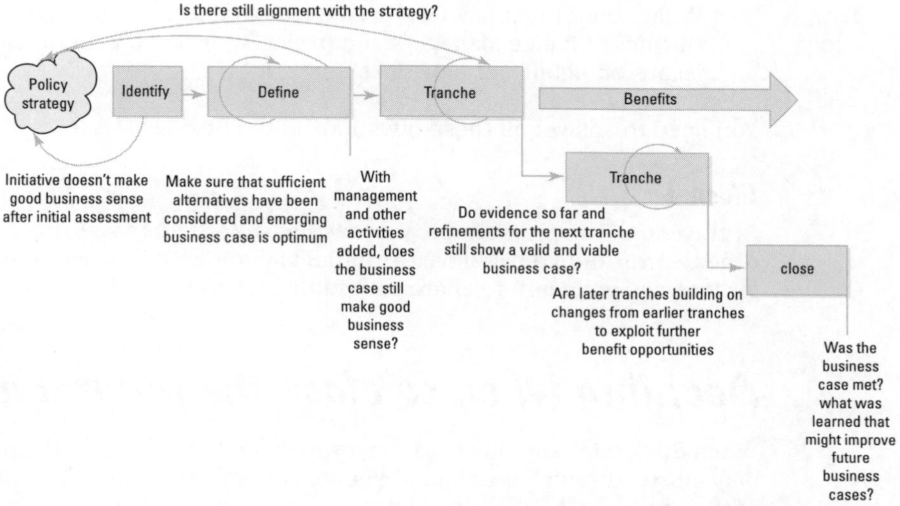
Is there still alignment with the strategy?
Policy strategy
Identify
Define
Tranche
Benefits
Tranche
close
Initiative doesn't make good business sense after initial assessment
Make sure that sufficient alternatives have been considered and emerging business case is optimum
With management and other activities added, does the business case still make good business sense?
Do evidence so far and refinements for the next tranche still show a valid and viable business case?
Are later tranches building on changes from earlier tranches to exploit further benefit opportunities
Was the business case met? what was learned that might improve future business cases?

Figure 8-4: Validating the Business Case.

Initial Business Case

During the Identifying the Programme and Defining the Programme processes (see Chapters 3 and 7, respectively), you need to test the emerging Business Case continually. Ask if the programme is still justified and whether you've considered enough options. You need to do so several times during these two processes.

Tranche boundaries

At a tranche boundary, you can ask whether you have historic evidence and a valid future projection. Do the costs and benefits to date mean that the programme is viable today and in the future? You learn from experience by recalculating figures and asking whether the programme is still the best possible programme that you can be running.

You want to discover whether the programme will realize the expected benefits and whether changes to the cost–benefit profile (the net benefit line; see the earlier section 'Examining the net benefit line and stakeholder engagement') are going to alter the status and relative priority of the programme when related to corporate objectives.

You can assess a few other things as well:

- What's the impact going to be of accommodating any strategic change or change business driver?
- What about proposed revisions to the programme's boundary and Blueprint and what will be the impact?

- What about the impact of revised benefit and cost estimates from the Business Change Managers and projects; or the impact of major new issues or significant new risks?

You need to answer all these questions in the Business Case.

Closure

At the end of the programme, you need to ask whether you succeeded. In other words, did you achieve the initial and updated Business Case and what lessons can you learn to share with future programmes?

Deciding when to close the programme

When discussing the Business Case you can reflect on when the programme may close. Although costs and benefits continue to accumulate after the end of the programme, it's still an interesting discussion. For one reason, a quick analysis shows that the programme closes some considerable time after the final delivery of the full capability, because benefits still have to accrue.

One useful definition for the end is 'when sufficient transition is achieved from old to new'. Another view holds that the end point is when changes are so embedded that the target outcome has been achieved again (quite useful if you have an outcome model).That could be in the Blueprint, which I describe in Chapter 6 or something you produce when modelling benefits, which I discuss in Chapter 15.

TIP

Personally, I use a simple but powerful test to determine when to close the programme. The last thing to flow is the benefits. Therefore, when benefits management is embedded in the business and is carrying on without any intervention from the programme, the programme has no more work to do. So that's when it closes.

HAVE A GO — Try This

If you're working in a programme, review your Business Case using the questions I pose in this chapter. Consider checking detail such as the composition and the types of cost.

If you aren't currently in a programme, look at a project Business Case you're familiar with and ask yourself what else you'd add if your project was being run as a programme.

Part III

Managing Multiple Projects

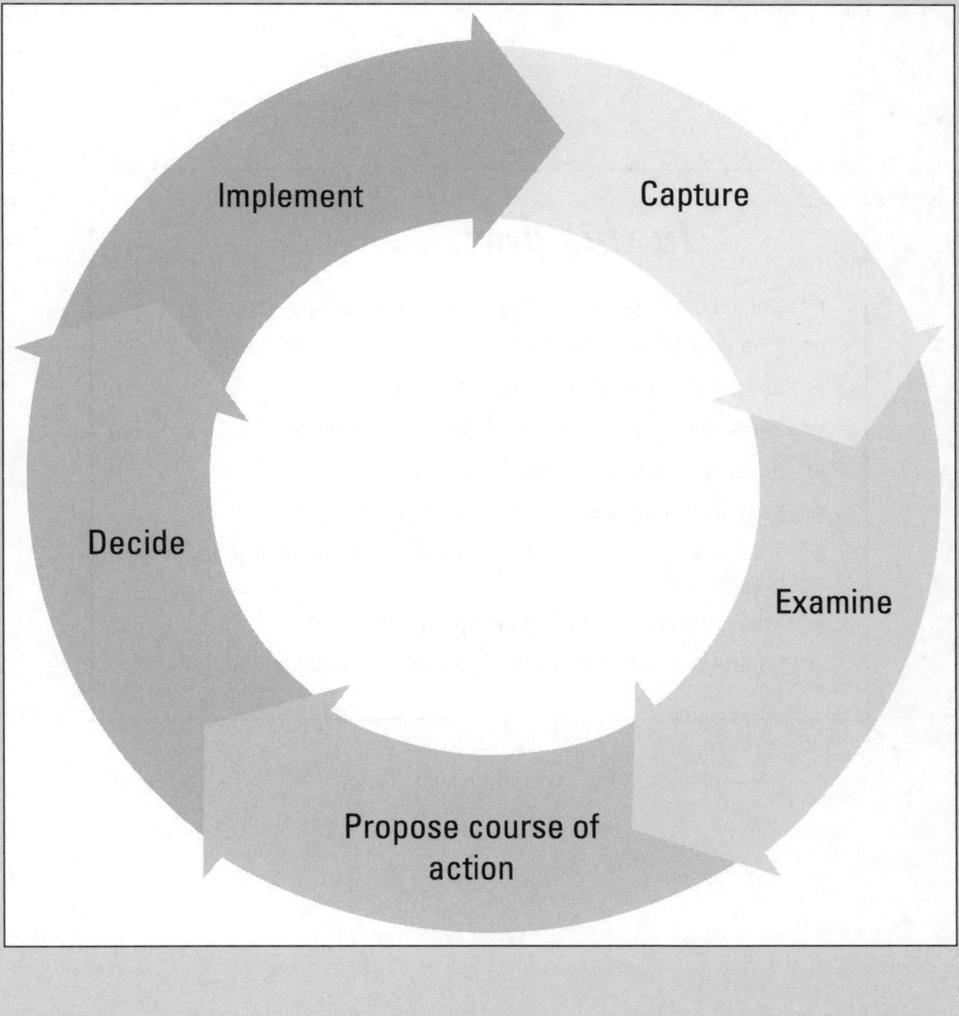

web extras

Go to www.dummies.com/extras/msp for free online bonus content about managing successful programmes.

In this part. . .

- Decide the organization structure for your programme.
- Plan your programme in projects and business as usual.
- Control your programme against your plans.
- Manage risks at the right level in your programme.
- Resolve issues, at the right level.
- Keep track of changes that occur in your programme.
- Track the configuration of all the different aspects of your programme.
- Manage quality throughout the programme.
- Control the information flowing through the programme.

Chapter 9

Organizing a Programme: Who does What

In This Chapter

- Understanding the basic roles in your programme
- Allocating responsibilities to each programme role
- Adjusting the relationships between roles
- Maintaining the power balance between roles

Each programme has its own organization with defined roles and responsibilities, and it is almost certainly supported by a Programme Office. The organization structure for a programme can be fairly straightforward, although as I discuss in this chapter, the relationships between the different roles become quite subtle in larger programmes, and you need to balance the power of these roles.

I lay out the responsibilities of roles such as the Senior Responsible Owner, the Programme Board, the Programme Manager, Business Change Managers, Business Change Teams and Programme Office. I also consider the attributes you need to look for in the people you ask to fill each of the roles: after all, people have different strengths, skills and experience, and you want the right person in the right role.

REMEMBER

Don't be fooled by the superficial simplicity in this chapter; the information I show you about how the programme organization is put together is crucial. The organization can become large and complex, particularly if you're working on a bigger programme, but it doesn't have to be – check out my ideas about loose and tight programmes, which I share with you in Chapter 3.

Considering the Basics

The basic organization model for a programme is simple.

The Sponsoring Group appoints a Senior Responsible Owner (SRO) as part of the Identifying a Programme process and a Programme Manager reports directly to that SRO. At the same time a number of Business Change Managers, who work in business as usual, also report to the SRO. The Programme Manager, or the team Defining the Programme, put more detail on the organizational structure. I explain this process in Chapter 7 and if you want to check out an organizational diagram, take a look at Figure 7-3.

Tightening up or hanging loose: The two extremes of programme organization

Before I describe the specific programme roles in the following section, here are two real-world examples for you to mull over. Note that the organization structure of a programme can range from being extremely simple through to very sophisticated, even complex. No standard right answer exists; you have to evolve a structure that works for your programme and its culture.

I once attended a briefing on a programme to return the headquarters of an iconic organization to the famous old building in which the organization had started.

Although the firm was keeping the front of the old building, managers were completely redeveloping and extending it. I don't want you to imagine that this was just a simple project to add a few new offices; a tremendous amount of technology was involved. (Just to give you a feel for the size of this programme, the building is so famous that I guess if you switched on a TV virtually anywhere in the world, within an hour or so pictures of this building would be broadcast.)

I went for a briefing on this programme. The Programme Manager drew the organization structure for me. He completely filled a flipchart with roles and structures (committees) with interlinking loops and swirls. It took the best part of an hour for him to describe the structure, and, frankly, by the end of it I simply didn't understand what was going on. It wasn't that he hadn't described the organization clearly; it was just that it was too complex.

In contrast, here's an example of a loose programme. While still big – the programme budget was of the order of £1 billion – what made this programme different is that the vast majority of the expenditure was in a single very large project. The rest of the programme still had its complexities; it affected organizations in 13 or 14 different countries. Yet just three people organized this programme. The Programme Manager had only two assistants, who were graduates on secondment for a year. Because it was a loose programme, the Programme Manager could keep in touch with all its different elements with this tiny team.

Create a programme organization structure that's appropriate for your circumstances.

Reading the role call

In this section, I look at the basic relationships between the main roles and provide a brief overview of each one. For a more detailed description of each role's responsibilities, check out the later section 'Taking Responsibility'.

Figure 9-1 shows the classic structure for a programme. Of course, this diagram is basic and your own programme may well require a much more complex structure. On second thoughts, complex is quite a negative term; I prefer to say that your structure may be much 'richer'.

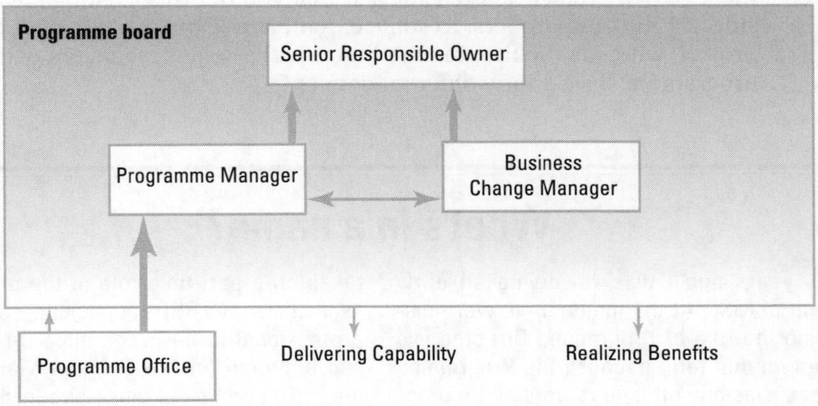

Figure 9-1: Senior Responsible Owner and the Programme Board.

I now give you a quick overview of each of these roles.

Sponsoring Group

A programme is of strategic importance, so you need the executive level commitment that comes from the Sponsoring Group.

TIP: Only rarely is a structure formed called the Sponsoring Group in reality. Usually your organization already has a structure that functions as the Sponsoring Group; it may be called the Board of Directors or the Senior Management Team or something similar. Please don't try and get the group to change its name.

Senior Responsible Owner

The SRO is one of the members of the Sponsoring Group. *Senior Responsible Owner* is a strange term, but it is widely used. If it doesn't fit with your culture, you can substitute the term *Programme Director* (see the nearby sidebar 'What's in a name?').

Be careful not to insert too many intermediate layers of management between those responsible for executing the programme and the organization's directors.

Programme Board

The SRO needs to get together with the other key managers within the programme, most likely called a *Programme Board.* The Programme Board reports to the SRO. The members of the Board can, for example, include Business Change Managers, and so the Programme Board gives a level of business involvement to the programme. Probably the Programme Board establishes the governance for the programme. Its purpose is to drive the programme forward and deliver outcomes and benefits.

If you come from a project management background, you may be familiar with the idea of a Project Board. I suggest that you put this existing idea to one side. A Project Board sits, to some extent, above the management of the project, whereas the Programme Board is the senior managers of the programme. It's a subtly different concept.

What's in a name?

Many years ago I was reviewing an early refresh of MSP. At the meeting we were discussing the role of Programme Director. We settled on that term because the Programme Director was one of the directors of the organization, who'd be accountable for the programme. We were told by a representative of the UK government department that owns MSP that it wanted to use a new term – SRO – because it emphasized ownership and taking responsibility. We argued for both terms to be included, but we were overruled. In recent years though, I've seen another interesting development. The SRO is a director who takes on a part-time role in the programme. I sometimes see SROs appointing a programme professional to be Programme Director who sits between the Programme Manager and the SRO. Perhaps in these circumstances the Programme Manager becomes something closer to a Programme Office Manager.

Also, a better term may be Senior Accountable Owner rather than Senior Responsible Owner. The SRO delegates most of his responsibilities down into the programme organization, but he always remains accountable for the programme.

As I say so often – do whatever works for you.

Programme Manager

The *Programme Manager* is at the heart of the programme and undertakes the day-to-day programme management. This person ensures delivery of the new capabilities on behalf of the SRO and plans, designs and monitors the programme.

Business Change Managers

The programme has to do more than deliver a capability: it has to exploit that capability in order to achieve strategic outcomes and benefits. Business Change Managers make this happen.

Note that I say 'managers'. Very rarely does a programme have only one Business Change Manager. Usually, each area affected by the programme has one Business Change Manager.

The *Business Change Managers* realize the benefits by embedding the capability the projects provide. In other words they facilitate business change by exploiting that capability. In a large programme you may have a large number of Business Change Managers. In that case, instead of sitting on the Programme Board, they may sit on some sort of Business Change Managers steering group.

Business Change Team

Despite having a number of Business Change Managers, even more people are likely to be involved in business change.

Each Business Change Manager is likely to be supported by a *Business Change Team.* Together they create new business structures, new operations and new working practices.

Programme Office

Almost certainly, some sort of *Programme Office* is going to assist with the administration and running of the programme. This Office is the nerve centre – the place you go to find out what's happening The Programme Office is likely to run an information hub. Indeed a hub is vital within a large programme, because so much information is flowing around.

The Programme Office is the custodian of the standards used to execute projects. But it also gives supporting and guidance to projects. Furthermore, the Programme Office may be the home of governance and control, and if so it needs to remain independent of initiatives.

Therefore, a large Programme Office can have a number of discrete elements.

Project Boards

Projects are likely to have *Project Boards*, from where a project is directed. A Project Board may exist for each project or perhaps look at several related projects. I don't examine the role of Project Board in any more detail here.

Taking Responsibility

This section describes the responsibilities and attributes of the following:

- Sponsoring Group
- Senior Responsible Owner
- Programme Board
- Programme Manager
- Business Change Manager
- Business Change Team

My hope is that these detailed descriptions of role responsibilities provide you with an extremely useful starting point when defining someone's terms of reference and a firm foundation for designing your own programme management structure (even if you don't want to read this section at one sitting!).

TIP: As you may expect, this section is a fairly detailed set of lists. When you first read these detailed responsibilities, have a brief look at them, just to understand the nature of the role. Then use them as template lists of responsibilities and tailor them to your needs.

Getting executives on-board: Sponsoring Group

The Sponsoring Group doesn't play a significant role in the monitoring and control of the programme, but it does have an absolutely vital role in leading the programme:

- It makes the executive-level commitment to the programme.
- It comprises the senior managers who are responsible for the investment in the programme.

- It has to establish and demonstrate the values and behaviours of the new world.
- It understands that normal reporting lines probably don't apply, such as individuals from one organizational unit reporting to senior managers from another.
- It acts as the overarching authority for the programme.
- Its members may have to display different leadership styles from the ones they use when running business as usual, for example:
  - More team working.
  - Greater empowerment of individuals within the programme.
- It encourages initiative by:
  - Taking risks itself.
  - Recognising when taking risks is appropriate in certain circumstances (and in a programme that may be all the time . . . just kidding!)

Leading the Programme: Senior Responsible Owner

The SRO is a member of the Sponsoring Group and ultimately accountable for the success of the programme. The SRO:

- Is an individual (that is, only one SRO)
- Is a peer member of the Sponsoring Group
- Has personal responsibility
- Is empowered to direct the programme
- Has sufficient seniority and authority
- Is probably part-time as SRO because they keep their day job
- Is ultimately accountable for success

Responsibilities

The SRO is a champion and leader of the programme, but each of the person's responsibilities is quite subtle.

TIP

If you're, say, a newly appointed Programme Manager, I suggest you find an opportunity to talk through these responsibilities with your SRO, so that you both understand what they mean in your organization.

You expect the SRO to have some responsibility for each of the *governance themes*. (How you manage the different aspects of the programme; refer to Chapter 1). You can use the comprehensive Contents or the Index to find more details on a particular aspect or term.

REMEMBER

The SRO is responsible for:

- Creating and communicating the Vision
- Providing clear leadership and direction
- Securing the investment required to set-up and run the programme and to fund the transition activities in order that the Business Change Managers can achieve the benefits
- Ensuring that the programme delivers a coherent capability, achieves its strategic outcomes and realizes its benefits
- Establishing the programme's governance arrangements and ensuring that appropriate assurance is in place
- Assuring the viability of the programme Business Case
- Engaging and informing key, probably senior, stakeholders
- Monitoring and managing the strategic risks facing the programme
- Maintaining alignment with the strategic direction of the parent organization
- Commissioning assurance and audit reviews
- Assuring the effectiveness and performance of the programme organization
- Appointing and chairing the Programme Board

This list may seem daunting, but in reality it's what any senior manager accountable for a strategic initiative would be doing naturally. So the SRO doesn't have to dedicate enormous amounts of time to managing the detail of the programme.

Attributes

You're unlikely to ever have to appoint an SRO, but you may find yourself being consulted about who can fulfil the role or why someone's doing a good or poor job.

With this in mind, here are the personal attributes of an ideal SRO:

- Has the seniority that goes with the accountabilities for the programme and for the detailed responsibilities the person needs to execute. To put it less formally, they need to be a big enough beast to carry the can when the brown stuff hits the fan. Is that enough mixed metaphors?
- Is proactive and visible as the driving force behind the programme without being aggressive or overbearing
- Possesses strong leadership and decision-making skills
- Has the right experience, character and personality for the particular programme
- Combines realism with openness and clarity of expression in order to be able to communicate the programme's Vision effectively
- Gives purpose and direction to the programme by taking strategic decisions where necessary
- Focuses on the delivery of benefits and the achievement of the end goal
- Builds productive relationships across the programme team
- Has access to and credibility with key, probably senior or influential, internal and external stakeholders

I have to say that I've met very few leaders with all these personality traits. The world would be dull if everyone was this perfect. I'm sure you'd agree that such as person would be quite a character!

Providing governance: Programme Board

The Programme Board reports to the SRO and gives business involvement and establishes governance for the programme. The members can help drive the programme forward to deliver outcomes and benefits.

At a minimum the Programme Board comprises:

- SRO
- Programme Manager
- Business Change Manager(s)

In addition to these core members, having some Project Executives on the Programme Board is useful, whether permanently or on an ad-hoc basis. You may also want to invite representatives of corporate functions, for example, finance, human resources or IT – but take care to ensure that they aren't at too junior a level. If the programme is buying substantial amounts of capability from another organization, including the lead supplier is also a good idea.

General responsibilities

The Programme Board's responsibilities go beyond merely monitoring projects, so take a look in Part IV in order to appreciate those wider responsibilities.

The Programme Board's general responsibilities include:

- Defining risk profiles and thresholds for the programme and for projects.
- Ensuring that the programme delivers within the agreed boundaries, including:
  - Cost
  - Organizational impact
  - Pace at which new capabilities are adopted
  - Expected and actual benefits
- Resolving strategic issues between projects or issues of direction that need the input and agreement of several stakeholders.
- Ensuring the integrity of benefit profiles and the realization plan.
- Maintaining focus on the development, maintenance and achievement of the Blueprint.
- Providing assurance that business as usual remains stable and effective even as the programme transforms the business.

Local responsibilities

Although the Programme Board meets as a group, individual members also provide support for the SRO in their own areas of work. The sort of local responsibilities they have includes:

- Helping their areas of work understand the impact of change and helping to manage change.
- Monitoring achievement of the previously defined benefits.
- Resolving issues and risks that relate to their area of work.
- Dealing with dependencies, for example between change projects or within business as usual.
- Ensuring the viability and integrity of the Blueprint in their areas.

- Representing local strategy back to the programme as expressed in, for example, medium-term local plans.
- Supporting the application of and compliance with standards that the programme is defining.
- Making resources available to plan and execute programme activities.

Running things day-to-day: Programme Manager

Briefly the Programme Manager leads and manages:

- Setting up the programme
- Delivering new capabilities
- Realizing benefits
- Closing the programme

Responsibilities

This Programme Manager's primary responsibility is successful delivery of new capabilities and establishing governance.

The Programme Manager is responsible for day-to-day management of the programme. Usually this person takes it forward from the Identifying or Defining a Programme processes and then carries out the supervision, control and closure of the programme. The Manager is the day-to-day agent of the SRO, carrying out planning and design of the programme and proactively monitoring its overall success. The Manger also resolves issues and initiates corrective action.

REMEMBER

Here are some more detailed responsibilities of the Programme Manager:

- Developing and implementing the programme governance framework.
- Ensuring effective co-ordination of the projects and dealing with interdependencies; for example, among projects or between projects and business as usual.
- Managing and resolving risks and issues.
- Maintaining the overall integrity and coherence of the programme.
- Developing and maintaining the programme environment in order to support each individual project within it.
- Managing the programme's budget, which means monitoring expenditures and costs against benefits as the programme progresses.

- Facilitating the appointment of individuals to the programme delivery teams.
- Ensuring that the delivery of outputs or services from the projects meet programme requirements in line with the programme Blueprint and Project Dossier, including ensuring that these outputs are of appropriate quality, on time and within budget.
- Facilitating the development of the Blueprint, including getting approval from the Business Change Managers.
- Managing the Blueprint and ensuring that the capabilities delivered are aligned with the Blueprint.
- Managing the performance of the programme management team.
- Maximising the efficient allocation of resources and skills within the Project Dossier.
- Managing internal and external suppliers to the programme.
- Managing communications with stakeholders.
- Reporting progress of the programme at regular intervals to the SRO.
- Initiating extra activities and other management interventions where gaps exist.

I just love that final responsibility of filling in the gaps; as if the Programme Manager doesn't have enough to do. But this list makes quite clear that the Programme Manager is at the heart of the programme.

TIP

Before you think that your Programme Manager has to be a superhero, able to leap tall buildings with a single bound, in a larger programme the Programme Manager defines a whole series of additional roles to help with all these responsibilities.

Attributes

Here are some of the key attributes of a good Programme Manager:

- The ability to work positively with the full range of individuals and groups involved in the programme.
- An ability to develop and maintain effective working relationships with other members of the programme management team, senior managers, project teams and third-party service providers.
- The seniority to be able to take on the responsibility associated with the role.
- Strong leadership and management skills.
- An understanding of the wider objectives of the programme.

- Credibility within the programme environment and the ability to influence others.
- A good knowledge of the techniques for planning, monitoring and controlling programmes, including risk management.
- A good knowledge of project management approaches, for example, PRINCE2.
- A good knowledge of budgeting and resource allocation.
- The ability to find innovative ways of pre-empting and solving problems.

Taking charge of change: Business Change Managers

The Business Change Managers, one for each area, carry out the following tasks:

- Facilitate business change in order to exploit capability.
- Create new business structures, operations and working practices.
- Realize benefits by embedding capability.

While you read the responsibilities and attributes of the Business Change Managers in this section, you can see that they need to be genuinely from the business and retain sufficient responsibilities within the business to keep in touch with what's going on there. Plus, they need a softer set of skills than you may find in people from a project background. Success isn't as simple as creating a plan and telling people to execute it. Business Change Managers really need to know the people they're working with and have a knack for persuading them to do things differently, as well as other change management skills.

TIP

I find that identifying credible managers in the business is pretty straightforward. From among potential Business Change Managers, you can always identify some with the helpful softer skills. The problem is finding people with the required change management experience, so quite often I have to put in place a mixture of training and coaching for them.

Responsibilities

Business Change Manager is a new role if you've not worked on a programme before. It has to be someone from within the organization who continues to hold responsibilities for business-as-usual operations.

Business Change Mangers have the following responsibilities:

- Focus on realizing beneficial change.
- Contribute to the development of the Benefits Management Strategy.
- Allocate responsibilities in the business for drafting and delivering Benefits Profiles and the Benefits Realization Plan.
- Identify, define and track the benefits and outcomes required by the programme.
- Design the future operating model, sometimes known as the 'to be' state part of the Blueprint, ensuring that it's contained in the Blueprint and maintained as the programme and the Blueprint evolve.
- Identify organizational changes that happen outside the boundary of the programme but which may affect the contents of the Blueprint.
- Prepare their own areas of work for change.
- Identify opportunities and realize new benefits that arise during the programme, which may not have originally been profiled, and ensure that the achievement of these extra benefits is recognized.
- Ensure effective communication with all areas of the business that they represent.
- Identify and monitor the performance metrics used to track the operational health of the organization.
- Implement mechanisms by which benefits can be realized and measured.
- Monitor business stability and the on-going capacity to cope with the level of change that the programme creates, which may involve establishing how far performance can be allowed to deteriorate while the change is being embedded.
- Report to the SRO the readiness for change, achievement of outcomes and realization of benefits.
- Advise the Programme Manager whether the work of the programme and of each project covers the necessary aspects required to deliver the products and outputs, the services and outcomes that will achieve the Blueprint and lead to benefits.
- Ensure that no double counting of benefits takes place for which they're responsible.
- Prepare the affected business areas for the transition to new ways of working so that they can implement new business processes.

- Ensure business stability is maintained during the transition to the new ways of working and the changes are effectively integrated into the business.
- Initiate business assurance reviews to ensure that capabilities are being embedded and optimized.
- Optimize the timing of the release of project deliverables into business operations.
- Notify delivery of the expected benefits.

Attributes

The key thing about Business Change Managers is that they have credibility. They:

- Are drawn from the relevant business areas in order to demonstrate detailed knowledge of the business environment and to have direct business experience.
- Almost certainly keep on-going operational responsibilities within their areas.
- May have participation in the programme as an integral part of the normal responsibilities, in order to ensure that the changes resulting from the programme are properly embedded in the organization.
- Have the confidence of senior managers from the areas to be changed.
- Understand the management structures, the politics and culture of their areas.
- Have the management skills to co-ordinate personnel from different disciplines and with different viewpoints.
- Have some understanding of change management and enough experience to bring order to the complex situations that the programme triggers.
- Maintain focus on the programme's objectives.
- Have negotiating skills.
- Have fluency in their interpersonal relationships, be comfortable with ambiguity and be able to prioritize in a dynamic way.
- Need access to specific skills, for example, process analysis, benefits identification modelling, and analysis and business continuity management.

Supporting change: Business Change Team

The Business Change Teams are the specialists who support each Business Change Manager. They prepare their areas for transition to the new ways of working and help their operational units to transition smoothly. The size and composition of the Business Change Team is likely to evolve over the course of the programme and individuals, say with particular expertise, may be members of multiple Business Change Teams.

Therefore, the skills they need include the following:

- Change management.
- Operational experience.
- Authority to influence the people in the area that's changing.

Reading about the Relationships between Roles

You can use programme management to run some really substantial change initiatives, which is why I include a fair amount of detail about the roles and responsibilities in the two earlier sections 'Considering the Basics' and 'Taking Responsibility'. Nevertheless, you still need to tailor these basic roles and responsibilities fairly radically in order to create an organization structure that suits your programme and culture.

In this section I share with you a number of different ways in which you can tailor the basic programme management structure, particularly as regards the relationships of the roles and responsibilities.

Linking project and programme management roles

Some form of structured project management is almost always necessary within an MSP programme, and although PRINCE2 isn't compulsory, it is highly suitable for MSP. (Have a read of *PRINCE2 For Dummies* by Nick Graham (Wiley) for more about this project management practice.)
To illustrate how programme management staff can fulfil project management roles, I show the MSP and PRINCE2 roles in Figure 9-2. The Programme Manager can also act as the Executive on a PRINCE2 Project Board and the Business Change Manager can also take on the role of Senior User.

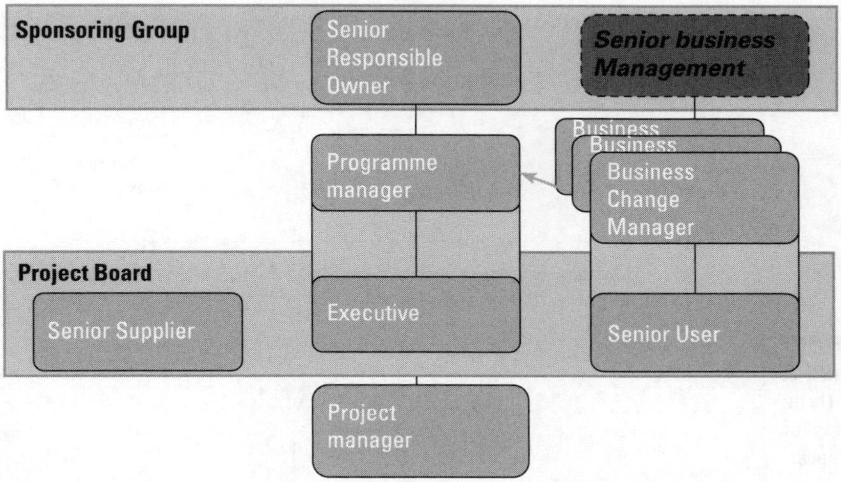

Figure 9-2: Linked programme and project roles.

The downside, of course, is that these busy programme people are taking on an additional set of responsibilities. But it's one way of making sure the programme stays in touch with particular projects. I don't suggest that the Programme Manager is the executive for every project, but it is often worth doing so for one or two key projects.

Integrating project organizations

Figure 9-3 looks at three different ways in which you can integrate programme and project roles:

- **Scenario A shows a dedicated Project Board.** The programme authorises the terms of reference of the Project Board and provides strategic direction. The Project Board is then free to concentrate on the project. This situation is particularly suitable when a project is large but not necessarily central to the programme.
- **Scenario B applies to projects that are central to the programme.** In this case the Programme Manager acts as Project Director and can maintain a tight, direct link between the programme and the project.
- **Scenario C shows the situation where a Business Change Manager acts as Senior User on a Project Board.** I look at this arrangement in the preceding section.

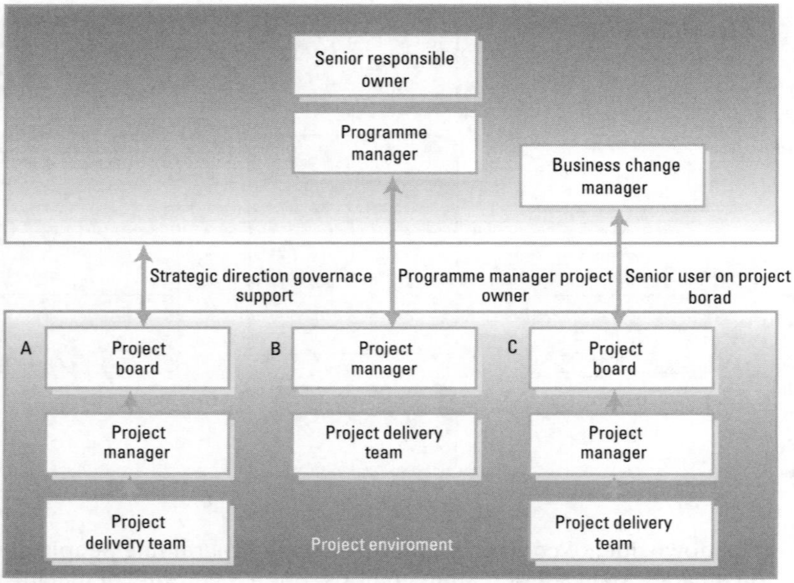

Figure 9-3: Three options for integrating project organizations.

Co-operating in cross-Organizational programmes

You can create a committee called the Sponsoring Group if you work on a multi-organization programme. In this situation several organizations have to co-operate in order to deliver a programme, as in Figure 9-4. That co-operation is a bit more intimate than where one organization simply has a supplier providing a range of technical services.

For a cross-organizational programme, the SRO chairs the Sponsoring Group. This body assists with the direction-setting and leadership of the programme and is an excellent venue for bringing together key stakeholders. In certain circumstances, the Sponsoring Group may decide to act as a Programme Board as well.

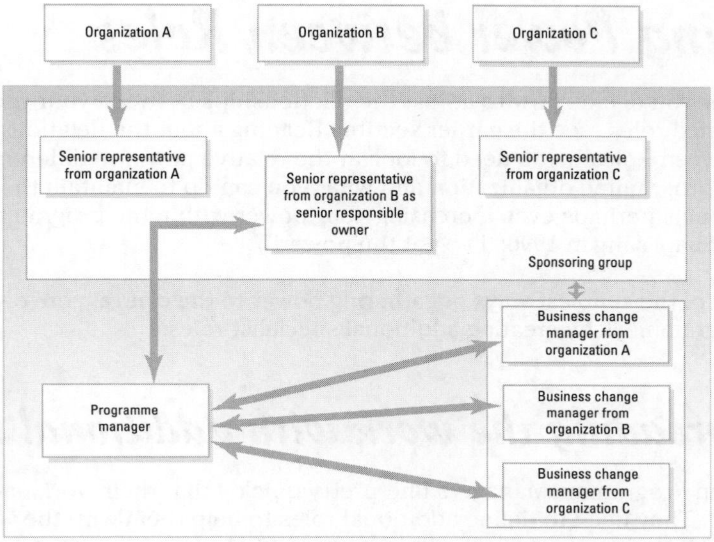

Figure 9-4: Cross-organizational programmes.

Copyright © AXELOS Limited 2011 Reproduced under licence from AXELOS

Handling multiple programmes

If an organization is running several closely related programmes, you may have considerable overlap between the Programme Boards.

TIP

In that case the organization can set-up a Corporate Portfolio Board to oversee all the related programmes. The Corporate Portfolio Board ensures the on-going strategic alignment and prioritization across the programmes.

Tracking programme evolution

Programmes change over their lifetimes because they typically last for so long. Usually the most significant changes are made at a tranche boundary. As a programme evolves it requires different skills: at the beginning design skills, later on project delivery skills and towards the end the focus moves to business change.

Therefore, as the programme evolves you need different leadership styles and different people in a significantly modified organizational structure.

Balancing Power between Roles

After you decide how to adjust the relationships between your programme's defined roles (see the earlier section 'Reading about the Relationships between Roles'), you need to look at the relative power in different parts of the programme organization and what you can do to maintain the power balance, perhaps even increasing your power within the programme (as Snap! sang in 1990: 'I've got the power!').

One of the simplest ways of gathering power to the central core of the programme is by creating additional specialist roles.

Spreading the work with additional roles

Often Programme Managers find pretty quickly that their workload is just too high. They need to define additional roles to help them with the work. You can place these roles in the Programme Office or they can report directly to the Programme Manager.

You can also delegate some of the Business Change Managers' responsibilities to additional roles within Business Change Teams or the Programme Office.

Table 9-1 features a few of the roles you may need, though I've seen an enormous range of roles defined in programmes. If you can justify the additional role, feel free to set it up.

Table 9-1 Useful Additional Roles

Additional Role	*Function*
Benefits Realization Manager	Reports to Business Change Managers with delegated responsibility to manage benefits management activities of the programme
Design Authority	Integrity of the Blueprint
Risk Manager	Risk management
Quality Manager	Quality management
Programme Accountant	Business Case development
Procurement Roles	Procurement advice

If you give any additional roles the grade of 'manager', other people in the programme may think that the individual manages the specialist topic. For example, they may think that the Benefits Manager manages all the benefits. If you find yourself having to counter this assumption, my own preference is to give additional roles grades such as 'facilitator' or 'co-ordinator'.

Many of these additional roles can sit comfortably in the Programme Office (which I describe in the later 'Looking at the Programme Office' section). Indeed, thinking functionally, you can have the staff in the Programme Office cover any of the specializations within the governance themes (for example, a risk co-ordinator to cover the risk governance theme), creating jobs such as planner or issue co-ordinator.

Bringing in HR management

Programmes last for such a long time that people may work within them for several years. Therefore, you may need a human resources (HR) function within the programme. I prefer to approach the HR department and persuade it to second someone to the programme.

This function helps you ensure that you have the right people in the programme at the right time and are using the correct HR policies. *Matrix management* is where you report to two bosses, which I think is quite hard to make work. You may have just that situation in your programme and the relationship between the losing line department and the programme can lead to tensions, so you need to work out how things such as annual appraisals are carried out.

If people are working part-time in a programme, you can expect that business-as-usual work tends to take priority. You have to live with this situation and make sure those people aren't given too many time-critical jobs, or tackle the problem with their bosses.

If people have been working in a programme for several years, they may not have a job to go back to and the experience they've gained in the programme may not be valued. You need to look after your people by helping them find appropriate work in the transformed organization after the programme ends.

Procuring effectively

You can also consider seconding someone from procurement. You may be procuring all sorts of items: buildings, services and people. One thing you may need to procure is programme management expertise. Organizations and governments sometimes have quite complex rules for procurement that you need to fit in with.

You may want to think about using existing contracts, if they give an opportunity for resources at a good price without constraining the programme.

Pondering programme assurance responsibilities and conflicts of interest

When you're designing your programme governance you need to think about how you integrate programme responsibilities in your organization structure while making sure that people carrying out assurance functions are sufficiently independent. I look in detail at assurance in Chapter 14.

At first sight the Programme Office is the obvious place from which to carry out programme assurance. Be careful to make sure that the three functions shown in Figure 9-5 – Programme Office, Project Support Office and Programme Assurance – are sufficiently independent. For more on the Programme Office, check out 'Looking at the Programme Office' later in this chapter.

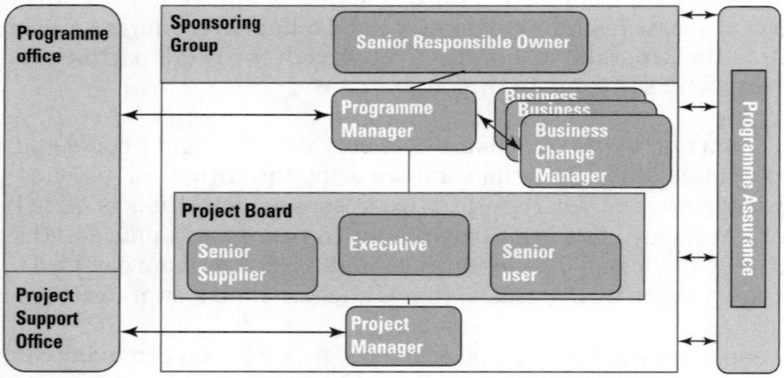

Figure 9-5: Programme and project support.

An example of a loss of independence that can occur is when you want to have a Design Authority providing one type of assurance. Such an authority within the Programme Office can come under pressure to compromise design in order to maintain the schedule.

Going with the (information) flow

Information is power. So ensure that you look often at the information flows in your programme and use them as a way of focusing power where you want it to be.

Figure 9-6 contains three examples:

- **Information flows via the Project Boards:** Makes those Boards powerful.
- **Information flows directly to the Programme Manager:** Can overload that person.
- **Information flows through programme support – the Programme Office:** Increases the power of the Programme Office, which may end up losing its objectivity.

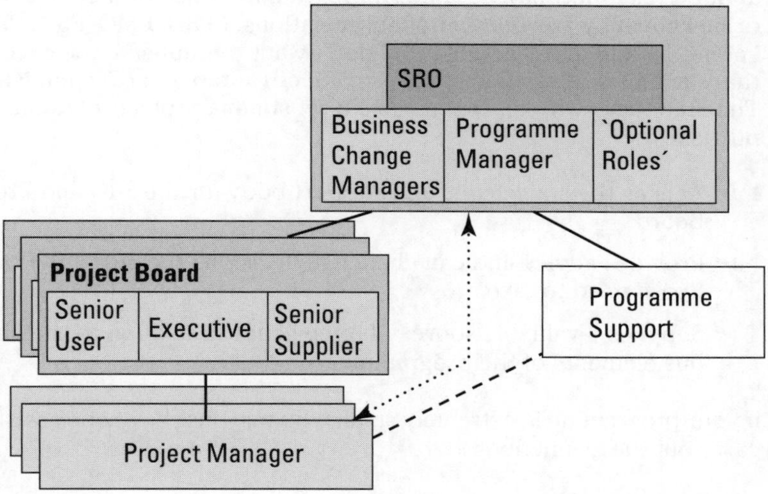

Figure 9-6: Three possible information flows.

Think about what power exists in the organization and where you want to reinforce or diminish that power. If you want to strengthen power, improve the information flow in that area. If you want to counterbalance power, strengthen other information flows.

Allocating programme staff to project teams

You may want to have some of your programme staff in project direction roles. I look briefly at this topic earlier in the 'Reading about the Relationships between Roles' section. For example, asking someone from your Design Authority to act as Senior Supplier on a Project Board improves the flow of information from that Board and helps to consolidate your power – though it may compromise the Board's independence.

This power-balancing all gets a bit tricky, doesn't it? But getting the balance of power right in a programme is important. Make sure you put aside a bit of time to reflect on the current balance of power and what balance you're trying to achieve.

Looking at the Programme Office

Many organizations use the services of an office to support the implementation and delivery of the changes in a business that the programme brings about. This office may be called a Programme Office or a Centre of Excellence or be known by any number of abbreviations: PPSO, PMO, P3O, C3PO (okay, I admit I made that last one up!) I don't want to duplicate the excellent advice that's available elsewhere on these offices (notably in *P3O* published by The Stationery Office), but here's a brief summary of a Programme Office's purposes:

- Acts as the conscience and support body for the SRO and Programme Board.
- Provides advice and can challenge decisions the SRO and Programme Board need to take.
- Supplies a valuable source of intelligence in relation to the health of various elements of the programme.

REMEMBER: If your programme is extremely small, you may just have one assistant to carry out these functions.

Linking to other offices

Your Programme Office may have to link with and complement other offices:

- A Portfolio Office can have oversight of all the organization's change initiatives and provide you with valuable context.
- A Centre of Excellence can set some relevant standards.
- An existing or newly set-up Project Office can provide services to your projects.

REMEMBER: The art of designing your Programme Office is to achieve sufficient integration to maximise efficiency without compromising independence. Unsurprisingly, integrating Programme Offices is a job I often get asked to advise on.

You can have a number of Programme Offices, perhaps in different locations or based with workstreams (I cover the latter in Chapter 10).

Adding information hub functions

I love having an information hub in my Programme Office. The hub provides a crucial but elegant function that can maintain a high degree of control of the programme without imposing onerous information-reporting requirements on projects in business as usual.

TIP

Your information hub can carry out tasks such as:

- Change control
- Financial accounting
- Information management
- Interface and dependency management
- Quality control
- Risk and issue tracking
- Stakeholders communication
- Tracking and reporting

Using additional expertise

The Programme Office can also provide other services that require more skill or experience and are valued highly by those working in the programme:

- Analysis
- Assistance with techniques
- Coaching and mentoring
- Establishment of infrastructures
- Information and standards custody

If the other offices that you link to are rough and ready (the fancy term for that is *immature*) or non-existent, you may have to provide some of these services:

- Consultancy-style reports
- Health checks
- Internal assurance
- Strategic overview and upward reporting

If no corporate-level strategic change office (often known as a *portfolio office*) exists, the Programme Office may have to keep an eye on what's happening in the organization at the strategic level and also report to the senior level. You may want to strengthen the Programme Office's consultancy function so that it can provide consultancy-style reports to others in the organization who need them.

Even though the Programme Office may be providing internal assurance, you still require independent external assurance that can take an overview of what the Programme Office is doing.

Testing your organizational knowledge

Now you get to put the information I provide in this chapter to use.

Sketch out the organizational structure for your programme or a programme with which you're familiar.

You may want to go even further and do one of the following:

- Draft the terms of reference for different roles based on the examples I give in this chapter.
- Compare your existing terms of reference with this chapter, identify differences and (most importantly) identify any risks arising from the omission or duplication of responsibilities.

Chapter 10

Planning and Controlling Your Programme

In This Chapter

- Moving step-by-step through the planning process
- Slicing your programme into tranches
- Taking control
- Working with planning documents

I can hear some of you thinking (yes, your thoughts are that loud): 'Hey, I'm a project manager. I've been planning and controlling projects for years, and a programme is just a big project. Surely this chapter can't show me much I don't already know.' Well, read on because I think you're going to find plenty of useful new stuff. And those of you who aren't familiar with project planning, don't worry; you don't need any prior knowledge to read this chapter.

In this chapter, I take a look at the difference between programme and project planning. I talk about how you develop the Programme Plan, how you control your programme against the Plan and how you split it into *tranches*(sections that can deliver a new capability to business as usual). I also discuss who deals with each of the documents associated with programme planning and control.

Contrasting Programme and Project Planning and Control

You have to plan your programme and then control it against the Plan. A programme covers transformational change in business as usual, so Programme Plans are much more comprehensive than project plans.

Covering the basic differences

The fact is that programme planning is different from other planning you may be familiar with, for example, project-level planning. Here are some reasons why:

- You have to process very large amounts of information; consequently programme planning isn't just a matter of gathering information from projects and publishing a vast amount of data.
- The large number of stakeholders within a programme means that extensive consultation is required.
- The Plan needs to be built carefully to ensure that it encapsulates all the key information without overloading people with data.
- During the early versions of the Programme Plan you may discover a high level of ambiguity within the Plan – don't worry, this is quite normal.

Controlling a programme also involves more than controlling a big project. To see how they differ from each other, ask yourself, 'Why are we controlling the programme?' Simply and endlessly exerting control against detailed plans is a trap that's all too easy to fall into, and it doesn't necessarily allow you to deliver the programme effectively.

REMEMBER

You carry out programme control in order to:

- Refine and improve delivery
- Minimise ambiguity
- Bring certainty wherever possible
- Justify the continuation of the programme

Planning your programme

In this section I ask you to think about the relationships between the Programme Plan and other documents and themes to help you understand how planning sits at the heart of the programme. See Figure 10-1 for an illustration. I provide cross-references to the chapters where I discuss the related themes where appropriate:

- **Vision Statement.** Look at the Vision Statement and make sure that you have a clear understanding of the objectives of the programme. The Programme Plan has to deliver against the Vision. (Flip to Chapter 5 for more about the Vision Statement.)

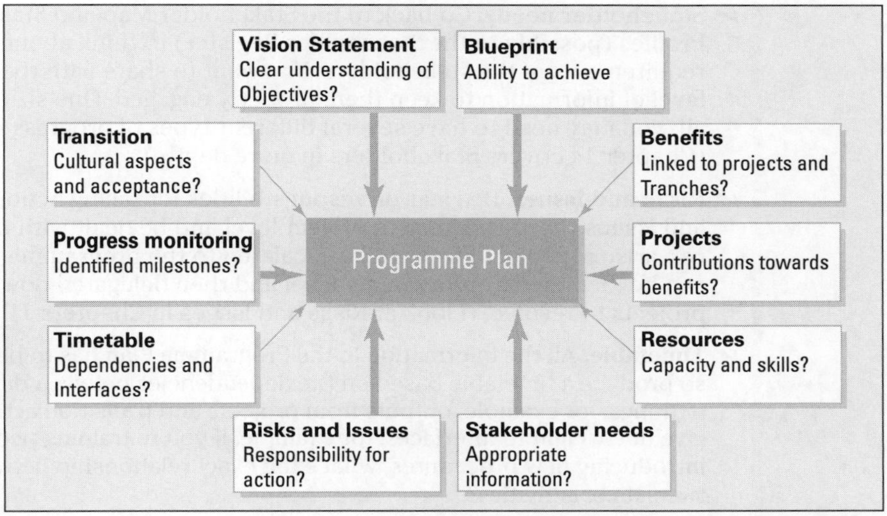

Figure 10-1: Contributions to the programme planning.

- **Blueprint.** Ensure that you look in detail at whether or not the outputs and capabilities that you're planning to create will result in the outcomes described in the Blueprint. Are you focusing on the right things? (Check out Chapter 6 for information on the Blueprint.)
- **Benefits.** Link benefits to projects. You also need to consider the timescale of benefits when putting together the tranches. (Benefits are covered in more detail in Chapter 15.)
- **Projects.** In an Emergent Programme a number of projects are already running and have their own stakeholder groups and supporters. But even a Vision-led Programme has projects that are running as you re-plan. Think vigorously about these projects and make sure that they're contributing outputs that lead eventually to achieving benefits. Indeed, examine projects more carefully than that: make sure that all the outputs being produced by projects ultimately contribute to benefits. (See Chapter 6 for more about Emergent and Vision-led Programmes.)
- **Resources.** Think carefully about the resources available and needed – the phrase *capacity and capability* is useful in this context. *Capacities* mean that you have enough resources and *capabilities* means that people have the right skills.

  TIP

  I've known many programmes that were limited simply because they tried to use all the available capacity and had no way of generating any more.

- **Stakeholder needs.** Go back to the Stakeholder Map and Stakeholder Profiles (possibly to the Stakeholder Register) to think about the requirements of the stakeholders. You want to share with them the right level of information to keep them properly engaged. One size doesn't fit all; you may need to have several different types of progress reporting. (Chapter 14 covers Stakeholders in more depth.)
- **Risks and Issues.** Be clear on responsibilities for taking action on risks and issues. They can arise at project level and be dealt with there. They can arise at project level and be escalated to the programme, or they can be identified at programme level and then delegated down for the projects to resolve. (I look at Risks and Issues in Chapters 11 and 12.)
- **Timetable.** All the information in the Programme Plan has to be scheduled, so produce a timetable based on the dependencies between different types of things, for example, outputs from projects and transition activities. Also, give due weight to interfaces; for example, if you're training people and introducing new procedures, what's the exact relationship between those two sets of activities?
- **Progress monitoring.** Too much information can be as much of a problem as too little when monitoring progress. Identify milestones that are truly significant to the programme. The detailed information can be monitored elsewhere.
- **Transition.** Capture transition activities in the Programme Plan. Transition is never as easy as you anticipate, so make sure that you consider things such as the cultural aspects of transition. Are staff prepared to alter their working practices? Something may seem like a wonderful idea to senior managers, but staff may be much more reluctant. Also consider what needs to happen for products to be truly accepted within business as usual. Make sure that you reflect all these aspects in the Programme Plan. (Transition is covered in Chapter 20.)

Pondering the Planning Process

At the very highest level the planning process is quite straightforward:

1. **Construct a schedule of projects that allows you to achieve benefits.**
2. **Integrate project plans as they're refined.**
   - Consider existing risks and the new risks from linking projects.
3. **Respond to project exceptions.**
   - An exception is basically when something goes wrong – big time. 'Houston, we have a problem,' was Apollo 13 reporting an exception.

4. **Monitor progress.**
   - Anticipate risks.
5. **Consider deadlines and constraints.**

The difficult part is in the first step: constructing a schedule based on benefits. I give you some useful ideas in this chapter, but you may like to look at the sequence I describe in Chapter 7 to see how each of the activities fit together.

Developing the Programme Plan

Simply taking all the project plans and publishing them together is too easy and just results in information overload. You require the level of detail necessary to provide progress information to allow you to identify pressure points and issues. You don't need any more information than that.

REMEMBER

When you think about the tools you're going to use to monitor and maintain your plans, you have to:

- Present the Programme Plan information to stakeholders in a variety of different ways.
- Distribute the Programme Plan to various people, again in different formats.
- Think about how you're going to integrate project-level information.

Prioritising activities

Focus on activities that are critical to the programme. These activities can be projects, such as procurement, that are prerequisites for other projects, or they may be activities that involve scarce resources.

Also give priority to early benefits realization, which provides funding and fosters commitment and enthusiasm.

Coupling and creating cohesion

When I'm planning the next tranche, I bear in mind a couple of ideas:

- **Coupling:** The overlap between projects.
- **Cohesion:** The way the elements in a project fit together.

In Figure 10-2, each circle is a project and the thin lines represent dependencies within the project. This is the cohesion within this project. The thick line is the coupling between two projects.

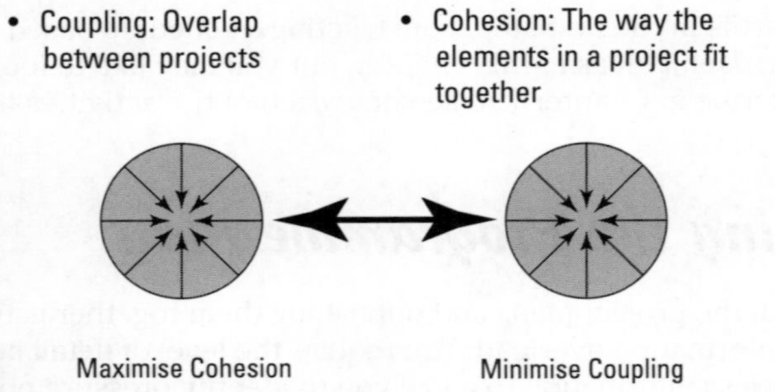
• Coupling: Overlap between projects
• Cohesion: The way the elements in a project fit together
Maximise Cohesion
Minimise Coupling

Figure 10-2: Coupling and cohesion.

The project environment is designed to deal with dependencies. So some cohesion within projects is entirely reasonable.

But when you have a lot of coupling between projects, issues and risks are constantly elevated from project level to programme level, which simply increases the workload at programme level.

REMEMBER

Your aim when reviewing the relationship between outputs and projects is to allow cohesion within projects in order to minimise coupling between projects.

Dependency management

When planning your programme, you want to focus on what's important, and quite often dependencies are vital at the programme level. Thinking about three classes of dependency is helpful:

- **Internal dependencies:** Can be managed within the boundary of the programme.
- **Intra dependencies:** Dependencies on other programmes or projects that are external to the programme but within the perimeter of the organization's programme and project management.
- **External dependencies:** Extend into other parts of the organization or other organizations and are probably outside the control of the programme.

Designing projects

If you have the power to change the scope of the projects in your Project Dossier, take the opportunity at a tranche boundary to slice and dice your projects. Here are some factors to consider:

- Create smaller projects if the task is big or complex.
- Combine small packages of work into a single project.
- Consider the availability of skills.
- Maintain existing team working arrangements (or perhaps even disrupt them).
- Make use of geography and the culture of teams by co-locating a project team or using an existing team to carry out a new project.
- Encourage *management by exception* (delegating an agreed tolerance and then reporting based on how close the project is to that predetermined tolerance level).

Reading about resources

A *resource* is any input required by a project or by the programme, including people, assets, materials, funding and services. You want to focus on shared resources: plan and manage shared resources at the programme level. You can delegate the management of other resources to projects or business as usual. Organizations tend to overestimate their capacity, and therefore you can end up with an unrealistic Programme Plan.

TIP

When you're setting about your planning activities, carry out assurance reviews and perhaps even maturity assessment (explained in Chapter 14) in order to understand the true capacity of the organization.

Here are the types of shared resource to consider:

- **Facilities:** Offices can be shared.
- **Information:** Projects update a shared repository. (In the old days, that was the office filing cabinet. Today it's some fancy cloud-based storage system.)
- **Staff:** Can work part-time on several projects.
- **Third-party services:** Several projects can use the same service provider.

When resourcing the plan, be realistic and bear in mind that:

- Resources have finite availability.
- Availability and capability limit pace.

Home, Home on the Tranche!

You need to organize the work going on within your programme into tranches, a key element in programme planning and control.

Arranging work into tranches

MSP SPEAK

A *tranche* (the French word for slice) is one or more projects and related transformational activities. The key characteristic of the tranche is that it delivers a step change in capability; in other words, something that is really noticeable in business as usual. It has to include the transition activities to achieve outcomes and provides an extremely useful control point for the whole programme.

A tranche ends when the transition stage of the Realizing the Benefits process is completed. In other words, outcomes are achieved and assurance reviews have been carried out, including reviews of the benefits realized to date. I describe that process in Chapter 20. However further benefits are realized in the post-transition phase, and that may happen in a subsequent tranche.

REMEMBER

This is a very precise definition of the end of a tranche. In the real world your tranche boundaries may be more blurred. Be pragmatic when defining your tranches in order to keep stakeholders comfortable and create meaningful control points. I cover the detail of the process in Chapter 18.

TIP

Sometimes splitting complex work, for example, long projects, is useful so that they don't run across tranches. Or you may want to combine small pieces of work to make management and reporting more straightforward.

Working with workstreams

MSP doesn't put a lot of emphasis on workstreams, although the term is used commonly in complex change initiatives. *A workstream* is a logical grouping of projects and activities to enable effective management. They can delineate projects against a whole variety of different criteria.

Practical considerations

Defining tranches is a judgement call. Think about factors such as the skills available to you, what technologies are being used and what facilities already exist. You may need to think about existing teams, so you can use them or break them up, and perhaps consider geography and culture as well. Plus if some existing projects are running (as is most likely), you want to provide a smooth transition between the current projects and the projects planned in the next tranche.

TIP

Although a reasonable description of a workstream, it doesn't really bring it to life. Quite often workstreams run the length of the programme, so if you're looking at a picture of a programme, the tranches are vertical slices and the workstreams are horizontal streams.

The simplest example of a workstream is just the grouping of projects with some natural interrelationship. Most frequently this grouping is by function. You may find an IT workstream with perhaps half-a-dozen projects all with an IT theme. You can also expect to find a human resources workstream and a facilities workstream.

Yes, I know IT projects should rightly be called business projects with a large IT content. But that's not the term used in the real world. The problem with just calling them IT projects is that you might group under an IT manager. It's the interaction with the business that's important from the perspective of the programme and therefore you may want to group those projects in a different way, perhaps by business unit.

Seeing tranches in a programme schedule

Tranches really only make sense when you can see a picture. Figure 10-3 features a simple schedule for a programme showing three tranches:

- **Tranche 1:** Includes projects A, B and C. Benefits are realized after the transition, and benefit reviews may happen sometime after the end of the tranche. But the tranche itself ends soon after transition, which is when any end-of-tranche review has to take place. I discuss reviews more in Chapter 14.
- **Tranche 2:** Includes projects D and F. You can see that project D starts during tranche 1 but logically is part of tranche 2.

- **Tranche 3:** Includes projects E, F and G. Project E has been running during tranches 1 and 2. Although acceptable, I sound a word of caution. In my experience a tranche lasts about six months, perhaps a little longer. That means that project E runs for well over a year. As a general rule, I become concerned when the duration of a project gets up to about one year. My preference, if at all possible, is to break it into a series of shorter projects, but that's a generalisation. In some industries the average duration of a project is much longer.

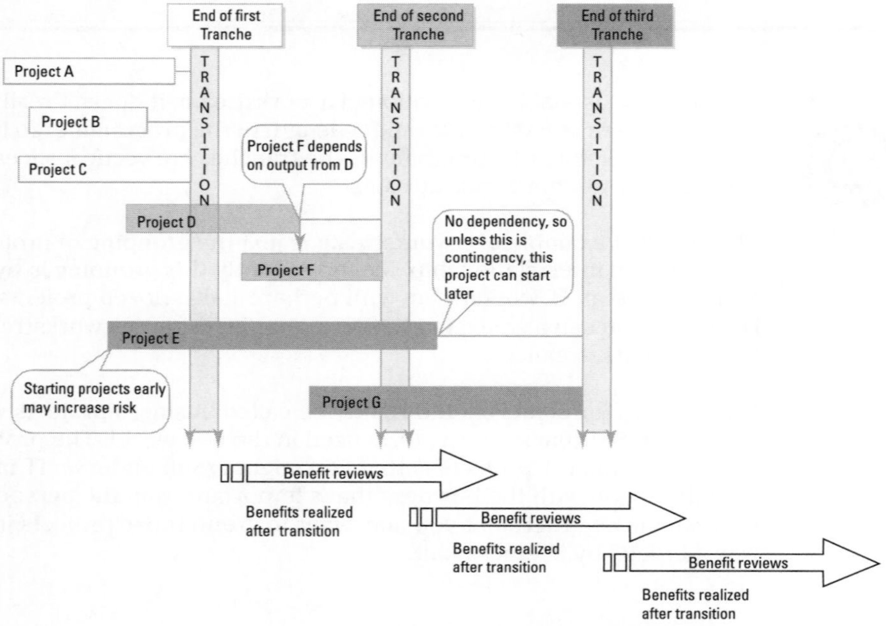

Figure 10-3: A sample programme schedule.

Given this schedule as a draft, I'd do my very best to break project E into two or even three smaller projects. I'd look in detail at the dependency network to see whether those smaller projects can be run in parallel as part of tranche 3, or if some of them can be moved to tranche 2 or even tranche 1.

Tales of the unexpected: Tranche boundaries

At each tranche boundary you hope to have a clear view of the Vision, or, to be more precise, a clear view of how you may get to the Vision. But if I can use a geographical analogy, you won't be able to see hidden valleys along the way. Figure 10-4 illustrates visibility across the tranches. At each subsequent tranche boundary you may get a clearer view – that is, see into more hidden valleys.

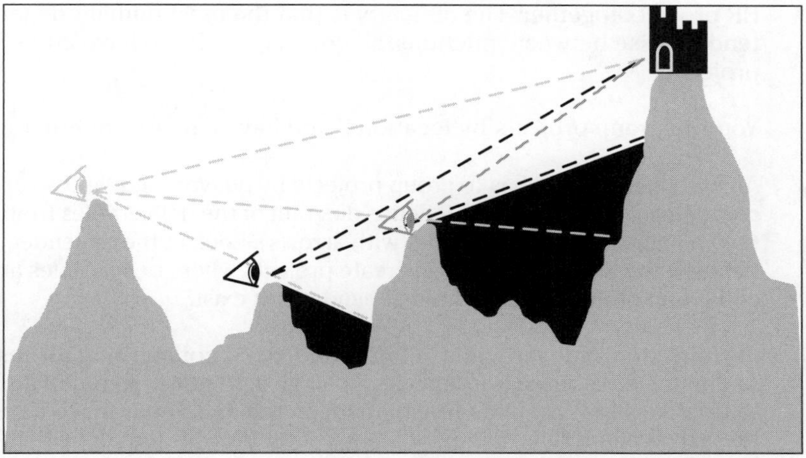

Figure 10-4: Visibility across tranches.

Figure 10-4 is a pretty little way of visualising tranches and getting a better appreciation of how much or how little detail you need in the Plan for the next and subsequent tranches. Notice the hidden valley to the right of the third peak. You can't see into that valley until you get to the beginning of the third tranche.

As a mountaineer on a mountaintop, with a number of hills and valleys between you and that Vision, what can you see? Well, if you look down into the second and third valleys, you can't see the valley floors; some detail is hidden from your view. So you can't plan how you going to cross those second and third valleys.

What you can do is plan how you cross the first valley. You can plan the tranche that's immediately in front of you. When you've done the first tranche and you look across valleys two and three, you still can't see enough detail in valley three, so you can plan only valley two. You know a lot more about valley two than you did at the beginning of the previous tranche, so you can now make a plan for the second tranche. Only when you reach the third peak can you see the third valley and plan the third tranche.

The lesson is not to plan too far ahead.

Grouping projects

When you group projects together, the obvious solution is to group by discipline. Programmes tend to be multidisciplinary, but grouping projects by discipline feels natural. For example, you can group IT projects together and

HR projects together. The difficulty is that the most difficult dependencies tend to arise between functions, so you may prefer to have cross-functional projects.

You can group projects by location if you have a multi-site programme.

TIP

An excellent approach is to group projects by deliverables, and so create some sort of logic network or precedence diagram of the deliverables from the projects (just a diagram linking things up with arrows). Look at the dependencies between the deliverables. Then create projects where deliverables are clustered and group projects again where dependencies exist.

In short, do whatever you can to try and avoid competition for resources and to minimise resource bottlenecks. I can give you only so much advice on how to do this, and it requires pragmatism. In the end you want to have a logic or precedence diagram that avoids tangles of inter-project dependencies; you want flexibility at the programme level.

Figure 10-5 shows a simple example. The five products are grouped into three projects. In the first option, all three projects have to communicate with each of the other two projects. As a result, six lines of communication operate. By regrouping the products, projects 1 and 3 have to communicate only with project 2. So the number of communication channels is reduced to four, without increasing the size of any projects.

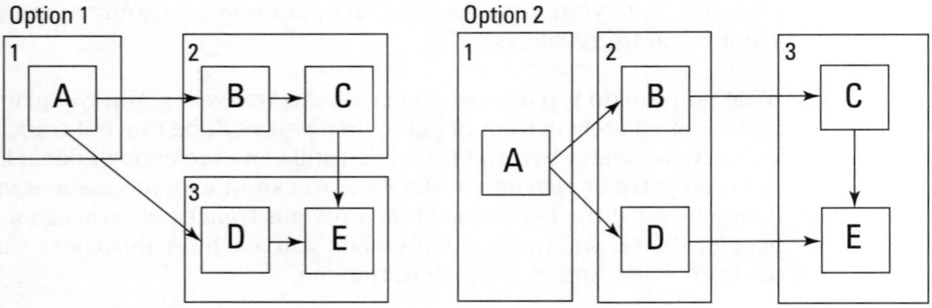

Figure 10-5: Example of a dependency network showing how projects depend on other project outputs.

Controlling Your Programme

As I discuss in the earlier section 'Contrasting Programme and Project Planning and Control', these planning tasks differ in a number of ways. The same is true of programme control.

Here are some typical questions you may ask when controlling a programme that you probably wouldn't ask when controlling a project:

- How will outputs enable change?
- What benefits will follow on?
- What enabling capabilities are also needed?
- On what projects are you dependent?
- What other projects depend on you?
- What's the state of these projects?

Programme control is quite different from project control. In a programme you want to be monitoring, reporting and controlling in order to achieve the Vision, Blueprint, outcomes benefits – that sort of stuff.

Overseeing a programme

Based on my personal experience, here are the aspects that you need to consider when you're overseeing progress at the programme level:

- **Review progress in order to make essential interventions.** You aren't second-guessing your project managers. Their job is to manage their projects and they report from the project perspective. Intervene when only you can see something because you have a programme perspective.
- **Use management by exception when dealing with projects.** Put in place some limits for each project (a tolerance). Deal only with individual issues that are escalated to you by the project manager because, for whatever reason, they feel they can't cope, or when the project exceeds the overall limit (known as an *exception*).
- **Manage dependencies that can't be managed within projects.**
- **Check and maintain alignment with the Blueprint.** The Blueprint is an evolving document both because the team puts more detail into it and due to changes in external circumstances.
- **Oversee quality.** I talk more about quality in Chapter 13.

And this programme was controlled just right

I was talking with a colleague about programme control and he made an insightful comment. He said that either the programme knows too much or it knows too little. So make like Goldilocks (of 'The Three Bears' fame) and reject the too-hot porridge and the too-cold porridge and go for the porridge (the balance) that's just right.

The key is to appreciate what you *must* monitor if you're going to oversee progress effectively.

Monitoring a programme's progress

When you're monitoring the progress of a series of projects, you can easily begin to drown in data. So cut back on what project information is reported to you. Ask for reports with less detail to make them clearer.

Let me put that another way. If I'm a project manager and you ask me if I'm happy with my progress I can answer yes or no. You're then quite clear if I'm happy or not. Or I can write a 3,000-word report that includes lots of ifs and buts and maybes and explanations. When you read the report, you may know more detail, but I doubt if the status of my project would be any clearer to you.

That said, projects must present certain key information in a summary form. The following aspects are crucial, starting with outputs being fit for purpose, then using whatever sequence makes sense for your programme:

- Outputs
- Timely completion against the agreed project plan
- Project risks, issues and assumptions
- Estimates
- Costs and benefits
- Resources
- Scope

Dealing with the Planning Documents

Programme planning and control involves a number of documents and someone has to deal with them. In this section I consider the purpose of each of the relevant documents, look at the composition of two key ones and discuss the areas of focus of each of the key players.

Discussing the purpose of the documents

Here are the purposes of a whole raft of strategies and plans:

- **Monitoring and Control Strategy.** Good Programme Managers know that they have to set up some form of internal control. Often they're quite charismatic characters (ha ha) and have a very clear way of doing things, such as holding a progress meeting every Wednesday morning in a particular room – that sort of thing.

  You let people know that these meetings are going to happen by publishing a *Monitoring and Control Strategy,* which records how the programme is to apply internal controls.

- **Programme Plan.** A comprehensive document used to control progress and track delivery of the programme and outcomes. Occasionally you may hear the word *programme* used to mean schedule and that's the case here.

- **Projects Dossier.** In contrast to the Programme Plan, the Project Dossier is a high-level document – a list of projects required to deliver the Blueprint with high-level information and estimates.

- **Resource Management Strategy.** Identifies how the programme is to acquire and manage resources needed to achieve business change. For example, you can negotiate with the finance director about how the programme can access funding – that goes into the Resource Management Strategy. Or you may have contracts with external companies that provide different types of resources.

  The more topics you can tackle proactively and record in the Resource Management Strategy, the less reactive resource management you have to do.

- **Resource Management Plan.** The arrangements for implementing the Resource Management Strategy. You can run the programme using crisis management – begging, borrowing and stealing resources when you need them. But the process is much more efficient if you've already negotiated ways of getting hold of resources and you have a plan for doing so.

Looking inside two documents

I look only at the composition of the Programme Plan and the Project Dossier. These two documents are central to your planning, while the composition of the other two documents (the Resource Management Strategy and Resource Management Plan) can vary quite widely.

Programme Plan

This list shows what the Programme Plan contains, but it gives no indication of its size or complexity, because that depends on the programme:

- Programme schedule
- Dependency network
- Cross-reference to the Risk Register
- Explanation of project grouping
- Transition plan
- Monitoring and control activities
- Programme tranches
- Effort and cost

Project Dossier

A useful idea is to record slightly more than a list of projects in the Project Dossier:

- List of projects
- Outline of outputs and resources
- Timescales and programme level dependencies
- Initial requirements from the Blueprint
- High-level budgets
- Contributions to outcomes and benefits
- Issues and risks

TIP

I often include a matrix that maps project outputs onto outcomes and then onto benefits.

Clarifying the planning areas of focus

This section covers the areas of focus for key roles in terms of planning and control. Flip to Chapter 9 for detailed descriptions of these roles and check out the earlier section 'Discussing the purpose of the documents' for more on the documents.

The Senior Responsible Owner focuses on the following:

- Consulting the Sponsoring Group and other key stakeholders and maintaining their buy-in, especially in preparing for and carrying out transition.
- Leading the on-going monitoring and review activities of the programme in mid-tranche and at end-of-tranche, including commissioning formal reviews such as audits or health checks, if required.
- Monitoring progress and direction of the programme at a strategic level and initiating management interventions where necessary.
- Authorising the Resource Management Strategy and the Monitoring and Control Strategy.
- Ensuring that adequate assurance is designed into the control mechanisms.
- Authorising the Projects Dossier, Programme Plan and the required monitoring and control activities.

The Programme Manager focuses on:

- Designing the Projects Dossier, Resource Management Strategy, Monitoring and Control Strategy and the required assurance activities.
- Designing of the Programme Plan.
- Ensuring that the Blueprint, Programme Plan, Benefits Realization Plan and Benefit Profiles are consistent and able to deliver the Business Case and remain aligned.
- Developing the Resource Management Strategy and deployment of the Plan.
- Developing and deploying the Monitoring and Control Strategy.

- Establishing and managing the appropriate governance arrangements for the programme and its projects.
- Ensuring that key programme documentation is current.
- Creating and issuing Project Briefs.
- Identifying and managing programme dependencies.
- Progress-reporting to the Senior Responsible Owner and the Programme Board on projects, Business Case, Programme Plan and Blueprint achievement.
- Adjusting the Projects Dossier, Blueprint and Plans to get the best flow of benefits.
- Managing stakeholder expectations and participating in communications activities to inform stakeholders of progress and issues.

The Business Change Manager has plenty to do in connection with planning and control, a lot of it focused around transition in business as usual:

- Consulting with the Programme Manager on designing the Project Dossier and scheduling the tranches and constituent projects to ensure that the transition aligns with the required benefits realization.
- Ensuring that changes are implemented in the business.
- Ensuring that the business continues to co-operate effectively during the period of change.
- Providing adequate and appropriate business and operational resources to the programme and its projects to ensure that outputs are designed, developed and assured to give them the best chance of enabling the scale of improvement required.
- Making sure that the operational functions are adequately prepared and ready to change when transition starts.
- Ensuring that plans are in place to maintain business operations during the change process until transition and handover are complete; also providing input to the reviews.
- Planning the transition within operational areas and accommodating requirements to maintain business operations.
- Ensuring that when transition is completed, the focus remains to establish the new ways of working and ensure that old practices do not creep back in (like an unpleasant insect you throw out the bedroom window during the night!).

The Programme Office is the information hub and involves:

- Supporting the development of planning, control and information management arrangements.
- Gathering information and presenting progress reports on projects.
- Supporting the Programme Manager in the development of reports.
- Providing the programme teams with information and resources that can assist with the design of documentation.
- Establishing and operating the programme's information and configuration management systems, procedures and standards.
- Collecting, monitoring and measuring data and keeping the information up to date.
- Collecting and presenting information on business performance.
- Ensuring that coherent and common project-level standards are in place for all document management arrangements for the programme.

Testing your programme planning and control knowledge

If you're in a programme, try a dummy end-of-tranche re-plan. Think about how you can slice and dice the projects.

Consider reviewing the information you use to control the programme. Check that you have neither too much nor too little information flowing to the centre.

Chapter 11

Managing Risk in Your Programme

In This Chapter

- Understanding the principles of risk management
- Taking a perspective on risks in different parts of the programme
- Using the risk-management approach
- Applying the risk-management process

By definition, any activity (such as your shiny new programme) that seeks to achieve benefits through change is going to include a certain level of uncertainty – in other words, risk. You can't avoid this reality. Risk isn't something to avoid at all costs (like saying, 'Do you want me to drive?' when your partner is fuming behind the wheel after taking yet another wrong turn), which is why I call this chapter 'Managing Risk in Your Programme' and not 'Avoiding Risk in Your Programme'.

Risk management is a big subject, and in this chapter I take a broad look at risks in the context of a programme. Plenty of risks can arise within a typical programme, so as well as covering the principles and terminology used, I also discuss the *perspectives,* which are the different parts of the business in which risks can appear (this practice is quite different from project risk management). When running a programme you're constantly judging whether you need to manage risk in one perspective or another.

In addition, I cover the risk management approach (another name for all the risk documents that you can use) and I look at the processes you can follow when you're managing risks.

TIP

Risk management is frequently linked with issue management, which I cover in Chapter 12. Therefore, to see the connection between risks and issues read that chapter while this one is fresh in your mind.

Introducing the Basics: Risks and Issues in a Programme Context

Crucial to dealing effectively with the risks that your programme faces is understanding the difference between a risk and an issue:

- **Risk:** An uncertain event or set of events that may affect you in achieving your programme's objectives. You state a risk in terms of the probability of the threat or opportunity. Don't forget *upside risks* by the way, which can be called opportunities. For example, if this book is very popular, I'll get lots of invitations to speak at conferences. It's still a risk, despite being a nice problem to have.

  You calculate the size of a risk as follows:

  Probability of Threat or Opportunity × Magnitude of Impact

- **Issue:** An unplanned event that occurs and requires management action because it affects the programme. An issue can be a problem, query, concern, change request or risk.

Sitting at the centre of the programme you're interested in are risks and issues that matter to you and come from those parts of the environment where the programme is having an effect. Here are a few examples:

- Benefits and transition.
- Dependencies, constraints and quality that don't affect just one isolated part of the programme but are common across a number of areas.
- Common and above-project risks and issues.
- Stakeholders including staff and third parties.
- Circumstances where operational performance can be degraded.
- Where ambiguity about states exists (*states* are a description of the future described in the Blueprint – refer to Chapter 6).

Viewing programme risk in context

A programme's context is necessarily complex, dynamic and uncertain. Indeed, you want to maintain a certain level of uncertainty within the programme in order to maximise innovation and allow for a flexible boundary (I discuss the boundary to the programme in more detail in Chapter 4 about principles, and Chapter 7, where I look at the documents where you describe the programme boundary). Therefore you need to manage and tolerate uncertainty, complexity and perhaps even ambiguity.

REMEMBER

Risk management helps you define a risk exposure and maintain it at an acceptable level. It avoids the occurrence of adverse events, militates against the effect of those adverse events and reduces the cost of dealing with risks. All these aspects come together to help increase the probability of you achieving your desired benefits.

Getting risk clear: Basic phraseology

I audit lots of *Risk Registers* (which I define in the later section 'Gotcha! Capturing risks with the Risk Register') and one of the largest and most common mistakes I see is that the risks aren't stated in a clear and unambiguous way. Therefore I find the basic language of risk, as shown in Figure 11-1, invaluable. If you're already an expert on risk, you can skip this section.

Figure 11-1 is called a *probability impact grid* on which you can plot the likelihood of the risk vertically and the impact of the effect of the risk horizontally. When you add the risks it's called a *Summary Risk Profile.*

You use a scale or standard, which you need to define, using terms such as very low, low, medium, high and very high. Each of those bands doesn't have to be of equal size. For example, very low probability can be from 0 per cent to 20 per cent, while very high probability can be a smaller band running from 95 per cent to 99.9 per cent. Also on the impact scale you need to have different standards for each class of risk. So reputational risk can have one set of definitions and financial risk a different set.

The stepped *risk tolerance line* indicates the point above which risks must be escalated to the next level of management.

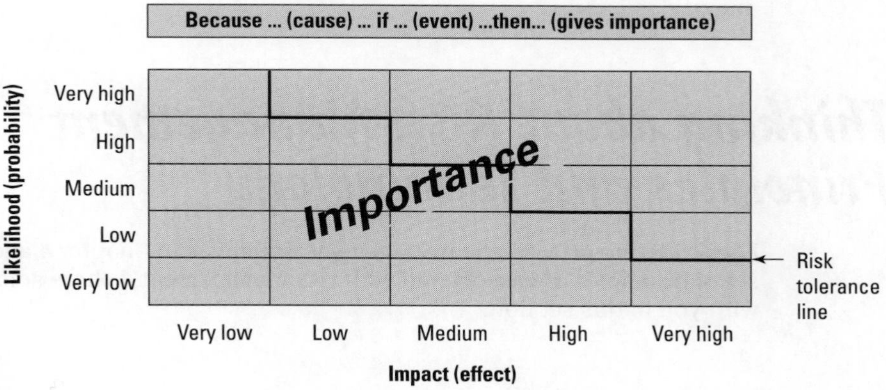

Figure 11-1: Risk – basic phraseology.

'Me talk clearly one day'

When writing about risk I prefer to use the 'if *x* then *y*' structure to one that goes 'there is a risk that *x*', because it's too easy to say only 'there is a risk that I'll write this paragraph incorrectly': in other words, to mention only one of the two elements of risk (probability) and leave out the resulting impact.

In addition, using 'because' before the details of the risk allows you to describe the existing circumstances, which are to some extent fixed. People find knowing the 'because' statement useful because it puts the risk into context: 'Because I have been working for a long time, I may write this paragraph incorrectly. If I write this paragraph incorrectly then I have to redraft it'.

I label the sloping line 'importance' rather than 'criticality' or 'expected value': the 'bigness' of the risk is what's important. 'Bigness' is a strange word that I use when I want people to think about the overall size of the risk. I don't like 'criticality' because it seems more appropriate for a threat than an opportunity and 'expected value' sounds technical and financial. The real danger is that instead of talking about the severity of the risk, people talk only about the severity of the impact.

You can say 'There is a high probability that I may write this paragraph incorrectly', but redrafting has a very low impact. The risk is medium-sized, because it's got a high probability and a low impact. If you look only at the impact you underestimate the significance of the risk. So make sure that you have clear language for the 'bigness' of a risk.

MSP SPEAK

At the top of the figureI include the format of the very simple language that I find is best used when writing about risks. I like to use the 'if *x* then *y*' phrasing (such as, 'If I write this paragraph incorrectly then I have to redraft it'), because it forces you to write down both an event (which has a probability) and an effect (which has an impact). To discover more about the importance of using precise language, take a look at the nearby sidebar 'Me talk clearly one day'.

Thinking about Risk-Management Principles and Terminology

I describe the programme management principles in Chapter 4 and a similar set of principles are associated with risk management. I share some of them with you in this section.

Meeting the principles: M_o_R

The principles of risk management are taken from a sister method to MSP called M_o_R (Management of Risk). These principles fit nicely with the way you want to run your programme and the principles of programme management as follows:

- **You need to make sure risk management is aligned with organizational objectives.** Clearly a parallel exists here with the MSP principle of remaining aligned with corporate strategy.
- **The Risk Management Strategy must be designed to fit the current context** (flip to the later section 'Defining required activities: Risk Management Strategy'). In other words, you need to put in place sufficient risk management to be appropriate for whatever you're doing, in this case running a programme.
- **Your approach to risk management needs to engage stakeholders and deal with the differing perceptions of risk from the different stakeholder communities.** As I cover in more detail in Chapter 14, you consider the different stakeholder groups with an interest in your programme (as you're aware, a diversity of stakeholder groups exists within a programme). Stakeholders have a good idea of what risk may appear in their area and be pretty good at judging the size of those risks. You can accept their opinions on new risks and their size without questioning them too much, and if their view is different from yours, a consensus will emerge as you go through the risk-management process.
- **You need to provide clear and coherent guidance to stakeholders on how to undertake risk management within your programme.** The document set within MSP makes aligning with this principle easy. You create a Risk Management Strategy and produce Risk Registers. Individual projects and business areas may even publish their own risk management strategies, so you can ensure sufficient local advice on how to carry out risk management.
- **The next principle is that risk management needs to inform decision-making.** Risk management can all too easily exist in a bubble. If it's seen as an end in itself, risk management rapidly becomes a tick-box exercise – an extra piece of bolt-on bureaucracy. You have to link risk management to decision-making across the programme so that better decisions can be made.
- **Risk management should facilitate learning and continuous improvement.** You need to use the historical data that you're accumulating about risk management to encourage continual improvement. Clearly a strong link applies to the programme management principle of learning from experience.

- **Risk management needs to recognise uncertainty and support considered risk-taking – a supportive culture.** If whenever you say to the boss 'I've spotted a risk', the boss tells you off and says, 'Risks aren't allowed to exist in my programme', you aren't going to achieve successful risk management. So you need to create a supportive culture that recognises the existence of uncertainty. A programme, remember, supports considered risk-taking.

  You can never mitigate all risks; all you can ever do is select certain risks and mitigate them even though some still occur.

- **The final and some argue the most important risk-management principle is that risk management needs to achieve measurable value.** You're only doing risk management in order to achieve the goals of the programme. Again a strong link can be made here to the programme management principle of adding value.

Talking the talk: Risk terminology

Several pieces of useful terminology exist in connection with risk management.

Risk appetite

Risk tolerance is the point above which risks need to be escalated (see the earlier section 'Introducing the Basics: Risks and Issues in a Programme Context'). It's a really useful mechanistic definition when putting in place procedures for escalating risks, but something cultural sits behind risk tolerance: the risk appetite of the organization.

A mechanistic approach

I use the term *mechanistic* quite a bit in this book, which just means, in MSP world, that you write down how to do something. If you want to alter the way people behave by just writing down what you want them to do and telling them to do it, that's a mechanistic approach. It's quite old-fashioned, but it works in simple circumstances. If you get into a more complex situation then you need to think about how you can also change cultures and behaviours. In a programme you sometimes do things in a mechanistic way; on other occasions you're more focused on the behavioural or cultural side of things.

Risk appetite is the amount of risk an organization is willing to accept. In other words, is the organization comfortable taking risks or is it risk averse? When you know the organization's risk appetite you can create your programme Risk Management Strategy (for detail, see 'Defining required activities: Risk Management Strategy' later in this chapter). The risk appetite steers risk management activities because it helps you define your delegation and escalation rules. This approach helps you insulate the programme from unwelcome surprises and define clear risk tolerances.

The risk tolerance thresholds:

- Translate the risk appetite into objective guidelines.
- Define the exposure that, if exceeded, requires escalation and reaction.
- Need to be in line with the programme objectives.

Assumptions

An *assumption* is just another way of stating that a risk has a very low probability. You can also use assumptions to describe uncertainties (which in essence is another word for risk) that are outside the influence of the programme.

Therefore, when you state a set of assumptions they help to clarify the boundary of the programme. You can consider assumptions to be potential sources of risks. Because assumptions are related to the programme boundary, you probably want to review the related risks at programme level.

Early warning indicators

Early warning indicators are performance indicators that lead, rather than lag, a change in the situation. They're used for all sorts of purposes throughout business as usual.

You can use early warning indicators as sources of risks. For example, staff sickness levels are a lead indicator of staff morale. If staff sickness levels begin to increase, you can identify some risks around forthcoming transition activities.

If you're going to take the time and trouble to track early warning indicators, remember that they're of value only if:

- You track valid indicators.
- You look at them regularly.
- They're accurate.
- You act on them.

Threats, opportunities, events and effects

When thinking about risks most people consider threats not opportunities. You may like to review any Risk Registers that you have and check how many opportunities are recorded in them (see the later section 'Gotcha! Capturing risks with the Risk Register').

The same event can be both a threat and an opportunity and therefore give rise to several risks. As you think more about risks you begin to separate events from effects. One event can trigger several effects, and an effect can be triggered by several different events. In the same way, the causes of a risk can lead to several different risks, or the same risk can arise from several different situations.

Also, an event can have different effects in different parts of the programme.

Proximity

You normally express risk in terms of two factors: probability and impact (as I explain in the earlier section 'Getting risk clear: Basic phraseology'). Sometimes, however, a third factor is useful: a time factor – the *proximity.* You use it when the risk is expected to occur at a particular time. So the severity of the overall impact of the risk varies depending on when the risk occurs.

Knowing the proximity and factoring it into the assessment of the risk has an effect on the urgency with which you take action, the nature of the response, what triggers the response and the timing of the response.

Proximity is particularly useful because a programme is likely to be long and some risks you identify aren't going to happen for a long time. If you give them a low proximity score, you record them but don't have to deal with them yet (check out the nearby sidebar 'Getting IT right' for a real-life example).

A statement such as 'something happens once in every 12 months' isn't a statement of proximity: it's a statement of the frequency of occurrence or another way of stating a probability.

Risk owner and risk actionee

As with so much in programme management, you want to be clear about terms:

- **Risk owner:** Named individual responsible for the management and control of all aspects of a risk.
- **Risk actionee:** Named individual assigned to implement the risk response action; this person supports and takes direction from the risk owner.

For more detail about who's responsible for the different aspects of risk (and issue) management, check out Chapter 12.

TRUE STORY

Getting IT right

I once helped a hospital move its IT department. I categorised risks using proximities of: before the move = 3, during the move = 2 and after the move = 1. The risk size was multiplied by the proximity to give the overall significance of the risk.

As a result earlier risks got a higher score and were considered first.

Risk aggregation

As risks pass up to the strategic level and down to projects some of them stick at programme level. You have to gather together the effect of risks from different sources at programme level.

MSP SPEAK

The generic term in this risk management activity is *risk aggregation,* which implies looking across all the risks and evaluating your overall risk exposure. Risk aggregation is a highly significant feature of programme risk management.

REMEMBER

As risks aggregate their effect can increase or diminish. So programme level risks can:

- Accumulate
- Grow (the sum is greater than the parts)
- Reduce (the sum is less than the parts)

Also, apparently independent risks can have a cascade effect: they can trigger other risks or increase or diminish the effect of other risks. As Programme Manager you're the right person to examine carefully the aggregated risks.

You need to consider factors such as the timing of related risks and their overall impact. You need to look at the overall cost of mitigation actions and think about whether mitigation is to be carried out at programme level or locally.

Dealing with Risk in Four Perspectives

Management of Risk (which I introduce in the earlier section 'Meeting the principles: M_o_R') looks at risk management from four perspectives: strategic (or corporate), programme, project and operational. See Figure 11-2 for an illustration of the hierarchy. You can add a fifth portfolio perspective if someone is running portfolio management in your organization.

I look at the types of risk that appear at each perspective and how in a programme you pass risks from perspective to perspective so that the right people can handle them.

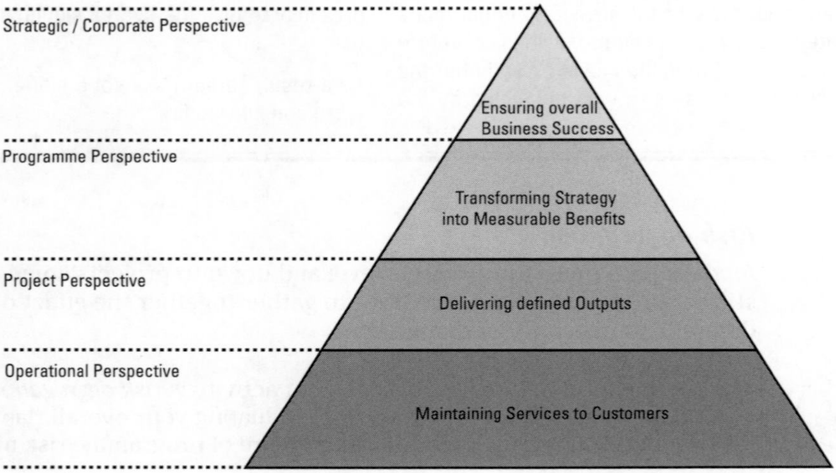

Figure 11-2: Organizational management hierarchy.

REMEMBER

Here are brief descriptions of each of the four perspectives and how they can interrelate:

- **Strategy.** The strategic perspective means looking outside the programme at the business or even outside the business at the external environment. It often has a longer-term focus. You may identify risks at the programme level that need to be escalated to the strategic level and you can also argue that the programme came into existence to deal with specific strategic-level risks.
- **Programme.** Your focus is on the programme perspective. Risks in this area are risks to the programme: for example, risks to benefits, outcomes, the Blueprint and execution of the programme. You can see this in terms of interrelationships: from the programme perspective you may need to escalate risks to the strategic level or pass them down to projects or the operational perspective.
- **Project.** The project perspective concerns risks relating to project delivery. You can think about typical project constraints such as time, cost, quality and so on. Project risk may have to be escalated to the programme or you may want to pass them across to the operational world. You hope that the relationships within the programme organization structure make doing so more straightforward.

- **Operational.** The operational perspective is concerned with risks to business as usual. You can if you like call this the 'business as usual' perspective. From the operational level operational risk owners may delegate risks to projects or they may escalate them to the strategic level.

Surveying the typical risks to a programme

Your programme doesn't have to deal only with programme risks; you may also need to get involved with risks that rightly sit in other perspectives. Here are some areas where different types of risks might arise:

- Strategic-level risks:
  - Other programmes
  - Political pressures
- Programme-level risks:
  - Changing requirements
  - Inter-project dependencies
- Project-level risks:
  - Changing requirements
  - Resource availability
- Operational-level risks:
  - Transfer to operations
  - Organizational acceptance

Thinking about programme risks and issues

Figure 11-3 is a simple diagram that allows you to consider the flow of risks and issues within the programme. But don't get too deeply into the detail of this diagram because it's not an explicit process model – it's just a set of concepts.

REMEMBER

You're trying to capture and log risks and issues in an appropriate way. Your focus is on programme-level risk and issue management, not necessarily risk and issue management that may be happening away from the centre of the programme. You should delegate that work.

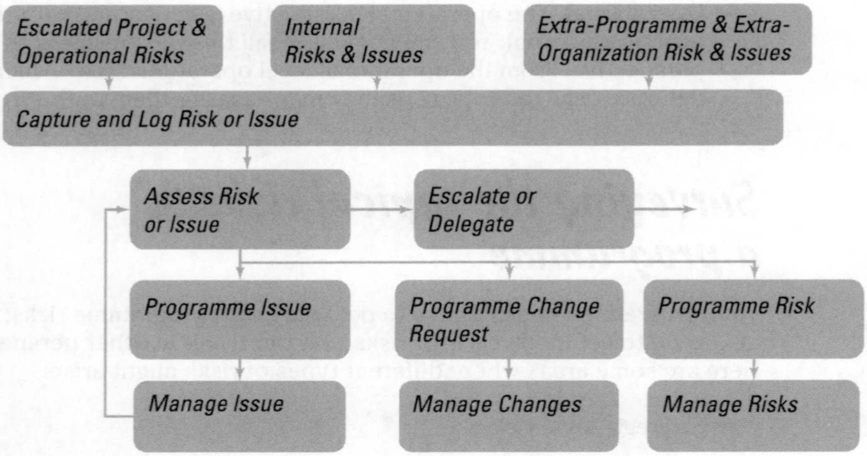

Figure 11-3: Risk and issue management.

I want to give you a feel for the complexity of risk and issue management at programme level. The following list gives you a little more insight into how risks move around within a programme:

- Risks may be escalated from projects or from business as usual.
- The people at the centre of the programme themselves identify risks and issues, and therefore some are internally generated from, say, the Programme Office.
- You also get risks from outside the programme but still within the business and perhaps even from outside the organization. So you also have to pick up risks and issues from these broader areas of interest.

You need a capability to assess all these risks or issues. Part of the assessment is considering where you can best manage the risks. You can deal with them at programme level or escalate them or delegate them. You can have a whole series of escalation and delegation routes that you have to document.

The risks and issues at your level can take different forms when assessed. Perhaps something is a programme issue that you need to manage, which may in turn trigger other risks and issues. This issue may be a change request that you need to manage, assessing it, considering it at the right body (a committee or working group, for example) and executing the change if action is approved.

If it's a programme risk, of course you use your risk-management process to manage it.

Distinguishing programme and project risks

You need to be absolutely clear on the difference between programme and project risks and ensure that your projects have the same understanding. In Figure 11-4, I envisage risks as being like satellites moving between the Earth's and the Moon's orbit. Sometimes you need to boost the satellite out of the Earth's orbit into an orbit around the Moon; sometimes a satellite in orbit around the Moon needs to come back to the Earth (if this doesn't make sense, read *Rocket Science For Dummies!*).

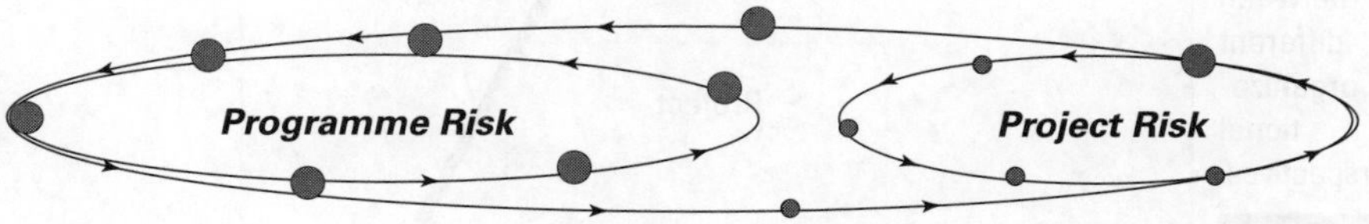

Figure 11-4: Programme and project risks: red circles represent individual risks.

REMEMBER

Here are a few examples of programme and project risks:

- Project risk: Within the span of control of a project that belongs to your programme, for example, time, quality or cost:
  - An intra-project, that is, one with no impact outside of the project.
- Programme risk: Outside the span of control of a project that belongs to your programme:
  - An inter-project, for example, dependencies.
  - An extra-project, for example, external factors.
  - Threats to the achievement of programme benefits.

Investigating interrelationships between different organizational perspectives

The whole idea of risks passing between perspectives gets more complex than even the preceding three sections may imply, because not all risks pass through the programme. So, for example, they may pass directly between the strategic and operational perspectives. Take a look at Figure 11-5, where the diagonal black line indicates the boundary between change and business as usual.

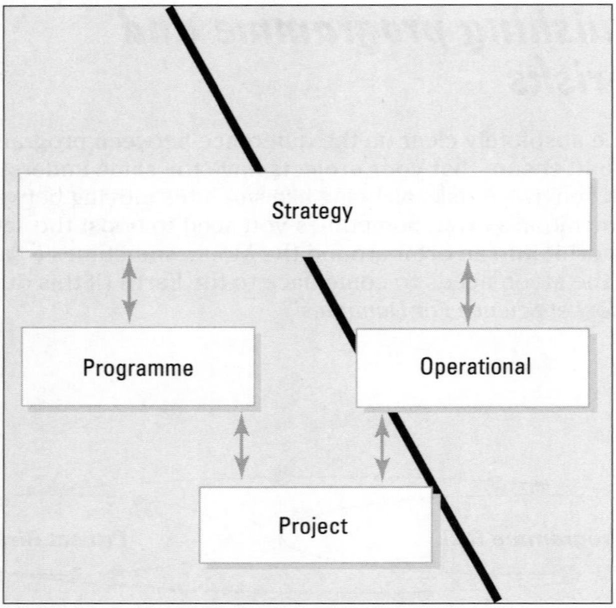

Figure 11-5: Interrelationships between different organizational perspectives.

I discuss the interrelations of the four perspectives in the following four sections.

Strategic risk and issue sources

Strategic risks and issues are going to be external to the programme. So they can be events that are externally triggered from beyond the business or just from outside your programme. If you're considering strategic risks from outside the programme, they can be triggered by other programmes just as you can be generating strategic risks for other programmes. Also certain risks and issues can occur between your programme and other programmes. Typically these involve inter-programme dependencies.

But other things that are going on in the business may not be as well structured as a programme. They may simply be cross-organizational *initiatives:* things happening across the business. For example, if the business is engaged with a third party and something happens in that third party, say a supplier goes bankrupt, that gives rise to strategic issues and risks that you have to consider within the programme.

Another category you need to consider is internal policies. By that I mean those internal to the business, internal to the organization if you like, not internal to the programme. For example, perhaps the finance director issues a new policy on accounting that gives rise to risks and issues in the way you carry out your financial management.

Programme risk and issue sources

Here's quite a long list of sources of programme-level risks and issues:

- **Aggregated project threats.** They may simply be individual project threats and opportunities or the total of a number of project threats.
- **Lack of senior management consensus.** If senior managers don't agree on the direction of the programme, they may find making decisions more difficult, or may take decisions that don't help the programme.
- **Lack of benefits clarity or buy-in.** Among those who should be owning and championing the benefits.
- **Cross-organizational complexity.** Perhaps the sheer complexity of what's going on across the organization – the complexity that you're triggering by carrying out the programme – gives rise to issues and risks.
- **Interdependencies.** A key source of programme issues and risks. Indeed, when you're controlling the programme you want to keep the closest track of interdependencies.
- **Funding uncertainty.** Perhaps over-funding.
- **Unrealistic timescales.** This can happen in project world or business as usual. An example from business as usual is if Business Change Managers underestimate the time taken to achieve transition, then benefit realization may be delayed.
- **Resource availability.** Non-availability of resources is a fertile source of programme-level issues and risks.

Project risk and issue sources

The sources of project-level issues and risks can be ones that you delegate down to the projects. Or they may occur in the project and you need simply to ensure that you deal with them within the projects.

Project risk sources can include:

- Lack of clarity on customer requirements within a project
- Lack of availability of resources within a project that affects one project but not a series of projects across the programme
- Timescales
- Quality expectations
- Project drifting off track because of limited visibility of the Blueprint within the project
- Procurement problems
- Scheduling problems
- Lack of visibility of programme-level risks

Operational risk and issue sources

Examples of operational risks and issues may be that business as usual managers, perhaps those who aren't Business Change Managers but are their colleagues, regard the programme as being their biggest source of risks and issues.

Operational risk sources can include:

- **Quality of benefit-enabling outputs.** The outputs that you're creating enable benefits to be realized that aren't of an appropriate quality.
- **Cultural issues.** Perhaps you're trying to change the culture more significantly then you appreciate.
- **Affecting business continuity.** If an output coming from a project works in the test environment in the project, but it isn't really suitable for the businesses, then existing business-as-usual operations may be disrupted.
- **Ability of operations to cope with outputs.** Overloading operations so that they don't have time to concentrate on business as usual while also coping with the capabilities you're providing.
- **Commitment.** Perhaps commitment to the programme within the operational area declines.
- **Stakeholder support.** Stakeholders who aren't really committed to the programme may not be a problem initially. But if, later on, you need them to really get behind the programme and make some changes in their environment and they're a bit lukewarm, then they won't make the necessary changes.
- **Industrial relations.** If you can't reach an agreement with trade unions they may take actions that prevent you from changing business as usual.
- **Availability of resources.** Within the operational area.
- **Track record in not managing change successfully within the operational area.** If the business hasn't been successful managing changes directly, you may face a fair amount of cynicism about your programme.

You can group several of these topics together under a heading of the *rate of change.* Maybe the rate of change that you're imposing on operations is just too great.

Documenting the Risk-Management Approach

The *risk-management approach* is just another term for the risk-management documentation. In this section I share with you the purpose and composition of three risk documents that you need in your programme.

For details on another document – the Probability Impact Grid/Summary Risk Profile – flip to the earlier 'Getting risk clear: Basic phraseology' section.

Defining required activities: Risk Management Strategy

The purpose of the *Risk Management Strategy* is to define and establish the required activities and responsibilities for managing the programme's risks.

The typical content covers: how to identify risks, responses and actions; how to handle risk ownership; how to make and implement decisions (for example, the tolerance you're delegating to others); how to monitor and evaluate actions and communication mechanisms.

More specifically, the Risk Management Strategy features the following:

- Assessing the effectiveness of risk management
- Early warning indicators (for an explanation, check out the earlier 'Talking the talk: Risk terminology' section)
- Escalation criteria
- How proximity is assessed
- How to calculate expected value
- Information flows and reporting
- Relevant standards
- Risk response category
- Roles and responsibilities
- Process
- Scales for estimating probability and impact
- Techniques

- The links between risk management and benefits management
- The templates you're going to use for documents like Risk Registers
- Timing of risk-management activities

Gotcha! Capturing risks with the Risk Register

A *Risk Register* lets you capture and manage actively the programme risks. Here are its typical elements:

- Risk identifier
- Risk description
- Probability
- Programme impact
- Proximity
- Response description
- Residual risk
- Risk owner and risk actionee
- Response type
- Current status
- Cross-reference to plan

Monitoring risks: Risk Progress Report

A *Risk (or Issue) Progress Report* is a tool to maintain oversight and monitoring of the overall risk and issue trends and to aggregate escalated key project risks and issues. I list headings in the Risk Progress Report below, starting with some pretty simple ideas and then going on to more sophisticated ones. Therefore you may not need those later headings:

- Action:
  - Progress
  - Effectiveness

- Trend analysis
- Contingency spend (money put aside to spend on dealing with risks)
- Number of risks emerging by:
  - Category
  - Project
- Anticipated risks
- The movement of relevant indicators against their target values

Following the Risk-Management Process

Figure 11-6 depicts the risk-management process, taken from M_o_R. The steps in this cycle and the transformational flow have no rigid links between them. I see each of these process steps happening on many occasions within each MSP transformational flow process. (I introduce the processes within the MSP transformational flow in Chapter 1.)

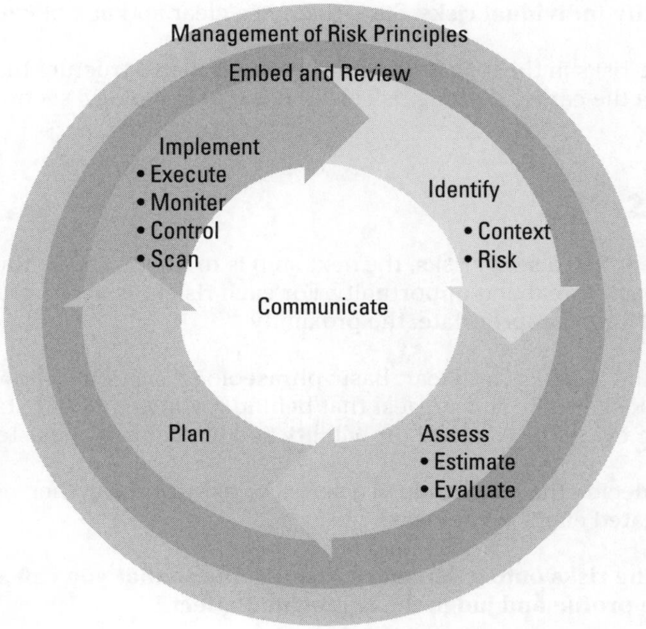

Figure 11-6: Programme risk-management cycle.

Communicate

Communication is an on-going activity during risk management. By communicating with the relevant stakeholders you're constantly identifying new risks that you can feed into the identifying, assessing, planning and implementing cycle.

TIP

Use *horizon scanning* when communicating, which involves imagining what the world will be like in the 'to be' state.

Identify

I suggest that you break identification into two steps:

1. **Identify the context within which you're looking for risks.** Think about the context of the programme, for example, its objectives and scope, any assumptions, stakeholders and the environment in which you're working.

   If you're carrying out risk identification within part of the programme, you want to examine in detail the context of that part of the programme. When you understand the context, you can move onto the second step.

2. **Identify individual risks.** State them in a clear and unambiguous way.

TIP

Record the risks in the Risk Register using the 'if then' structure that I describe in the earlier 'Getting risk clear: Basic phraseology' section.

Assess

Having identified a set of risks, the next step is to assess them. You need to estimate each threat and opportunity. For each risk look at the probability, the impact and, if appropriate, the proximity.

Earlier in the 'Getting risk clear: Basic phraseology' section, I show you a Summary Risk Profile and suggest that behind it you need clear standards, which help everyone estimate probability and impact in a consistent way.

After you decide the magnitude of a series of risks, you can then evaluate the net aggregated effect of the risks:

1. **Plot the risks onto a Summary Risk Profile so that you can simply look at the profile and judge the aggregated effect.**
2. **Add up the financial effect (expected value) of the risks, if they can be expressed in financial terms. This total is the *expected monetary value.***

TIP

If risks are expressed in different terms, for example, some are financial and some are reputational, you're probably going to have to use some form of risk modelling. Time to call in a risk specialist!

Plan

REMEMBER

You gain very little value in identifying and assessing a whole series of risks if you do nothing about them. The key is to put in place real, workable plans to address a specific number of risks. You'd rather see a programme properly addressing one risk than attempting and failing to address dozens of risk!

So for each risk that you decide you need to deal with, prepare a specific management response to remove or reduce the threat or maximise the opportunity. The aim is to make sure that the programme isn't taken by surprise.

Implement

Your goal is to make sure that the risk-management actions are implemented and then monitored to ensure that they're having the effect you anticipate; that way, you can take corrective action if necessary.

TIP

Make sure that roles and responsibilities are appropriately allocated. You may want to look at the definitions of risk owner and risk actionee in the earlier section 'Talking the talk: Risk terminology' just to check you know what I mean by 'roles and responsibilities'.

When you implement risk-management actions, you're entering into an execution, monitoring, controlling and scanning cycle that can go on for a long time. That cycle may happen as part of the implement step or it may trigger re-identification of risks: the next step in the process.

WARNING!

I think the implement step is a badly-designed process step because it occurs at different times. The important thing to remember about implement is that it can go on for a considerable length of time.

Embed and review

Risk management is cultural: people have to want to do it. In the embedding and reviewing process you can ensure that risk management is used appropriately and that risks are successfully handled. Carry out some form of *health check* on your risk management (a questionnaire that asks if you have all the different bits of risk management in place) or perhaps even a *risk management maturity review* (a more sophisticated assessment that looks at how repeatable each of the elements of risk management within your organization is).

The important thing about both of these techniques is that after you've assessed where you are, if you're not happy with the situation you get some pointers on what actions you can take to improve your risk management.

Another element of embedding and reviewing is to make sure that you're looking at the post-action risk magnitude (the residual risk) and feeding that back into risk assessment to see whether you need to take more actions.

Therefore, embedding and reviewing can take place at several levels from the detail of individual risks to the overall effectiveness of your risk-management cycle.

Responding to risks

You can use several types of risk response as part of the risk-management process. You may have the same or difference response types for threats and opportunities. I look first at the threat responses:

- **Avoid a risk.** You decide that you must remove completely the cause of the risk. You can avoid all the risks in a programme if you stop the programme. The avoid response is the most dramatic response and so you rarely use it. After all, you can avoid getting hit on the head by falling blue ice from an aeroplane, but do you want to spend the rest of your life indoors?
- **Reduce the risk.** You take action now to change the probability or the impact of the risk. This is one of the most common mitigation actions.
- **Transfer the risk to a third party.** For example, you take out insurance.
- **Share the risk with multiple parties.** For instance, in the supply chain. A common example is a contract with shared profit or shared pain and gain.
- **Accept the risk.** You say, 'All right, there's a risk but the cost of mitigation would be greater than the cost of the risk factored by its probability'. So you simply live with the risk and take the chance.
- **Prepare contingency plans.** You prepare plans now that make taking action later easier. In other words, you prepare a plan that reduces the impact of the risk after it has happened.

I regard contingency plans as being one of the poorer ways of dealing with risks. I reserve them for high impact, low probability risks.

The great value of risk management is that it enables you to look into the future and modify what's going to happen; in other words, to mitigate the risk. Contingency planning doesn't really mitigate the risk. Agreeing a contingency plan doesn't have any effect on the probability, it just slightly reduces the impact after the event. The only circumstances in which using a contingency plan makes sense is when the probability is already low, but the very large impact makes it necessary to do something. For lots of high impact risks, a better approach is to reduce that high impact, which brings down the overall size of the risk.

Here are a couple of risk responses that apply only to opportunities:

- **Exploit the risk.** You implement the risk that you've seen. You make the risk happen. If I advertise this training course, we get more delegates. So I exploit the risk by buying advertising for that course.
- **Enhance the risk.** You may be able to take the same action in several different places, so that multiple opportunities come to fruition. If exploiting the risk works once, then I can enhance it by taking out advertising for every course I'm going to deliver. (If you think of risks as being negative, try replacing the word risk with opportunity in the last couple of paragraphs and it makes a bit more sense.)

Table 11-1 provides a quick overview of the response options that apply to threats and opportunities.

Table 11-1 Generic Risk Response Options

Threat	*Opportunity*	*Explanation*
Avoid	Exploit	Remove the risk by removing/implementing the cause.
Reduce	Enhance	Action now to change the probability or impact.
Transfer		Pass part of the risk to a third party (an insurer?).
Share		Multiple parties (supply chain) share pain/gain.
Accept		Take the chance.
Prepare contingency plans		Prepare plans now to take action later.

Chapter 12

Resolving Issues and Keeping Track of Detail

In This Chapter

- Dealing with issues
- Controlling changes
- Keeping track of your assets with configuration management
- Allocating responsibilities

Issue management has a lot in common with risk management, both in general and within programme management, because many issues are risks that have happened. I cover managing risk in Chapter 11 and suggest you read that chapter in combination with this one. Inevitably certain topics overlap between risks and issues: for example, here I cover which programme individuals need to be responsible for which tasks.

In this chapter I look at the specifics of resolving issues. I also consider the associated subject of change control: issues can lead to unexpected changes; therefore you need to control these changes. Doing so is much easier if you understand the *configuration* (or versions) of the different assets in the programme. If configuration management is a new term to you, for the moment just think about it as version control.

TIP: I consider configuration management alongside issue management, rather than as part of quality management (which I cover in Chapter 13), to reflect the way that the MSP manual and exam syllabuses are laid out. But you can consider the subject as sitting here or with quality management: it doesn't really matter. In reality, all these subjects have a strong connection between them.

Resolving Issues

Issues are anything that's happened in your programme that you haven't planned for. Therefore you need to do something about them; you need to resolve the issues.

Think about the types of issues you're going to be dealing with and describe your approach to issue resolution in your Issue Management Strategy document (see the later section 'Describing your Issue Management Strategy'). You also need to share with your colleagues a standard process or cycle for managing issues and to record issues in an Issue Register (check out the 'Using the Issue Register' section later in this chapter.

You can probably guess that the issue strategy and register and the equivalent risk strategy and register that I describe in Chapter 11 have a lot of similarities.

MSP SPEAK

You may like to use the term *issue resolution* rather than 'issue management', because it emphasises that when an issue pops up you need to deal with it – resolve it.

Recognising the sources of issues

Of course issues can come from anywhere, but the following are typical sources:

- Escalated from projects
- From external to the programme
- From within the programme
- Generated by stakeholders
- In operational areas
- Programme constraints
- Related to benefits management

Describing your Issue Management Strategy

Your Issue Management Strategy document describes the mechanisms and procedures for resolving issues as follows:

- How issues are identified, captured and assessed
- How issues are managed
- Responsibilities – at programme level
- Responsibilities – at project and operational levels

- Change control process
- More detailed change control procedures (if you have any)
- How you plan to handle exceptions, particularly those triggered by issues
- Impact assessment
- The difference between project and programme issues
- Severity criteria
- Categorisation
- Monitoring and evaluation
- How you plan to judge effectiveness
- Associated strategies; for example, a cross-reference to the Risk Management Strategy

Setting up an issue-management cycle

Figure 12-1 shows a simple issue-management cycle, and I discuss the various aspects in this section, moving clockwise around the figure (if you start to feel dizzy, you're reading too fast!).

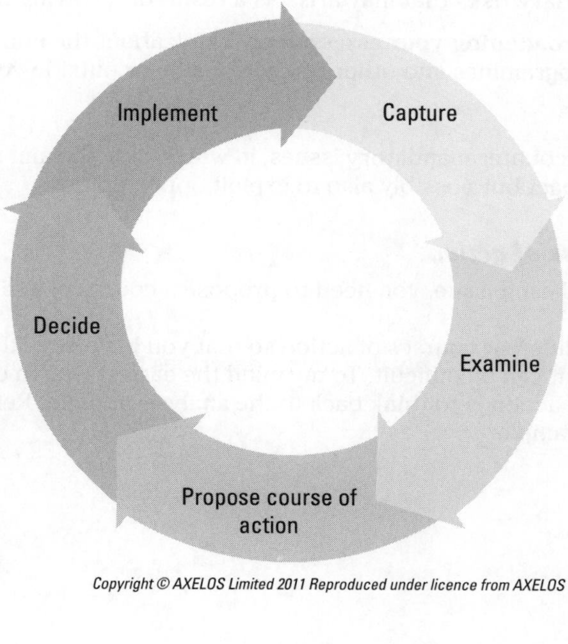

Figure 12-1: Issue-management cycle.

Capture

The first thing to do is to capture the issues.

REMEMBER

You have to go further than writing the issues down: you need to analyse them to determine the type of issue. You can have someone in the Programme Office do this task.

You need to categorise issues in some way so that you can assess their severity and the impact. Then, if significant, you allocate the issue to someone. If the impact is sufficiently high, you may need to escalate it.

Examine

Here's a checklist of things to bear in mind when examining an issue:

- **Consider enough alternatives.** If business as usual says an output isn't fit for purpose, you can put it back into the project to be changed; you can replace it with a manual procedure until you create something better in the next tranche; or you can delay that whole piece of change to the next tranche. A surprising number of alternatives is always available.
- **Balance the following:**
  - The advantage of dealing with the issue against the impact of dealing with the issue on cost, time and possibly on risk.
  - Secondary risks that may arise as a result of resolving the issue.
- **Consider broadening your assessment.** Think about the impact on other programmes and other projects inside or outside your programme.

TIP

You're sure to encounter mandatory issues, in which case the aim is to minimise the impact but possibly also to exploit opportunities.

Propose a course of action

Having examined each issue, you need to propose a course of action.

TIP

Thinking about different courses of action so that you have a good range of options to present can be difficult. To my mind the easiest way to envisage different courses of action is to think back to the analysis you did. Reflect on the impact on, for example:

- Blueprint
- Business Case

- Operational performance
- Programme performance
- Projects Dossier
- Risk Profile
- Stakeholders
- Suppliers

Next, propose a course of action that minimises the impact in each of these areas. I propose one course of action with no or minimal impact on the Business Case, another one with no or minimal impact on the Blueprint and so on.

In each case the impact on other aspects of the programme probably increases. But by taking this approach you get a good range of possible courses of action.

Decide

Having assembled a set of options, you simply make a decision. At this point you need to look at the Issue Management Strategy to understand who has the appropriate authority:

- Is it the Programme Manager?
- Is it even the Senior Responsible Owner (SRO)?
- Do you have some specialist individual or group of people who can make the decision, such as the Business Change Managers?

After the right person makes the decision, you need to plan the change. Consider aspects such as:

- Contingency within the plan.
- Allocating resources to carry out this change.
- Having a fall-back if the changes are more complex than planned.

You can then use the change control procedures that I discuss later in this chapter in the section 'Taking Control of Changes'.

Implement

Of course, you need to implement the action. The Programme Manager or someone delegated by that person has to communicate what you're going to do:

- So that actionees (see Chapter 11 for a definition; you can have an issue actionee just like a risk actionee) are aware of what to do; they in turn inform those who raised the issue that you are indeed taking action.
- To inform stakeholders so that they're aware that something is going to happen in their area of interest.
- To demonstrate effective management.

You also need to update various documents. I suggest:

- Issue Register
- Any affected plans
- Benefits Profiles
- Configuration management information
- Business Case

Using the Issue Register

The purpose of the *Issue Register* is to capture and manage actively the programme issues. It's the central log of all reported issues facing the programme, and you use it to assist with managing the issues so that they don't affect the programme adversely. Look at Table 12-1 for the make-up of an Issue Register.

Table 12-1 Issue Register Composition

Identifier	*Categorisation*
Dates	Owner
Who raised	Issue actionee
Description	Status
Cause and impact	Cross-reference to change control
Severity	Resolution
Response	Lessons learned

In the smallest programmes the Issue Register is just a simple spread sheet. In a more reasonably sized programme you may require a series of delegated Issue Registers (managed, for example, by Project Managers) as well as a central Issue Register.

TIP

Think about the level of access that central Programme Office staff members have to Issue Registers. You can undermine the Project Managers' authority if Programme Office staff look regularly at their Issue Registers. On the other hand, Project Managers may not be best placed to consider the wider programme impact of their issues, so Programme Office staff members do need to have some oversight of project Issue Registers.

Taking Control of Changes

MSP SPEAK

Change control is a mechanistic subject linked to keeping track of different versions of anything that's important to the programme. Don't confuse it with *change management,* which is the softer human side of change that I discuss in Chapter 20.

Your organization may already have sophisticated change control procedures in place, in which case these need to be the starting point for your programme change control procedure. However, if the subject is new to you, this section provides a straightforward change control procedure that gets you started.

Taking steps to control change

Here are the all-important change control steps to follow:

1. **Capture and define the change.** You need to record the change and why it's needed in order to deal with it in an orderly way.
2. **Allocate priority to the change.** You do so to help people understand the urgency and the significance of the change.
3. **Assess the impact of the change.** Make sure that the impact assessment is broad-ranging. You have to assess the impact across the whole of the programme; therefore you may need to look at documents such as the Programme Plan, the Blueprint, the various Benefits documents and the Project Dossier in order to be able to assess the overall impact across the programme. (Chapter 7 describes the programme documents.)

4. **Analyse your options.** You have to identify and analyse a sufficiently wide range of options and test the potential solutions that emerge from the options analysis.

5. **Authorise resolution.** At an appropriate level, as described in the governance structures, you have to obtain authorisation to resolve the change.

   Don't forget that one possible resolution for a change request is to do nothing.

6. **Implement the change.** Only now do you implement the change and subsequently monitor the effects of the change for deviations from what you anticipated. Bear in mind that one change may trigger a series of other changes.

7. **Review effectiveness.** Step back and review the effectiveness of the individual changes and your overall change control procedure.

Considering change control and issue management

The change control procedure in the preceding section is very similar to the issue management cycle (see the earlier Figure 12-1). Some organizations combine the processes and others prefer to keep them separate. In the latter case, everything goes through issue management, but only those issues identified as changes are passed across to change control. Combining or keeping separate these two processes is just a matter of what the people in the programme are familiar with. My preference is to leave well alone, unless the boldness of the change that the programme's going to bring about means people need to be shaken out of their existing ways of thinking, in which case I deliberately put in place a different way of working.

Getting to Grips with Configuration Management

I'm an aeronautical engineer by training, so I've been managing configuration since I left school; to me it's second nature. But most programme professionals aren't configuration management experts, so in the programme management world I'm considered a little strange (at least I think that's the reason!). When you start to implement changes you need particularly strong *configuration management,* which is just the way in which different versions of different assets sit together in a configuration (I'm working on a laptop with a second screen attached, remote keyboard and a fancy mouse. Together they are a configuration. If I wanted to give it a fancy name, I could call it my desktop computing environment).

In this section I provide a few definitions around configuration management, in case you're unfamiliar with the concept, and a simple process you can use. If you're already experienced with configuration management, for example, if you're a project manager or an engineer, by all means bring more sophisticated local procedures into your programme.

My goal is to give you just enough information about configuration management so that you can appreciate its significance to your programme. After that you almost certainly need to go out and recruit, part-time or full-time, someone with experience of configuration management.

REMEMBER

Configuration management isn't just about managing one class of asset; it's about managing all the assets in the programme. So, for example, if as an IT professional you're used to managing the configuration of software and IT equipment, don't forget that other people in the programme are managing the configuration of everything from offices to people's skills. Instead of imposing your configuration management approach on others, you may need a range of configuration management approaches across the programme.

Configuring assets

Configuration management looks at the configuration of sets of assets. The purpose of asset management is to identify, track and protect the programme's assets including:

- **External assets:** Exist outside the programme but can affect it.
- **Internal assets:** Interfaces between projects and the programme, for example, project progress reports.
- **Programme assets:** For example, the Blueprint and Programme Plan.
- **Project outputs:** the things that the project bills and delivers into business as usual.

If you go into an organization to set up a programme, you're certain to find people in business as usual who already carry out asset management. Just look at the serial number on your office computer for an example of how someone tracks assets. So asset management is a straightforward way to communicate with business as usual when carrying out configuration management.

MSP SPEAK

An asset that's subject to configuration management is called a *configuration item*. It may be a component of a product, a product or a set of products in a release.

I cover quality management in detail in Chapter 13, but for now I just want to note the two-way relationship that exists between quality management and configuration management. See Figure 12-2 for an illustration of this relationship.

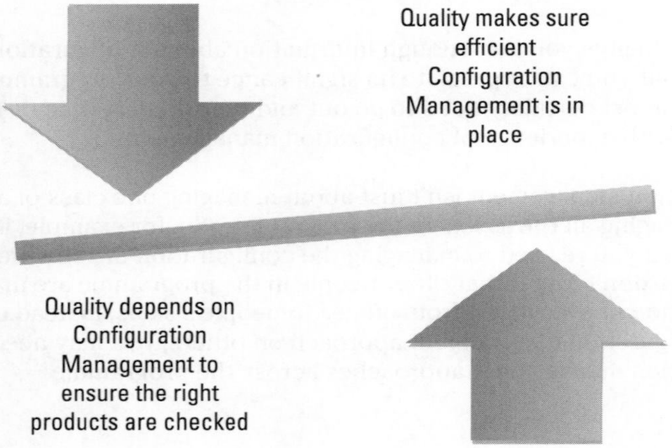
Quality makes sure efficient Configuration Management is in place
Quality depends on Configuration Management to ensure the right products are checked

Figure 12-2: Quality and configuration management.

Moving beyond asset management into configuration management

With configuration management, your aim is to control the development of and changes to items important to the programme:

- Programme management documentation
- Assets, for example, products or services
- Programme dependencies
- External items

Configuration management tracks interrelationships between assets as well as the assets themselves. In your programme you live in a world of change; you don't just need to know the status of the assets, you also need to know how those assets work together in a configuration.

Carrying out configuration management

You undertake five activities when doing configuration management, as I describe in the following sections.

If you find yourself thinking that this process looks too sophisticated and beyond what you need for your programme, bear in mind that most programmes require detailed and rigorous configuration management. Although not a high-profile activity, it can be a vital one.

Planning

The first step, inevitably, is planning. Based on the Blueprint and the organization's approach to configuration management, you need to decide what level of configuration management is appropriate for the programme and plan how to achieve it. Carrying out configuration management at a very precise level of detail can be extremely expensive.

You need only to carry out configuration management of assets where it's essential. I'm always amused when I see a document that's going to be valid for only a few days, but contains one page of information and several pages of configuration management data: in other words, much too much configuration management.

Identifying

Having decided the level at which you're going to exercise configuration management, you set out the requirements for configuration management that all projects should adopt.

Identify all the programme-level configuration items that are to be created during the programme and the dependencies between assets and between configurations. Set up a system for describing configuration items (which I define in the earlier section 'Configuring assets').

In fact, you're already familiar with systems for describing configuration items. The part number on anything from your kettle to your jacket is part of just such a system set up by the manufacturer.

Controlling

Having identified configuration items, you need to control them. When the Programme Definition Document is agreed the configuration of the programme itself is baselined. This happens at the end of Defining a Programme stage as I describe in Chapter 7.

Baselined means you take a snapshot of the version at that time which never changes. So if anything does change, you create a new version. Most programmes change over time, and any changes to the configuration must be properly version controlled, following procedures described in the Information Management Strategy.

Version control also includes managing the programme's management information. The programme needs to set out how to manage dependencies on external assets in the event of external assets being revised. Control over an asset passes to business as usual when that asset is agreed to be no longer the responsibility of the programme.

Accounting for status

You need to be able to account for the status of those items that are under configuration control. This task involves maintaining current and historical information for the following:

- Each configuration.
- The configuration items (assets).
- All relevant dependencies (external to the programme as well as inter-project dependencies).

Verifying the status

As the process is getting quite rigorous, you need to verify the status of configuration items. This job includes auditing the programme to ensure conformity between documented configurations and the actual status of products and configuration items before delivery to operations. You also need to verify dependencies as part of an audit, because they may have moved or changed over time.

Confirming Risk and Issue Areas of Focus

Getting clear the areas of responsibility for risk and issue management avoids duplication, and more importantly prevents some tasks falling between the cracks. Here's a checklist for you (to discover more about these roles, flip to Chapter 9):

- **Senior Responsible Owner:**
  - Authorises the Risk and Issue Management Strategies.
  - Controls risks and issues that affect alignment with Organizational Objectives.

- Initiates assurance reviews of risk and issue management effectiveness.
- Owns strategic risks and issues.

- **Programme Manager:**
  - Develops and implements the Risk and Issue Management Strategies.
  - Designs and manages the risk and issue-management cycles.
  - Manages the aggregate level of risks and issues.
  - Assures adherence to the risk-management principles.
  - Allocates risks and issues as appropriate.
  - Ensures that people with the right authority undertake change control.
  - Ensures that stakeholders understand the impact of risks.
  - Defines clear rules for escalation, cascade and thresholds. (Another word for cascading is delegation – the circumstances when you push something down to, say, a project. You also need to be clear about the threshold for those escalations and delegations. For example, projects have to escalate issues with a budget greater than five per cent of the project budget.)
  - Owns programme-level risks and issues.
  - Rolls out consistent language for risk management.
  - Communicates progress on the resolution of issues.
  - Escalates items that cross programme boundaries to the SRO.
  - Designs and implements the configuration-management system.

- **Business Change Manager(s):**
  - Manages risks linked to operational performance and benefits.
  - Ensures that operational risks, including opportunities and issues, are managed.
  - Manages risks that impact on business performance and transition.
  - Identifies operational issues to the programme.
  - Identifies opportunities from the business operations to the programme.
  - Contributes to impact assessments and change control.
  - Monitors and reports on business performance issues during transition.

- **Programme Office:**
  - Manages and co-ordinates information and support systems.
  - Maintains the programme Risk and Issue Registers.
  - Establishes, facilitates and maintains the risk and issue-management cycles.
  - Provides support and advice on risks and issues to projects.
  - Co-ordinates risk and issue-management interfaces with projects.
  - Maintains the configuration management system.
  - Helps with the change control steps.

Putting your risk management and issue resolution knowledge to the test

I don't want to recommend that you set up a change control, risk, issue and configuration management systems for your programme all in one go – it's a lot of work. But you may like to try verifying the status of a range of configuration items in your programme.

Establish the status and change history of an important document, a project product and something significant in business as usual. Doing so lets you see whether your programme is keeping track of the detail.

Consider also tracking a risk from its initial identification, through a bit of escalation and implementation of some mitigation actions, to its eventual residual state, in order to get an insight into how risk management is happening in your programme.

Chapter 13

Achieving Quality in Your Programme

In This Chapter

- Considering the scope and diversity of quality management
- Linking quality management to other parts of the programme
- Managing information in your programme
- Applying quality management to specific parts of your programme
- Documenting your approach to quality management

Quality management within a programme can be a large and complex subject. If you're building, for example, a piece of safety-critical infrastructure that a wide range of stakeholder groups are going to use, quality management runs through everything you do within the programme. But this complexity doesn't mean that quality management has to be a difficult subject to understand.

This chapter provides a sound start on the journey towards mastering quality in your programme. I take a look at the scope and nature of quality and its management. I come over all practical and examine what you need to do in the real world as part of quality management, in order to align the programme with MSP principles. Quality management affects many other aspects of programme management, so I discuss the relationship between quality management and topics such as your suppliers and any standards with which you have to comply.

In order to achieve quality, you need to control properly the information in the programme, which is why I cover information management, from the critical success factors through to definitions of the types of information you need. I also discuss the purpose and composition of the documents in which you describe how you plan to manage information and quality in your programme.

All in all, this is a quality-filled chapter!

Understanding the Scope and Diversity of Quality Management

Quality means different things to different people, and you have to accommodate all these definitions when managing quality within your programme.

You may want to read this definition now, but if you want to ease yourself in gently, skip down the page to my two core questions. You can always come back to this definition later.

As a useable definition, I suggest that *quality* is:

> The totality of features and inherent or assigned characteristics of a product, person, process, service or system that bears on its ability to show that it meets expectations or stated needs, requirements or specification.

This description allows me to state the following about *quality management:*

- Quality management ensures that management aspects are working appropriately and the programme stays on target.
- The focus of quality is a set of goals that may change during the life of the programme, so the manner in which you manage quality may change during the programme.

If these ideas seem a bit abstract, don't worry: I expand on and clarify them in this section.

Answering two core quality questions

To help understand this issue, please consider two simple questions about the nature of quality:

- **What is quality?** Jot down on a piece of paper what you think the term 'quality' means.
- **What do you measure the quality of?** This question is more difficult to pose than to answer. Note down on your piece of paper the things whose quality you measure.

Take a little time to consider those questions and bear them in mind as I share with you my views on the nature of quality.

I've heard many definitions of quality over the years, and in a diverse programme you can find stakeholder groups with differing views on what quality is.

TIP

If a stakeholder group has a particular definition of quality, they're right. In this case, perception is reality. Your task at programme level is to build a consensus between stakeholders' views on the different, acceptable definitions of quality.

WARNING!

I'd like to clear up one confusing usage: 'excellence' isn't a definition of quality, even though quite often the marketing staff talk about 'a quality product', meaning that it's excellent or expensive. In the world of programme management, try and stay clear of this definition because excellence can be very expensive.

In the following list I present some terms that define quality. You may be familiar with them, and you're certainly able to manage them:

- **Fitness for purpose.** If something is quality, it does what it needs to do.
- **Meeting stated requirements.** Assumes that you can document the requirements for a product.
- **Meeting implied needs.** This broader term leads to the question of how you understand and document those implied needs.
- **Conformance and compliance.** I don't intend to differentiate the meaning of those two words in detail, but quality is sometimes defined by carrying out a piece of work in a particular way, *conformance* if you like, or the work may be certified against a standard, which is *compliance.*

Measuring quality . . . but of what?

The first thing that springs to mind when considering what you measure is products (or outputs) from projects. If you move along the programme chain from products, you can measure the quality of capabilities and the quality of outcomes.

When you talk about benefits reviews, which I cover in Chapter 16, perhaps you're measuring the quality of benefits. Going a bit further, you can look at the fitness for purpose (the quality) of the processes within the programme.

You can also consider the quality, the fitness for purpose, of programme personnel, which can be contentious territory. You can end up recommending that a person isn't suitable for a role in a programme, and if you're talking about senior roles, your life can become very interesting.

Finally you can measure the quality of the activities you carry out within the programme. Indeed, you can measure the quality of anything that may be classed as a programme asset.

'So what?' I hear you say. I'd like you to have reached two conclusions. First, programme quality is not about measuring just one thing in only one way. Second, programme quality is about assessing lots of different aspects of the programme in a range of ways, that your stakeholders will be comfortable with. That means the programme needs to put together a patchwork quilt of quality and assurance checks that covers you completely but doesn't smother you. If you get the patchwork quilt, you get programme quality.

Comparing quality management in projects and programmes

Quality management involves much more than project quality management. If you come from a project background, you may find reflecting on the differences between quality in the project and programme worlds reassuring:

- **Project.** You don't have to come to quality management in a programme environment from the project perspective. Nevertheless your programme has lots of projects, and people working in projects are familiar with the project view of quality management.

  In a project, quality management is about outputs that meet acceptance criteria or meet the specification. In other words, outputs that are fit for purpose.
- **Programme.** In a programme you have a much broader focus than in a project. You focus on management, that is, the quality of management. You focus on processes and on alignment with the environment. Have you as a programme remained aligned with the external environment?

You're bound to face changes to the environment over the length of the programme, so you need to be prepared to change your approach to quality management. You also need to be aware of and indeed understand the corporate priorities, for they're going to change as well. Overall you're demonstrating that the Blueprint and plans are remaining aligned with corporate priorities.

Providing assurance

This governance theme in MSP is called quality and assurance management, so I'd like to be clear on the meaning of assurance as the term is often misused. I frequently hear of people talking about carrying out quality assurance (QA) when in fact they're carrying out quality checking or quality control (QC).

The definition of programme *assurance* is:

- A systematic set of actions necessary to provide confidence to the Senior Responsible Owner and stakeholders that the programme:
  - Remains under control
  - On track to deliver
  - Aligned with strategic objectives

The key idea is to provide confidence, reassurance if you like, that you're on track.

Instead of discussing assurance management in this chapter, I do so in Chapter 14 because I think that you get an interesting perspective by looking at it while considering stakeholders.

Running through quality management principles

Any discussion about quality management can easily become overly abstract. To avoid this problem and make quality management in a programme more real, I look at each of the principles. Looking at quality management in comparison to each of the programme principles is a powerful tool. Chapter 4 describes these principles and may well help you clarify your ideas about quality management.

This section contains a powerful set of ideas relating quality to principles and some useful questions to ask yourself. I hope that it gets you thinking practically about quality management.

TRY IT YOURSELF

You may like to ask yourself how you'd reinforce each programme principle using quality management before you read on.

Aligning with strategy

In order for quality management to assist with achieving this principle, you check on the validity of documents such as the Vision, the Blueprint, the Business Case and the Benefits Realization Plan.

Ask yourself the following questions to be true to (remain aligned with) the strategy principle:

- Are the right projects running?
- Are the governance strategies still current and still relevant?

Leading change

Leading change is where you get into assessing the quality of behaviours in the programme:

- Is the leadership being shown by leaders fit for purpose?
- Is it appropriate?

- Are senior people, your key players, exhibiting the behaviours that are needed in order to trigger the transformational change?
- Are you having an appropriate effect on the stakeholder landscape?
- Is your interaction with stakeholders such that they're supporting the programme or at least not actively interfering with it?

Envisaging a better future

Linking to this principle is about more than checking whether a Vision has been published. It involves assessing whether the levels of engagement within the programme are appropriate and whether people have a true understanding of what you intend to deliver and the benefits to come.

Think about subjects such as the following:

- Quality of leadership
- Behaviours being exhibited
- Effect of the stakeholder landscape

Focusing on the benefits and the threats to them

Quality management can do simple things, such as ensuring that 'benefits' is an item on the programme board agenda. Other aspects of benefits quality are covered if you ask questions such as:

- Is all the benefits information current?
- Are the projects properly aligned with the benefits to be realized?
- Does the Risk Register illustrate the sensitivity of the benefits to various variables?
- Are business performance indicators being tracked?

Taking things further

When trying to get your mind round quality management in a programme, you can take the idea of linking quality to other aspects of programme management a little further. You can look at how quality management may work in each of the governance themes or in each of the processes within the transformational flow.

This exercise is a useful one to undertake when carrying out a health check of quality management in your programme, but it can take some time. So instead of discussing the results, I leave you to carry out that audit in your programme when convenient.

Adding value

The quality management question around added value comes down to the following: is the programme still justified in its current form?

Delivering coherent capability

One principle is to design and deliver a coherent capability. You can check the fitness for purpose of the capability and its coherence by asking questions around the following:

- Validity of the Blueprint
- Ability of projects to deliver capability
- Ability of the business to adapt
- Effectiveness of management of project-level quality (remember that projects deliver the outputs that become that capability)

Learning from experience

Connecting to learning from experience, you can ask questions such as:

- How are reviews being carried out?
- Are they effective?
- How well are lessons being used?
- What effect is learning from experience having on the performance of the programme?

Investigating Interdependencies with Other Disciplines

The preceding section reveals the nature, scope and sheer diversity of quality management within a programme. But the scope of quality activities is broader than just the principles, because the latter are overarching. Another set to linkages (dependencies) are identified in MSP, which give you a further insight into how all-pervasive quality management can and should be.

You may be wondering why I don't include many figures in this chapter. I'm a great fan of diagrams when the included relationships add value, but that's not the nature of quality management, I'm afraid: it's more abstract. Figure 13-1, however, is one diagram that successfully illustrates the relationships between quality management and other aspects of programme management.

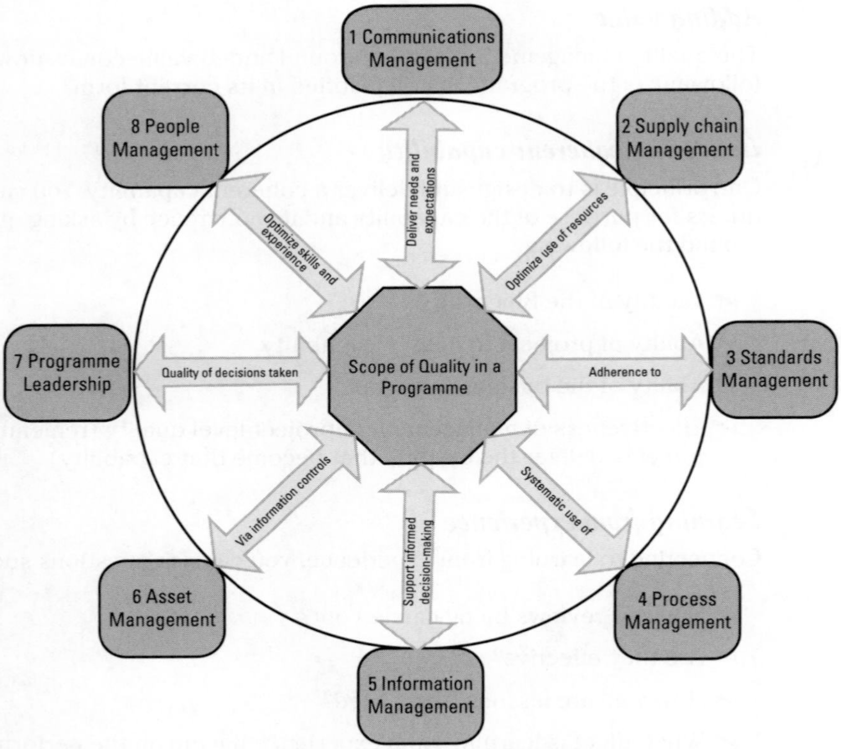

Figure 13-1: The scope of programme quality: Relationships to the rest of programme management.

Figure 13-1 illustrates the process areas that require management review of their effectiveness in supporting programme objectives. Process areas are just aspects of programme management. Management review in this way is another way of saying quality.

MSP SPEAK

Before I describe the eight areas shown in the figure, please note how I use the following terms:

- **Process:** A set of related activities carried out in a defined order.
- **System:** Contains several processes and has management and control mechanisms.

The quality management you set up in your programme needs to look at the effectiveness of all the processes and systems that exist within the programme. In business as usual, the effectiveness of process and systems is (I hope) in place. You need to put in an equal and appropriate level of rigour in the processes and systems that you're setting up.

Here are the elements in Figure 13-1, moving clockwise around the figure. I don't get specific about who does each of these actions – whatever works for your organization is fine.

- **Communications management.** Quality activities need to test the perceptions of success of the stakeholders and the soundness of the relationships the programme has with them.
- **Supply chain management.** Suppliers have to apply quality management to their processes to ensure that they deliver their obligations and are effectively aligned with the programme.
- **Standards management.** Changes delivered by the programme need to continue to be aligned with corporate standards and policies, and you need some way of having a dialogue with the people who set those policies.
- **Process management.** You need to create programme processes with the right level of specification and rigour.
- **Information management.** The right information is provided in the right format, to the right people, at the right time. I write more on information management in the following section.
- **Asset management.** Assets that can range from programme information to software or the contents of buildings are protected when subject to planned or unplanned changes. This requirement almost certainly means that they need to be under configuration control, which I cover in Chapter 12.
- **Programme leadership.** Quality activities must ensure that good, effective leadership is taking place throughout the programme. I look at leadership in Chapters 9 and 14.
- **People management.** You need to apply principles such as leading change, envisioning and communicating a better future, and learning from experience, to get the best out of the people deployed onto the programme. They may be working in the programme for a considerable time.

Managing the Flow of Information

Information management may sound like a dry and boring subject, but I've seen programmes lose control of change simply because they didn't manage the information about the programme sufficiently carefully.

A programme commonly has to prove itself to business as usual. After all, it's the new kid on the block (ahh, where are *they* now!). Business as usual, and perhaps even projects, are reluctant to cede power and authority to the programme, which makes it difficult for the programme to demonstrate that it's adding value.

The neatest way I know of establishing the credibility of a programme, without challenging the power of business as usual, is to take control of the information about the changes that are taking place and make that information available to those who are interested in it.

If you're the source that people contact to find out what's going on, you rapidly gain power and authority. Often when I go into a programme the first thing I look at is information management.

Looking at information baselines: Types of programme information

To be honest, in one sense I talk about information management throughout this whole book: every time I mention a document, it's a location where you manage information. In Chapter 7, I give you an overview of all the documents you may need in a programme, grouping the documents into several classes. Here are the official MSP definitions of those different classes of documents.

When you look at the process chapters (Chapters 3, 7 and 18 to 21) and in particular the process diagrams that I include in each chapter, you often see references to *information baselines.* These are the current versions of the sets of documents that go under each of these three headings:

- **Boundary:** Sets out the direction and scope of the programme.
- **Governance:** Sets standards and frameworks for delivery and how the programme is to be managed.
- **Management:** Used to manage delivery and what activities are to be undertaken by whom.

Addressing critical success factors in your Information Management Strategy

To achieve quality of documentation, you almost certainly have to state your Information Management Strategy. I identify some critical success factors that go with this Strategy.

Before you look at these headings, you may want to jot down what you see as being the critical success factors. What's critical if you're going to manage information successfully?

- **Availability.** Make information available. Give decision makers access to the information and documentation they need without making them put in too much effort.
- **Confidentiality.** Set the levels of confidentiality within the programme so that documents are allocated appropriate levels of sensitivity and limit their distribution accordingly. In other words, don't let people get at documents they don't need to see. You may need to set up audit trails and certification of confidentiality.
- **Compliance.** Make sure that information storage and retention is compliant with organizational policies and applicable legislation. In particular, consider data protection and freedom-of-information legislation and requirements, such as retention periods for personnel and financial records.
- **Currency.** Information being used should reflect the current situation. Acknowledge any gaps in reporting from projects or concerns about the accuracy of business performance data. Note the limitations that these problems can bring to decision-making.

  At a more basic level, you need to avoid information being held in discrete documents and then being copied from one place to another, being duplicated and left to sit in an apparently current document which is in fact out of date. You need to think about how you manage the Information Hub in order to maintain a database of current information.
- **Integrity.** Bring important information under change control and release management control; in other words, treat it all as configuration items (which I discuss in Chapter 12). You can ensure that the right versions of information are in circulation and use. Consider commissioning audits that check that the distribution systems are working.

  I recall asking to see the Vision of one programme I was looking at. The people showed me one, and another, and another, and another, and another! They had five different visions in circulation, all substantially different – not great information management!

Understanding the information documents

In your programme you're probably going to set up a new way of managing information. You're going to have to write down and tell people how you're going to do that. That means you have to create some documents that explain what you're going to do. In this section I cover a few strategies and plans related to information management.

Information Management Strategy

Here are the details of an Information Management Strategy:

- **Purpose:** To measure systems and techniques to control information
- **Composition:**
  - Audit scope
  - Confidentiality
  - Configuration management
  - Effectiveness criteria
  - Information security and standards
  - Integrity
  - Release management and availability
  - Responsibilities
  - Storage systems

Information Management Plan

Below the Information Management Strategy you need an Information Management Plan:

- **Purpose:** To produce a timetable and arrangements for implementing the Information Management Strategy
- **Composition:**
  - Information assets
  - Monitoring and reporting
  - Responsibilities
  - Schedule for templates
  - Schedule for providing information to support reviews
  - Timetables

Describing Quality Documentation and Areas of Responsibility

In this section I grab a large lasso and round up the quality and assurance management documents that I haven't already covered in this or other chapters and give details of who needs to do what. You may notice that I'm using the term quality *and assurance* management. Assurance management is an extremely important complement to quality management. I discuss it in more detail in Chapter 14 and describe only the documents here.

Explaining the Programme Quality Processes: Quality and Assurance Strategy

At the top of the pile sits a Quality and Assurance Strategy. This is the first document to read if you want to know how quality is going to work:

- **Purpose:** To define and establish activities for managing quality
- **Composition:**
  - Aspects subject to review and control
  - Assurance results processing
  - Audit and health-check guidelines
  - Continual improvement mechanisms
  - Corporate systems and interfaces
  - Functions and roles
  - Integrated assurance arrangements
  - Internal audit interfaces
  - Links to independent assurance
  - Monitoring and control interfaces
  - Performance and tracking processes
  - Post quality check action
  - Programme success criteria
  - Responsibilities
  - Standards and experts
  - Triggers

Detailing what to do: The Quality and Assurance Plan

The Quality and Assurance Strategy from the preceding section is supported by a Quality and Assurance Plan:

- **Purpose:** To produce a timetable and arrangements for carrying out the Quality and Assurance Strategy
- **Composition:**
  - Assurance arrangements
  - Effort and costs
  - Responsibilities
  - Schedule
  - Schedule of assurance reviews
  - Timing and conduct of audits, reviews and health checks
  - Timing and conduct of quality monitoring and analysis

Allocating responsibility for quality

Here are the main areas of responsibility relating to quality and assurance management. Check out Chapter 9 for more about these roles.

Senior Responsible Owner

The Senior Responsible Owner is that very senior individual accountable for the success of the programme. This person is responsible for the following areas:

- Consulting with the Sponsoring Group on the approach to programme assurance.
- Ensuring that an adequate assurance regime is in place for all aspects of quality in the programme.
- Signing off the quality and information management strategies.
- Initiating assurance reviews and audits.
- Maintaining focus on the programme management principles.

Programme Manager

The Programme Manager runs the programme day-to-day, and is responsible for:

- Developing and implementing the Quality and Assurance Strategy and Plans (of the preceding section) and co-ordinating delivery of outputs from the projects that are fit for purpose and are capable of achieving the desired outcomes and benefits.
- Developing and implementing the Information Management Strategy and Plan (see the earlier section 'Managing the Flow of Information').
- Initiating assurance reviews of project and supplier performance.
- Ensuring that lessons learned are implemented.

Business Change Managers

Business Change Managers bed down the changes in their part of the business. They're responsible for:

- Implementing transition and realizing and reviewing benefits derived from the outputs of the projects.
- Initiating assurance reviews of business performance and change readiness.
- Ensuring that business change lessons are learned and implemented.

Programme Office

The Programme Office looks after the administration of the programme and is responsible for:

- Establishing and maintaining the programme's Quality and Assurance Plan and ensuring the establishment of the appropriate audit, assurance and review processes for the programme in accordance with the Quality and Assurance Strategy.
- Establishing and maintaining the programme's Information Management Plan and ensuring the establishment of the appropriate audit, assurance and review processes for the programme in accordance with the Information Management Strategy.
- Providing information to support assurance reviews.

HAVE A GO — Try This

Working on your quality management know-how

Here are my suggestions for how to try out this chapter's ideas in your existing programme:

- Look at product quality in projects. Do what's written down, what people say they're doing and what's actually happening align?
- Follow the chain through capabilities, outcomes and benefits to strategic objectives and check whether quality assessment links up.
- Talk to different stakeholder groups to see whether each of them is happy with the way quality is being managed, in their own language.
- Choose a piece of information and check whether it's being managed in accordance with the Information Management Strategy and Plan and the critical success factors.

These assignments give you something to get your teeth into. If you're setting up a programme rather than auditing one, turn these questions and tasks around and put in place systems that would subsequently sail through an audit with flying colours.

Part IV

Out in Business as Usual: Exploiting Projects' Capabilities

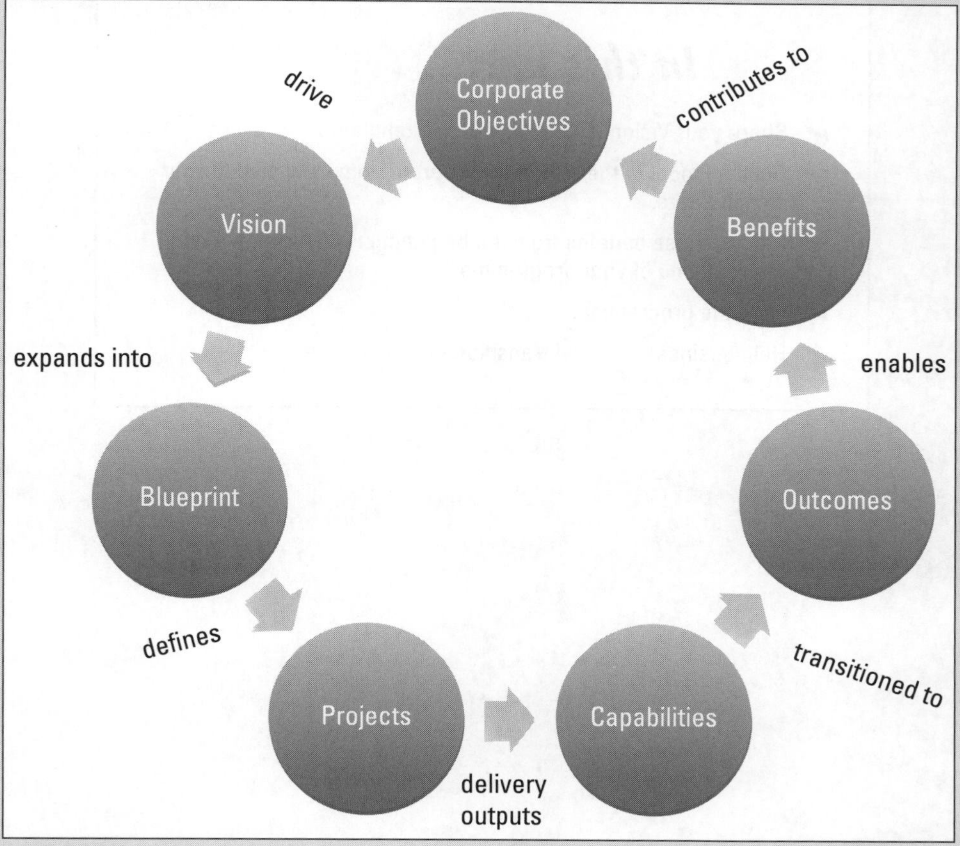

Go to www.dummies.com/extras/msp for free online bonus content about managing successful programmes.

In this part. . .

- Share your Vision with all of your stakeholders.
- Build a model of the benefits your programme will give to your stakeholders.
- Realize those benefits from the beginning right through until after the end of your programme.
- Lead the programme.
- Help business as usual transition to a new state.

Chapter 14

Keeping 'em Sweet: Engaging Your Stakeholders

In This Chapter

- Defining a stakeholder
- Understanding your stakeholders
- Connecting with stakeholders
- Reassuring stakeholders

A programme can have a diverse range of stakeholders. Particularly in a large programme, or one that involves fundamental transformational change, stakeholders are naturally extremely interested in how the programme is going and whether or not it's going to be successful.

In this chapter I help you discover your programme stakeholders and describe the relationship they have with your programme's Vision. Thinking about the Vision allows you to understand who the stakeholders are – including their interests and influence – and then communicate effectively with them. I also discuss the documents and areas of focus for different roles relating to stakeholders.

In addition, I look at assurance, because you need to provide reassurance to the diverse range of stakeholders in a programme. As I note in Chapter 13 on quality, I choose to discuss assurance here rather than there because it's done on behalf of stakeholders. I delve into assurance principles and some of the techniques you can use.

REMEMBER

I'm taking about stakeholder *engagement,* by which I mean talking with and listening to stakeholders in a style that works for them, and not something as narrow as just communicating with people or as invasive as managing them (or indeed proposing marriage). I don't know about you, but I get upset when people try and manage me without my permission – stakeholders in your programme are likely to take a similar view. Therefore, engage with your stakeholders; don't try to control them.

Holding an Identity Parade: Finding Your Stakeholders

Before I go any further, I'd like to set out a clear definition of a stakeholder. In the context of a programme, a *stakeholder* is:

> Any individual, group or organization that can affect the programme, be affected by it or perceives itself to be affected.

The next section explains why this definition has to be so wide-ranging.

Appreciating different stakeholders

Although you may not have a particular interest in a potential stakeholder group, its members may experience the effects of the programme strongly. In fact, you may not even think that a particular group contains stakeholders, but if the members perceive themselves to be such, they are stakeholders. Their perception is the important criterion.

Stakeholders act in all sorts of ways as regards the programme:

- They can support or oppose it.
- They may ultimately gain or lose.
- They may be indifferent to the change.
- They can end up supporting or blocking it.

In addition, certain stakeholders may see only a threat in your programme while others may see an opportunity.

As a result, you need to take different, appropriate approaches with different stakeholder groups.

Grouping stakeholders

Programme stakeholders can include the groups that I show in Figure 14-1 and list as follows:

- Customers or consumers
- Internal and/or external audit
- Owners, shareholders, management and staff who are sponsoring, affecting or supplying goods or services

- Political interests or regulatory bodies
- Project management teams
- Programme management team including the Sponsoring Group
- Security
- Trade unions
- Wider community

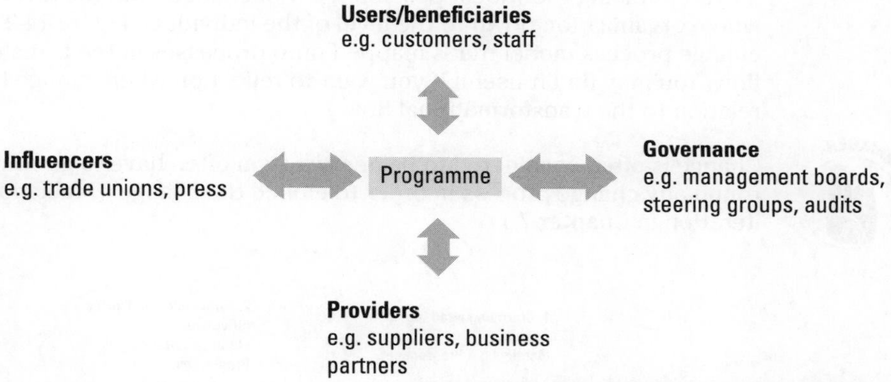

Figure 14-1: Possible stakeholder groups in a programme.

REMEMBER: When you get together with colleagues to analyse your stakeholders, be innovative in identifying stakeholder groups; don't just use the lists that I give. The best way to identify stakeholder groups and give them relevant names is to have someone from the stakeholder group present at the stakeholder analysis workshop (look at the later section 'Modelling your stakeholders').

MSP SPEAK: A stakeholder *interest area* is a place within your programme where a potential benefit needs to be managed. When you understand your stakeholders, identifying benefits becomes that much easier for you.

Using the Vision to Understand Your Stakeholders

Engaging with stakeholders is one of the ways you help them to change, so it's part of the wider subject of business change management (which I define in the next section). One of the most powerful tools you can use to encourage change in people is to give them a clear Vision of the future (flip to Chapter 5 to find out more about the Vision).

Managing business change

MSP SPEAK

You hear the phrase *business change management* a lot in connection with programmes. To me, this term means the way in which change happens within individuals, teams and the organization. Put another way, it's how people can be led through change, but note that by 'led' I mean 'travel with'. Like many others, I prefer the idea that you travel with people through change as opposed to pushing them through change.

So you're taking the widest possible view of change from the level of the whole organization down to the level of the individual. Figure 14-2 is a simple change process model that's mapped onto processes in the transformational flow. You may find it useful if you want to reflect on when change happens in relation to the transformational flow.

REMEMBER

Change is often considered to be *iterative;* you often have to go round and round any change process in order to embed the change. (I talk more about iteration in Chapter 7.)

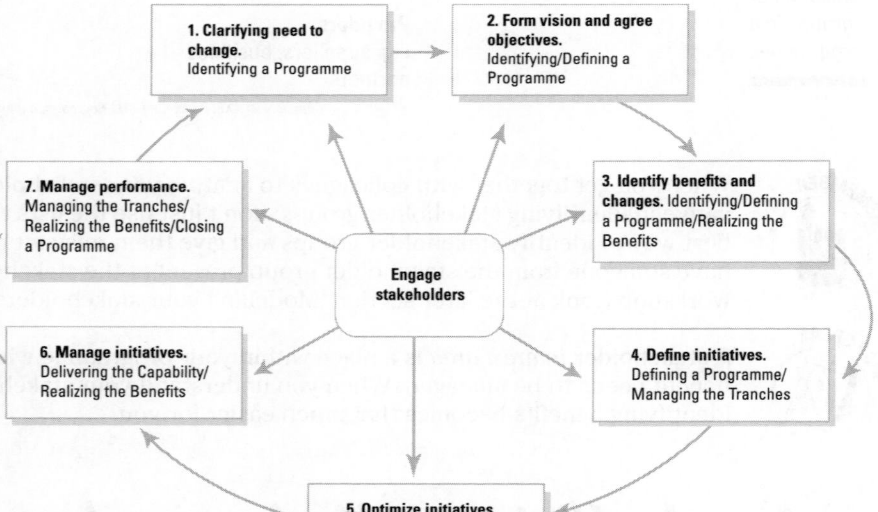

Figure 14-2: A change process model and programme processes.

Bringing stakeholders into the Vision workshop

One of the most important occasions in which you use stakeholder engagement is when you're creating the Vision. Engaging with stakeholders early on in creating the Vision is vital, because doing so ensures joint ownership.

The worst thing you can do is to present stakeholders with the draft Vision and then simply ask them to endorse it.

The engagement is best done at the Vision workshop. Make sure that you understand fully the nature of the current situation; the positive and more importantly the negative impact of staying as you are. I suggest considering two ideas:

- **Do-nothing Vision:** The positive impact of staying put.
- **The negative result of staying put is often referred to as a burning platform (or burning bridge):** The idea is that if you stay where you are, you burn, so you need to jump off the platform into the river. In other words, it's worth going somewhere else.

An examination of the do-nothing Vision or the burning platform allows you to appreciate the nature of the current reality. From there you can look at the beneficial future. The workshop can explore the tension between the two ideas.

That tension is what you want to encapsulate in the Vision. The aim is to build and maintain the impetus and commitment to change.

Leading change: Engaging stakeholders

Effective leaders use the Vision to help influence stakeholders. So, for example, Business Change Managers can engage with operational stakeholders to help them through transition.

Connect the change to benefits (which I cover in Chapters 15 and 16). A benefit is an outcome that a stakeholder perceives to be advantageous, so use the language of benefits to engage and help lead stakeholders. Don't think of stakeholders as just passive recipients of change; some stakeholders are the resources who deliver capability.

Understanding the importance of stakeholder engagement

You may like to pause before reading on and jot down some notes on why you think stakeholder engagement is important. Doing so can be extremely useful later, because a colleague may well ask you this question when you're trying to describe the significance of programme management.

The main aim of stakeholder engagement is to encourage buy-in, by having managed involvement with stakeholders instead of mere ad-hoc involvement. You can expect such buy-in to improve stakeholders' co-operation and assist with the co-ordination of tasks within the programme and with those outside it.

In addition, stakeholder engagement is an important tool for leaders. The people involved in the programme are going through change and therefore you need strong leadership. Another interesting aspect of good stakeholder engagement is that it helps to avoid unexpected surprises, which stakeholders may think you haven't anticipated (see the nearby sidebar 'No news is good news').

If, say, an international regulator takes an interest in a programme and its involvement hasn't been anticipated, stakeholder engagement wasn't working properly.

Stakeholder engagement provides a basis for better communication, because messages are consistent to each stakeholder group. Stakeholder groups talk to one another, so don't give one message to one group and a different message to a different stakeholder group.

Good stakeholder engagement maximises the possibility of good benefits realization.

No news is good news!

I provide consultancy on a lot of programmes, often very large ones of national significance. When I read the newspaper or watch television, my programmes sometimes appear as items of news. Quite often this appearance is due to some unexpected intervention in the programme, usually because of a failure of stakeholder engagement.

Newspapers prefer to report bad news. So if you see a programme reported in a newspaper, something is probably going wrong. Sometimes stakeholders do something that the programme wasn't anticipating and isn't in the interests of the programme. If the programme is properly engaging with the stakeholders, what the stakeholders want to do and more importantly why they want to do it are understood. Then perhaps the programme can change the stakeholders' opinions or, at the very least, take action to tone down bad news.

Engaging and Communicating with Stakeholders

Figure 14-3 displays the stakeholder engagement cycle, which I lead you through in this section. At first sight stakeholder engagement can look like a complex process, but breaking it down helps you to carry it out in a logical way. The perceived complexity is only because of the frequent feedback from one process step to another. If you ignore that feedback for the moment and just look at the purpose of the six process steps, it's pretty straightforward.

In this section I cover each of the steps in the stakeholder engagement cycle.

Modelling your stakeholders

You can do much better than simply engaging with stakeholders on an ad-hoc basis whenever you happen to come across them.

TIP

Set aside some time to work out who your stakeholders are: that's the first couple of steps in Figure 14-3. The ideal opportunity to do this is at the beginning of the Defining a Programme process (flip to Chapter 7 for more on Defining a Programme).

Figure 14-4 is an example of the Stakeholder Map (which happens to be for a sports programme).

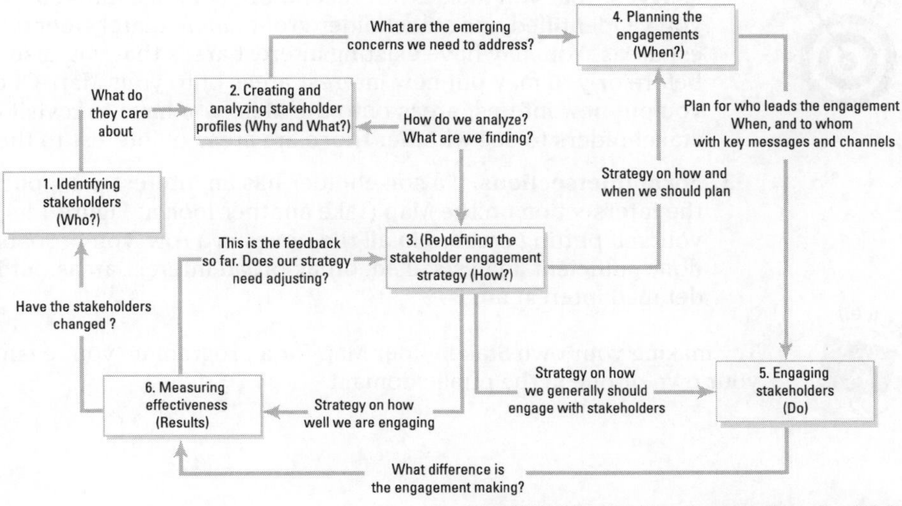

Figure 14-3: The six process steps in the stakeholder engagement cycle.

Stakeholders \ Interest Areas:	Sports Facilities	Transport Infrastructure	Public Transport Service	City Image/ Prestige	Local Economy	Housing	Hotel Accommodation	Local Environment	City Taxes
Planning Department		×			×	×		×	
City Mayor	×	×	×	×	×	×		×	×
City Government	×	×	×	×	×	×	×	×	×
Transport Department		×	×		×				
Sports Minister	×	×	×	×			×	×	
National Government	×	×	×	×	×	×	×	×	×
Local Residents	×	×	×		×	×		×	×
National Sports Council	×						×	×	
Tourists	×	×	×	×			×		
Athletes	×			×			×		
Rail Company		×	×		×				
Local Businesses	×	×	×	×	×	×		×	×

Figure 14-4: Sports programme Stakeholder Map.

Here's the stakeholder modelling process in a bit more detail:

1. **Create a simple list of stakeholders, perhaps grouping them as well.** The stakeholders can begin to look like a *decomposition diagram* (a model that shows one thing consisting of several other things below it, for example, the organization diagram for a typical company).

2. **Identify each stakeholder's areas of interest.** In a workshop, people tend to name lots of stakeholders before thinking about their interests.

   TIP: I suggest that you tackle the Stakeholder Map in a different way. When you've identified one stakeholder group, immediately identify their interest areas. You may have existing interest areas that you discussed before or you may put new interest areas onto your Map. Of course, if you put new interest areas onto the Map, you have to revisit existing stakeholders to see whether those are areas of interest to them as well.

3. **Form intersections.** If a stakeholder has an interest area, put a cross in the intersection on the Map (take another look at Figure 14-4). If you find yourself putting crosses in all the boxes in a row, you probably haven't done sufficient analysis: if so, break broad interest areas out into more detailed interest areas.

HAVE A GO: Try making your own Stakeholder Map for a programme you're familiar with – your own or one in the public domain.

Figure 14-5 shows the Influence/Interest Matrix, which illustrates the interest that stakeholders have in the example sports programme against the influence they have on the programme:

- **Interest.** The vertical axis is the interest of the stakeholder in the programme. You can think of this as the impact the programme has on the stakeholder: if a programme has more impact the stakeholder is probably going to be more interested in the programme. But I emphasise 'probably'. Some people may be very interested in the programme, even though you think the programme doesn't impact on them.
- **Influence.** The horizontal axis is how much influence stakeholders have over the programme. To put it crudely, how much power they have. Again, the relationship may be more subtle. A stakeholder group may have a great deal of power but choose not to use that power in relation to a programme. If they ignore the programme, do they really have influence?
- **Banding.** In the figure I give some simple examples of different types of interaction with different types of stakeholders. So you simply keep a low interest, low influence stakeholder informed of progress. Whereas a high interest, high influence stakeholder needs to be closely involved in the programme. You need to work very hard at achieving and maintaining strong buy-in.

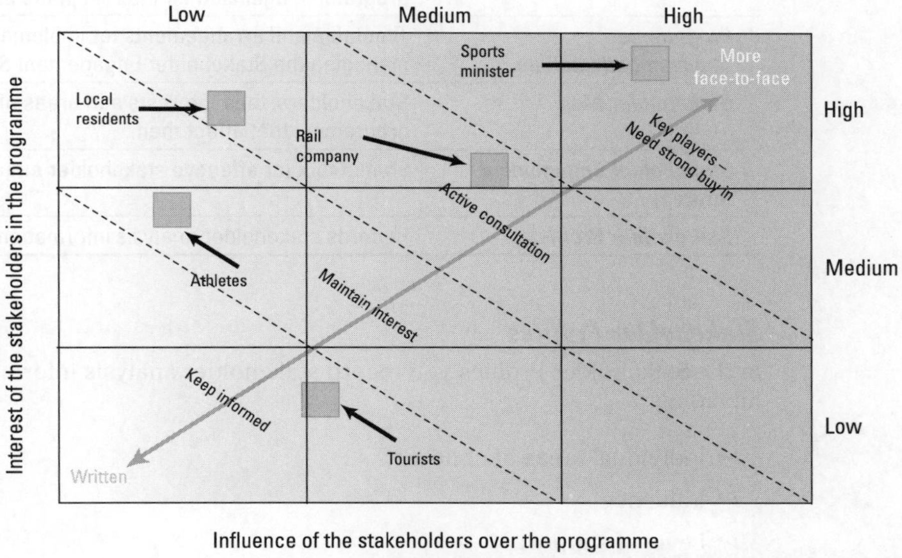

Figure 14-5: Influence/ Interest Matrix of a sports-complex programme.

WARNING!

The weakness with the banding in Figure 14-5 is apparent in the high-low and low-high corners (top left and bottom right). You need to be treating people who have high interest and low influence differently from those who have low interest and high influence. Those with high interest have lots of time to talk to you, but you don't really want to spend time on them. In the other corner it's the opposite: you want to get to the high influence people, but they may not have time for you.

Documenting your decisions

Having enjoyed the delights of the stakeholder identification workshop in the preceding section (oh, what fun you'll have! No really they are quite fun), you need to document what you've decided. I present an overview of the documents and their purposes in Table 14-1. I describe the Influence/Interest Matrix and the Stakeholder Map in the preceding section, Stakeholder Profiles and Stakeholder Engagement Strategy in this one and the Programme Communications Plan in the next.

Table 14-1	Purposes of Stakeholder Documentation
Influence/Interest Matrix	A plot of the influence of stakeholders in your programme against their interest in the programme.
Programme Communications Plan	Timetable and arrangements for implementing and managing the Stakeholder Engagement Strategy.
Stakeholder Map	Stakeholders, their interests and areas of the programme that affect them.
Stakeholder Engagement Strategy	Framework for effective stakeholder engagement.
Stakeholder Profiles	Records stakeholder analysis information.

Stakeholder Profiles

In the Stakeholder Profiles you record stakeholder analysis information, including:

- Individual areas of concern
- Influence
- Level of support
- Programme areas interested
- Trends

In a single document you can include the Stakeholder Map and the Influence/Interest Matrix, plus a profile for each stakeholder on the Map. You can also include a distribution of benefits by stakeholder and highlight key influencers. You can summarise all this information in a Stakeholder Register.

Stakeholder Engagement Strategy

The formal purpose of this document is to define the framework that enables effective stakeholder engagement and communication. Informally, people think of it as encapsulating the right message received by the right people, at the right time, in the right form, from the right person, with the right authority.

The document can answer questions such as:

- How will the programme effectively engage with stakeholders?
- What are the key messages?
- Who takes on particular roles?
- How are we going to identify, categorise and group stakeholders?
- Who's responsible for particular stakeholders/stakeholder groups?
- How are we going to manage interfaces between programme and project stakeholders?
- How are we going to process feedback?

Here's the composition of the Stakeholder Engagement Strategy:

- Communications guidelines
- Engagement mechanisms
- How to assess importance and impact
- How to assess analysis
- How to change the Communications Plan
- How projects will interface
- Key message delivery
- Negative publicity
- Policies
- Responsibilities
- Review cycle
- Stakeholder tracking
- Success measures

Communicating with your stakeholders

When you've worked out at a high level how to engage with your stakeholders, you can drill down to the detail of the tasks involved in communication.

The purposes of communication are as follows:

- Raising awareness
- Gaining commitment
- Maintaining consistent messages
- Keeping expectations in line with delivery
- Explaining changes
- Describing the future end state

You want to turn communication into a process that can run in the background in your programme, with the following objectives:

- Keeping awareness and commitment high
- Ensuring that expectations don't drift out of line with what's to be delivered
- Explaining what changes will be made and when
- Describing the desired future state

You need to include the following core elements in your communication process:

- **Stakeholder identification and analysis:** Sends the right message to the right audience.
- **Message clarity and consistency:** Ensures relevance and recognition and engenders trust.
- **Effective message delivery:** Gets the right messages to the right stakeholders in a timely and effective way.
- **Feedback collection system:** Assesses the effectiveness of the communications process.

Communications Plan

The objectives of the Communications Plan, which put some flesh on the overall purpose of communication, are as follows:

- Raising awareness
- Gaining stakeholder commitment
- Keeping stakeholders informed
- Promoting key message
- Demonstrating and gaining commitment
- Making communications truly two-way
- Ensuring that projects have a common understanding
- Maximising benefits

Composition of the Plan

Consider putting the following information in your Communications Plan:

- A schedule
- The objectives of each communication
- The key messages and information
- The audience for each communication
- The timing of each communication
- The channels you plan to use to communicate
- Responsibilities
- The feedback process
- The estimated effort
- Supporting projects and activities
- Information storage
- Possible stakeholder objections

TIP

Although this list can seem rather daunting, just keep it simple. It's only a plan for how you'll communicate.

Communications with projects

The programme needs to control project communications, so the Programme Office may well have to vet all communications. You may decide always to refer certain stakeholders to a specific custodian and perhaps direct certain sensitive topics to the programme each time.

To make this happen, you need to hold regular briefings for projects to keep them involved. You may also need to check that project communications align with the Programme Communications Plan.

Communication needs to start early in the programme. Take a look at Chapter 3 where I mention the need to include stakeholder engagement in the Programme Preparation Plan.

Engaging stakeholders: Areas of responsibility

Here are the main areas of responsibility relating to stakeholder engagement. Chapter 9 has lots more detail on these roles.

Senior Responsible Owner

The Senior Responsible Owner (SRO) is responsible for the following:

- Engaging key stakeholders early and at appropriate milestones throughout the programme.
- Leading the engagement with high-impact stakeholders and anticipating stakeholder issues that may arise.
- Briefing the Sponsoring Group and gathering strategic guidance on changing business drivers.
- Showing visible leadership at key communications events and ensuring the visible and demonstrable commitment of the Sponsoring Group.
- Ensuring the creation, implementation and maintenance of the overall Stakeholder Engagement Strategy.

Programme Manager

The Programme Manager is responsible for:

- Developing and implementing the Stakeholder Engagement Strategy.
- Day-to-day implementation of the whole stakeholder engagement process.
- Developing and maintaining the Stakeholder Profiles.

- Controlling and aligning the project communication activities.
- Ensuring effective communications with the project teams.
- Developing, implementing and updating the Communications Plan.

Business Change Manager

Business Change Managers are responsible for the following in their areas:

- Engaging and leading those operating new working practices through the transition, generating confidence and buy-in from those involved.

  Active stakeholder engagement is a major part of discharging this role.
- Supporting the SRO and taking specific responsibility for stakeholder engagement in their parts of the organization.
- Supporting the Programme Manager in the development of the Stakeholder Engagement Strategy and Communications Plan.
- Alerting the Programme Manager to the new winners and losers (if any) in their area of changes.
- Providing information and business intelligence for Stakeholder Profiles.
- Briefing and liaising with the Business Change Team.
- Communicating with affected stakeholders to identify new benefits and improved ways of realizing benefits.
- Delivering key communications messages to their business operations.

Programme Office

The Programme Office administers the programme and is responsible for:

- Maintaining information relating to the stakeholders.
- Maintaining an audit trail of communication activity.
- Collating feedback and ensuring that it's logged and processed.
- Facilitating activities specified in the Communications Plan.

Reassuring Your Stakeholders

In this section I tackle the vitally important subject of stakeholder assurance, discussing the principles and techniques and defining some of the terms you need to know along the way.

Programme assurance has to be independent of the programme management team, to meet the principle of independence that I discuss in the next section. The team can be internal or external to the organization, and different types of programme assurance can cover different aspects of the programme: all this assurance may not be happening on your behalf. You aren't asking the programme assurance team to look at what someone else is doing and report back to you; you are asking the assurance team to look at what you're doing and report to someone else. If you're the Programme Manager, your task is to integrate the assurance to cover all aspects of the programme while avoiding gaps and overlaps.

You may also like to refer to Chapter 13, because assurance is closely linked to quality.

Pondering assurance management principles

Taking a principles-based approach within programme management in general can be helpful, as I discuss in Chapter 4, and you can do the same with assurance management. *Assurance* means giving stakeholders confidence and reassurance that things are working properly.

Principles have to be universal, self-validating and empowering.

The following five principles for guiding your behaviour when carrying out assurance management are a really useful addition to programme management:

- **Independence.** Assurance needs to have a degree of independence from what's being assured. So, for example, assessors should have no direct line management for the programme team if they're carrying out assurance reviews on the team. Assessors need to be impartial and have no control over project outcomes or service operations. Independent assurance can then be a powerful tool.
- **Integration.** You need to make sure that assurance is integrated into a programme.

  Integrated assurance requires the planning, co-ordination and provision of assurance activities from the start of the programme to the delivery of benefits, in a way that provides greater assurance but with less effort. The Programme Manager's job is to make sure that someone is doing that. You can achieve this through the provision of an agreed plan that indicates how assurance reviews, of all types, are scheduled to support decision-making and inform investment approvals while avoiding duplication of activities that don't add value.

I once carried out an assurance review of a programme and was told that it was something like the fourth assurance review that had been held that month. Project managers weren't spending any time managing their projects; they spent all that time attending a series of overlapping and fragmentary assurance reviews.

- **Linked to major decision points.** A key way of achieving value is to link assurance to major decision points.

  Plan assurance activity to support major events. Examples are achievement of outcomes, tranche ends and key approval points (for example, funding decisions). These occur throughout the transformational flow, from the Mandate to the realization of benefits.

  For example, consider your end-of-tranche reviews. Make sure that you hold an assurance review before the end-of-tranche decision-making, and that the results of that assurance review feed into the end-of-tranche decision-making.

- **Risk-based.** Assurance needs to be risk-based. Base your assurance activities on an independent risk assessment and make sure that they focus on areas of greatest risks to commercial, legal, regulation, trading, investment and performance requirements. You may also want to look at specialist areas such as financial, delivery, technical, social, political, programme, operational or reputational risks.

  Places with more risk require more rigorous assurance; those with less risk need less assurance.

- **Action and intervention.** Often the assurance reviews work pretty well: they identify what's going and what's gone wrong. The relevant managers receive the reviews. . . and then they're ignored! Therefore, you need another principle of action and intervention.

  Assurance is most effective when appropriate follow-up actions are taken to resolve any serious issues identified as a result of the planned assurance activity. These consequential assurance actions may involve further reviews. Link your reviews of action plans, case conferences or more detailed reviews to ensure that appropriate actions are taken. This process includes clear escalation routes that need to be used if appropriate to the highest organizational levels of the organization for resolution of issues.

  In an ideal world, assurance reviewers should only make observations. If they make recommendations for action, they may well be limiting their independence for subsequent assurance reviews. It's convenient if the reviewers also make recommendations. So as part of your planning (as part of your integration of assurance), you need to consider whether you want people carrying out assurance reviews to make observations or recommendations. The most important factor is whether you'll ask the same reviewers to come back and do a subsequent review. In those circumstances, I suggest they just make observations.

Assessing assurance management techniques

In the preceding section I talk about carrying out an assurance review, but that's only one of a number of different techniques you can use when carrying out assurance activities.

When discussing assurance techniques, I use some terms that may be new to you. I find that being clear on the following definitions is helpful: audit, verification and validation, health check and review.

Audit

Audit means assessing the management and conduct of a programme and involves examining its activities to see whether the work has been carried out in accordance with an external procedure or standard. In practice, most audits check whether or not you're doing the thing right.

The weakness is that the audit may not be checking if you're doing the right thing. They aren't thinking about whether whatever you are doing is appropriate.

Although audits can be proactive, they tend to be reactive in that they're looking back on the previous performance of an aspect of the programme. Furthermore, audits tend to focus on conformance and compliance: have you done the activity correctly (sometimes known as a *validation activity*). I'm not criticising the auditing profession (some audits are very comprehensive and wide-ranging), but an audit may, for example, check carefully that you filled in the form without checking that the form makes sense. Therefore, they can be of limited value.

Audits can be carried out by internal audit staff or by external audit bodies. Indeed, anyone can carry out an audit. No particular skills are required in order to carry out an audit, other than some knowledge of the subject matter. Aim to ensure that the range of programme audits consider all aspects of the programme, its management and ability to deliver – although individual audits may cover only one aspect.

I think of *assurance activities* as having almost the opposite characteristics to audits. I hope that they're outward-looking and innovative. They need to provide evidence that quality-related activities are being performed effectively. They need to do whatever they need to do in order to reassure the people who are responsible for the activity.

Your programme undoubtedly needs to ensure that the projects are managed effectively, so you definitely need to put in place some project audits. One approach is to make use of programme staff on project boards (as I discuss in Chapter 9). But although in Chapter 10 I encourage you to put in place less control and reporting in order to reduce the burden, don't think that I'm soft on projects. If you reduce the overhead of reporting on projects, you need to put in place more rigorous reviews.

Verification and validation

You may come across the following terms on the Internet in the context of audits. I use these generic definitions:

- **Verification.** Doing the thing right. For example, does the product meet the specification?
- **Validation.** Doing the right thing. For example, are you building the right product?

Try to aim for a good mix of verification and validation. They can be combined in a single review, or you can ask one group to verify what's happening and another team to validate what's going on.

Health check

A *health check* means assessing whether a programme is meeting its objectives. The strength and weakness of a health check is that it's a series of yes/no questions. If you answer yes and no to the questions on a health check, you do get a very quick insight into the status or the health of the programme, but you may get only a black-and-white answer with no shades of grey.

Here's a simple sequence for carrying out a health check. You can apply the same sequence to any of the assurance techniques I discuss:

1. **Prepare by deciding on the scope, selecting and briefing the team members and agreeing how you document the health check.**
2. **Decide on your information requirement, such as which records or process descriptions you look at.**
3. **Undertake the review by reading the various documents and talking to people.**

4. **Analyse the review findings by drawing some conclusions about the health of the programme and putting them in a draft report.**
5. **Agree a corrective action plan between the team that carried out the health check and those who asked for it to be carried out.**
6. **Follow up to make sure the actions have happened.**

Assurance reviews

Whereas audits tend to focus on conformance and compliance (or verification) as I say earlier in this section, reviews take a broader look and may be used as a programme assurance tool by senior managers to determine whether the programme continues.

Key areas to consider within an assurance review are based on the elements of quality, scope and the programme management principles (take a look at Figure 14-1 in Chapter 13, which looks a little like a wheel).

Here are some specific areas of focus that often form topics of assurance reviews:

- How well is the programme controlling and enabling its projects?
- Is the level of overhead appropriate?
- How well are the Business Change Managers preparing the organization for changes and are benefits truly being delivered?
- Are the internal processes and governance strategies working effectively and optimally for the purpose of the programme?

Effectiveness of measurement

Effective decisions are based on accurate measurement of data and analysis of reliable information, which is why the Information Management Strategy and Information Management Plan are so important (check out Chapter 13 for more on these).

Therefore, looking at the effectiveness of measurement is another form of assurance. You can consider measurements in a programme in two ways:

- Measurements may be concerned with the management and control of the programme (for example, cost and budget reports).
- Measurement of the programme's outcomes may be a way of assessing whether acceptable benefits are materialising.

P3M3 assessments

P3M3 stands for Portfolio, Programme and Project Management Maturity Model (I show the model in Figure 14-6). A P3M3 assessment looks at the level of organizational maturity in portfolio, project or programme delivery and has a direct bearing on how well an organization can support its programmes.

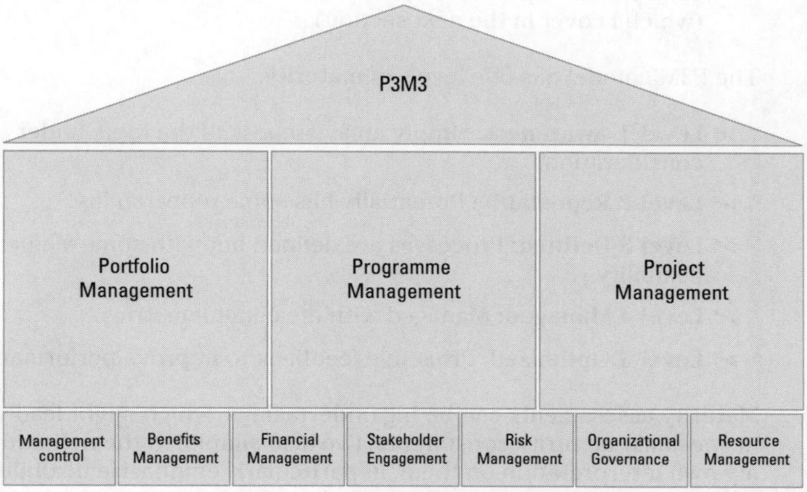

Figure 14-6: P3M3 model.

A simply way to explain *maturity* is to talk about repeatability. Within the programme are you able to have repeatable projects (project maturity)? Across the organization are you able to run repeatable programmes (programme maturity)?

REMEMBER

The P3M3 model views an organization's maturity through seven perspectives:

- Benefits management
- Financial management
- Management control
- Organizational governance
- Resource management
- Risk management
- Stakeholder engagement

The management and engagement terms will be familiar to you (if not, turn to Chapters 8, 10 or 11 as necessary), so I just put the other two into perspective:

- **Management control:** Internal control such as plans, monitoring and progress reporting.
- **Organizational governance:** Sits at a slightly higher level. It's external control, and is perhaps typified by things such as gateway reviews (which I cover in the next section).

The P3M3 model has five levels of maturity:

- **Level 1 Awareness:** Simply an awareness of the topic under consideration.
- **Level 2 Repeatable:** Potentially has some repeatability.
- **Level 3 Defined:** Processes are defined but with some element of flexibility.
- **Level 4 Managed:** Managed with meaningful metrics.
- **Level 5 Optimised:** Proactive feedback to improve performance.

Maturity assessments can be big undertakings, which might lead you to call in specialist maturity consultants. I've also simplified the definitions and put my own interpretation on them. In particular, I emphasise flexibility or tailoring more than some writers on the subject.

Note: The P3M3 model is being updated at the time of this writing. I anticipate that another process perspective – commercial or contract management – is likely to be added, but the fundamental concept will be unchanged.

Gated reviews

Gated reviews (sometimes called gate reviews, gateway reviews or independent reviews) are an ideal way of applying assurance control to a programme. The programme isn't allowed to progress to the next stage unless it's undergone a gated review.

Gated reviews check that the programme is under control and on target to meet the organization's needs. They are also applied to projects to ensure that the projects are properly under control and aligned to the programme's Blueprint and the programme objectives.

The decision gates below were originally for a procurement project. These terms may also apply in your programme if a lot of procurement is involved:

- **Gateway 0 – Strategic Assessment:** Why are we doing this?
- **Gateway 1 – Business Justification:** Do the costs, benefits, timescales and risks stack up?
- **Gateway 2 – Procurement Strategy:** Are we buying in the right way?
- **Gateway 3 – Investment Decision:** Now we've selected a solution, does it still make sense?
- **Gateway 4 – Readiness for Service:** Is the solution really ready to be used?
- **Gateway 5 – Benefits Evaluation:** Did we get the benefits we promised?

Testing your assurance knowledge

When I go into a programme to carry out an audit or review, one of the first things I do is have a chat with the Programme Manager and ask that person to explain to me how the assurance environment is set up.

Would you be happy answering that question if I popped into your programme?

Chapter 15

Getting Started with Benefits Management: Modelling the Benefits

In This Chapter

- Understanding the central role of benefits in a programme
- Discussing the importance of benefits management
- Identifying and describing your benefits
- Documenting your approach to benefits management

Programme benefits – how you measure the achievement of outcomes – are what a transformational change programme is all about. As I discuss in this chapter, you have a wide range of modelling techniques available to help you create a sensible map of the benefits to be achieved in your programme; additionally, you can document these benefits in a variety of ways.

Benefits management is an important subject to which I devote two chapters. In this one I describe the concepts behind benefits, including some key definitions and useful documentation as well as several figures that help put benefits into context. I also discuss how to identify, test, map, categorise and model benefits, useful tasks that I suggest you undertake in a benefits management workshop. I cover the benefits life-cycle in Chapter 16.

Considering the Concept Behind Benefits

In this section I look at the rationale for benefits, and I take this important subject nice and slowly: you encounter some extremely useful ideas here.

Placing benefits front and centre

The trigger for any change initiative needs to be the desire to realize benefits, some value if you like. I'm using the term *change initiative* at the moment, because at the very early stages you may not know whether the initiative is going to be a project or programme.

Benefits occur as a result of change; they don't occur while the status quo is in place. Therefore, I argue that benefits are the fundamental reason for undertaking a programme. Later on when you're defining benefits you have to make sure that you're measuring change, not the status quo. Of course benefits can trigger any initiative, but the real test is whether the organization wants to manage benefits in a structured way, co-ordinated with structured management of projects.

Consider re-reading the above paragraph because it contains some important ideas: in particular, I want you to get really comfortable with the idea that you do change in order to achieve benefits. Think of some changes you've been involved in, what the benefits were and whether they were properly managed.

If the organization does want to manage benefits and projects within the same initiative, you probably want to take an outcome-driven approach to planning. If the main focus is on achieving change, then only a benefits- or outcomes-related view can help you understand and manage change.

Of course, some people stick resolutely to a project view of the world. They think that a project builds things and exploitation is someone else's responsibility. If that's the case, you aren't going to be able to deploy all your programme management: sometimes the organization's culture is just too strong. But I assume in this chapter that the culture accepts a co-ordinated project-delivery and benefit-realization approach and therefore look at what that means.

Here's how I suggest you view the benefits rationale:

- Benefits are the trigger for an initiative.
- You realize benefits through change – they're the fundamental reason for a programme.
- Change results in outcomes.
- Benefits are quantifications of (that is, they measure) outcomes.

If you can understand each of those bullet points then you've got it; you understand the central role of benefits in achieving change. In essence, programmes are about co-ordinating delivery from a set of projects and integrating with that capability delivery (the realization of a set of benefits).

Benefits are the driver:

- The programme is driven by benefits: no benefits, no programme.
- Modelled benefits are a key input to the Business Case: its performance improvements justify the investment.

Defining benefits

You know what a benefit is, right? Well, I just want to be clear with a precise definition.

A *benefit* is a measurable improvement resulting from an outcome that one or more stakeholders perceive as an advantage, and contributes to one or more organizational objectives. Notice how subjective this definition is: if something is *perceived* as an advantage by a stakeholder, any associated measurable improvement can be a benefit.

You limit benefits to measurable improvements that contribute toward one or more organizational objectives, which some people may consider quite a contentious statement. This limitation suggests that some outcomes, perceived to be important by stakeholders, can be ignored because they can't be linked to an objective. My advice is simple. Don't ignore benefits that stakeholders are passionate about just because you can't see a link to organizational benefits.

For example, if you look at a dis-benefit (a decline resulting from an outcome; see the later section 'Discovering the dark side: Dis-benefits'), perhaps reduced staff morale, some may argue that this isn't connected to an organizational objective. However, it's really dangerous to ignore the effect of a transformational change on staff morale.

A good organization has an organizational objective of maintaining staff morale. Therefore, a drop in staff morale is relevant to an organizational objective, and so can be counted as a benefit or dis-benefit.

I also want to define an output and a capability, which make up an *outcome*, which, after all, results in a benefit:

- **Output:**
  - A tangible or intangible artefact
  - Produced, constructed or created as a result of a planned activity
- **Capability:**
  - Completed set of project outputs
  - Required to deliver an outcome
  - Exists prior to transition (check out Chapters 10 and 24 for a full description of transition)
  - A service, function or operation

Managing Programme Benefits

As I describe in this section, *benefits management* is the identification, definition, tracking, realization and optimisation of benefits within and beyond a programme.

Accelerating the programme: Benefits management as the driver

Benefits management sits at the heart of programme management and drives many (indeed most) aspects of the programme, including the following:

- Aligning and validating the Blueprint and projects
- Comparing with costs to test viability
- Prioritising to maximise value
- Planning the programme
- Engaging stakeholders
- Defining fit-for-purpose capability
- Informing tranche reviews
- Balancing costs and value
- Monitoring risks and issues

If the programme needs active benefits management, that management needs to include:

- Identifying of benefits
- Baselining of benefits
- Measuring of benefits

In essence, these points reflect the standard management activities, applied to benefits.

Identifying the areas of focus of benefits management

When you adopt benefits management, the focus is on enabling benefits realization and not just delivery of capability: it runs all the way from identification of the benefits through to their measurement and is continuous. It even goes beyond the end of the programme. In the Benefits Management Strategy (which I cover later in 'Deciding on your strategy for managing benefits'), you record when the programme stops counting benefits and responsibility transfers across to business as usual.

Figure 15-1 provides an illustration of the interfaces between benefits management and other aspects of programme management, as follows:

- **Plans.** Benefits can highlight dependencies that need to be reflected in the plans.
- **Risks.** Looking at benefits helps you to identify risks.
- **Blueprint.** Benefits qualify the Blueprint. The outcomes in the Blueprint have to be measurable by benefits.
- **Business Case.** Benefits, along with costs, inform the Business Case, allowing you to test the on-going viability of the programme. Costs must be balanced against benefits. They help the programme make trade-offs to achieve maximum value.
- **Quality.** Quality criteria are ultimately defined by benefits. Fitness for purpose can be considered as fitness for benefits.
- **Stakeholders.** Benefits sit within stakeholders' areas of interest. They're a great aid to engagement.
- **End-of-tranche reviews.** Benefits drive these reviews. If benefits aren't being realized, the programme has to change direction.

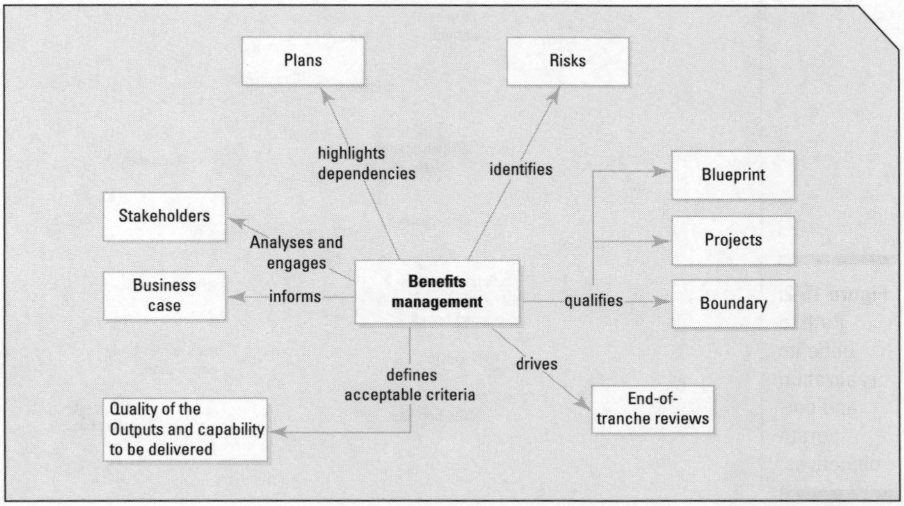

Figure 15-1: Benefits management interfaces.

REMEMBER

Of course you need to ensure that the programme is focused on the right benefits. Benefits management also increases the awareness of the positive and negative impacts of the programme activities on business as usual, and these impacts can be cast as benefits.

Naturally, benefits management helps ensure that benefits are indeed managed and that the programme is aligned to the transformational flow, because one of the key processes within the flow is Realizing the Benefits (flip to Chapter 20 for more on realizing benefits).

Aligning with corporate strategy

Benefits management can help ensure that the programme is aligned with corporate strategy. Figure 15-2 depicts the relationships between outputs, capabilities, outcomes, benefits and corporate objectives:

- **Capabilities.** Outputs is a term used in the project world: people working in projects see them as the end of the project. When you think of those outputs from the business-as-usual perspective, you can see that they aren't the end – they're the beginning. They're capabilities that can be used to achieve outcomes and benefits. Outputs are usually grouped into capabilities: although not a hard and fast rule, in general I think of outputs as being at a lower level of detail than capabilities.

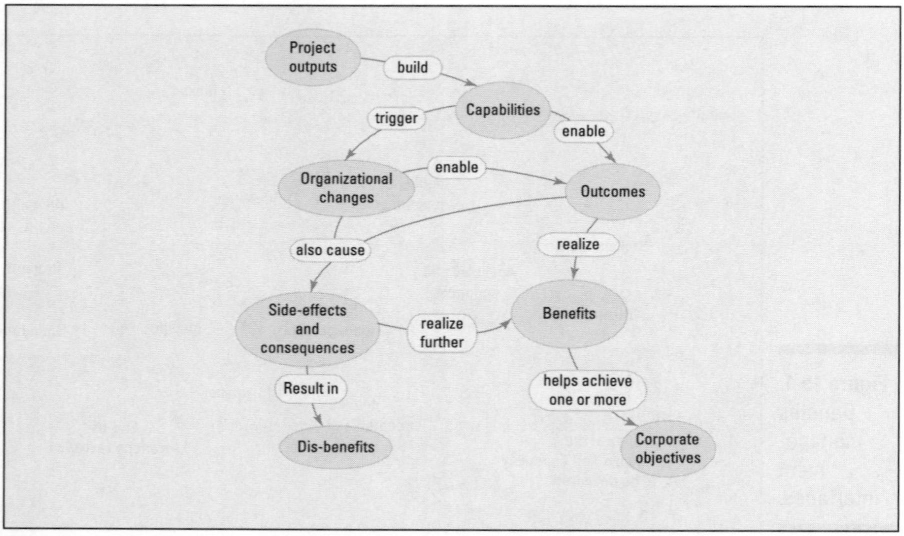

Figure 15-2: Path to benefits realization and corporate objectives.

- **Outcomes.** One of the most common phrases when considering transformational change programmes is that 'capabilities are exploited in order to achieve outcomes' (remember that *outcomes* are the effect of change). They're visible in the real world, what happens when you, to put it very simply, use capabilities.
- **Benefits.** How you measure outcomes. I don't mean as simple as one benefit being the measure of a single outcome, though: you have a many-to-many relationship between benefits and outcomes. When you understand these relationships, the benefits give a picture of your progress towards achieving the outcomes.
- **Corporate objectives.** From a programme you can't dictate the format of corporate objectives: the organization decides how it wants to state these. But benefits almost certainly feed into the breakdown of corporate objectives or key performance indicators (see the later sidebar 'Benefits and key performance indicators'): those outcomes and benefits are what enable you to achieve transformational corporate objectives.
- **Organizational changes.** You can take a slightly more nuanced view of what's needed on the journey from capabilities to outcomes. Almost certainly you have to make some detailed changes in business as usual in order to enable outcomes. That mixture of capabilities and organizational changes, in the real world, is what leads to the outcomes.
- **Side effects and consequences.** Organizational changes and outcomes are likely to have side effects that weren't your primary intention. For example, if you aim to get more business via your website, you may find that you get less business in your high-street shop. As well as side effects, you also have to deal with consequences (knock-on effects). For example, if business goes down in your shop, you may find that your reputation suffers.
- **Dis-benefits.** If you're very lucky the side effects and consequences give rise to further benefits, but also recognise that they may lead to dis-benefits. As I say in the next section, you need to manage dis-benefits.

Benefits and key performance indicators

You may be able to link benefits pretty closely to your organization's key performance indicators, but you may need to adjust or supplement them. Be careful if you're adjusting performance indicators, because they may also be written into contracts. If performance indicators are highly variable, they may not be particularly effective as benefits measures because they have too much 'noise' associated with them.

Discovering the dark side: Dis-benefits

In the simple world of a project, you can sometimes imagine that everyone is pleased to have the output and that all users are happy. In the complex world of the programme, however, you're dealing with a more diverse set of stakeholders, some of whom welcome the change and others who're unhappy with it. Consequently, you need to recognise the existence of dis-benefits within a programme.

A *dis-benefit* is the measurable decline resulting from an outcome; it detracts from one or more organizational objectives. One or several stakeholders perceive it as negative, but that's not to say that all stakeholders do. Dis-benefits are inevitable when change is involved. Some people resist change and some end up in a worse situation compared to if no change had happened. In addition, some changes are seen as a benefit by one stakeholder group and a dis-benefit by others.

If you simply ignore dis-benefits, they go unmanaged and surprise you (probably unpleasantly) in the future. You can't predict and manage the effect of the dis-benefits, so you have to model and manage them just as rigorously as you manage benefits.

Dis-benefits aren't risks. Although dis-benefits happen in the future, they're certain to happen whereas risks have a probability associated with them. For example, if you change the job descriptions and responsibilities of a group of staff, you will see a reduction in morale: it's not a risk, it's a dis-benefit. Similarly, managers may welcome redundancies because they reduce staff costs, but employees probably regard redundancies as a dis-benefit.

That said, you may not identify all the dis-benefits at the beginning of the programme. Just as with side effects and consequences, often partway through a programme you become aware of additional dis-benefits. Therefore you need to revisit your benefits model and properly plot new dis-benefits and manage them.

You're almost certain to have a many-to-many relationship between each of these pairings of outcomes, benefits, capabilities and outputs; Figure 15-3 illustrates these relationships. For example, an outcome is measured by many benefits and benefits measure many outcomes. In even a slightly complex programme, you need to get your mind round all these many-to-many relationships. You need to put your outputs, capabilities, outcomes, benefits and projects into a database so that you can keep track of the relationships.

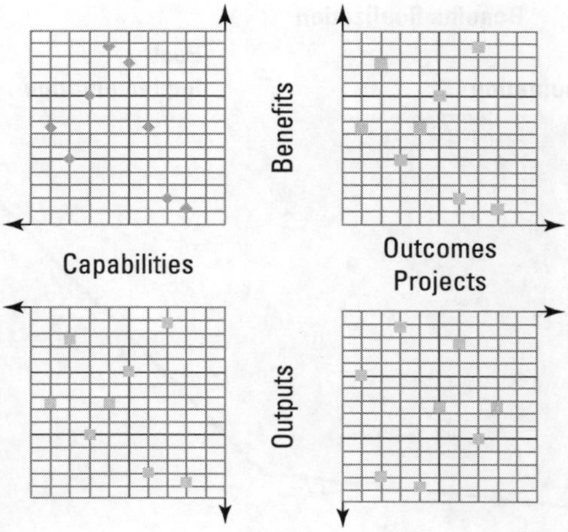

Figure 15-3: Many-to-many relationships in a programme.

Looking at the big benefits picture

The preceding sections include a number of new ideas around benefits management, so perhaps your head is spinning. If so, I provide Figure 15-4 to help sort things out.

Here's how the figure works:

- **Dotted line:** Shows what used to happen when you simply delivered a project: nothing until the end of the project – no performance improvement and no benefits while the output was being developed. The output was handed over to the user community (to business as usual). Perhaps you didn't have adequate communication between the project and business as usual, or perhaps even experienced a drop in performance after delivery of the output (sometimes called a *learning dip*).

  Only after a significant amount of effort in business as usual (possibly unplanned effort) did performance return to the original level. And only then did benefits start to be realized.

- **Thick line (your goal):** To have a smooth increase in performance (realization of benefits) after the output or capabilities are delivered. But also the hope that initial benefits can be realized in anticipation of the delivery of capabilities (which can be called *quick wins*).

  You may say that this situation is getting something for nothing – and you'd be right! It certainly requires considerable communication and trust between the business and project communities, which is the whole reason why you set up a programme organization.

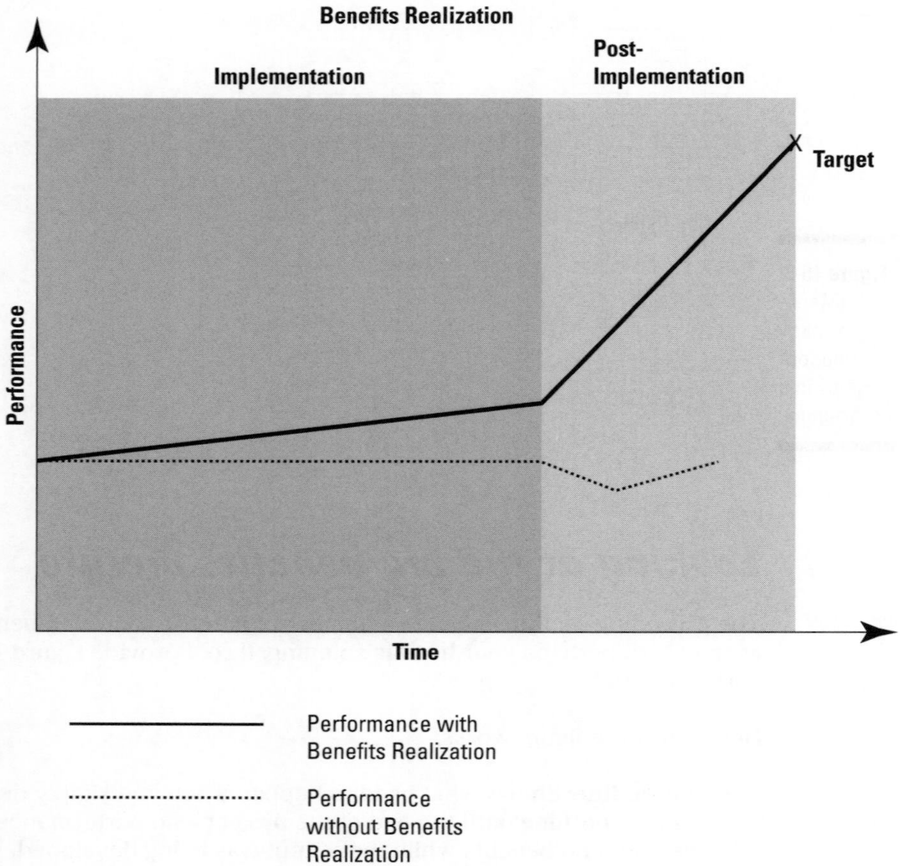

Figure 15-4: Benefits realization.

Imagine you wind down a facility to maintain outdated equipment in anticipation of the delivery of replacement equipment. The staff that you used to maintain the old equipment can be redeployed, which is a benefit and occurs before you have the new equipment. But you have to be pretty certain that the new equipment is going to arrive on schedule.

Being Clear about Each Benefit: Your Benefits Identification Workshop

In Defining a Programme, a process I cover in Chapter 7, you model the benefits. At the heart of that is a benefits workshop, benefits modelling workshop or benefits identification workshop. Don't get too hung up on the precise name for your workshop, the key is to choose a name that makes your stakeholders comfortable. Here are some of the techniques to use. The sequence in your benefits workshop is to:

1. **Brainstorm benefits and check that they're measurable.**
2. **Apply the critical tests to the benefits.**
3. **Categorise the benefits using one of the many available categorisation criteria.**
4. **Plot the benefits onto a map.**
5. **Document the benefits.**

REMEMBER

Benefits are all about measurement: make sure when you describe the benefit that you describe something that's measurable in a meaningful way.

You can think about benefits as being analogue or digital (see Figure 15-5):

- **Analogue benefits:** Vary continuously across a range of values. The example I take is of a more secure site (Internet site or a physical location; it doesn't matter for this example). When you talk about 'a more secure site', you can discuss the number of breaches that happen over time.
- **Digital benefits:** A less useful description, because a digital (binary) description can have only values of zero or one, yes or no. If you simply say you want 'a secure site', you're defining a digital benefit. A site is secure until a breach occurs, at which point it's no longer secure: measuring, managing or monitoring the benefits doesn't help you.

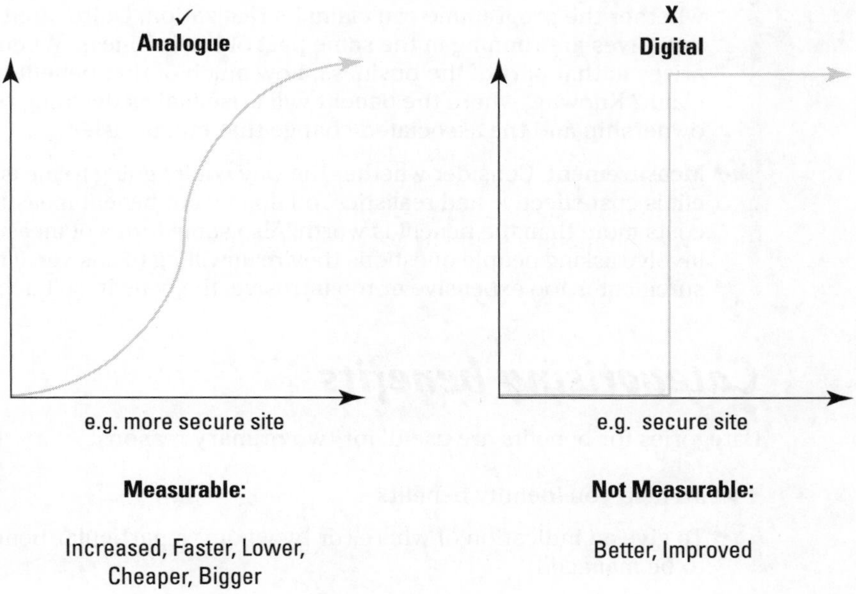

Figure 15-5: Progressive measurable benefits.

TIP

Another way of thinking about this issue is that measurable benefits are good: they employ terms such as 'increased', 'faster', 'lower', 'cheaper' and 'bigger'. But words such as 'better' or 'improved' are so vague that they may not be measurable in any meaningful way.

In this section I give you a whole range of different ways in which you can categorise benefits: some are straightforward, others are more sophisticated. I find some very useful (my favourite is to split benefits into direct financial, direct non-financial and indirect categories) and others just too clever by half (for example, the precise definitions of cashable and non-cashable benefits). Your task in your programme is to choose one or more ways of categorising your benefits that helps you: an approach that makes benefits management easier, not more complex.

Confirming real benefits: Critical tests

While you're identifying your benefits, you do so by brainstorming possible benefits. The best way to ensure that you've identified a real benefit is to apply critical tests in the following four areas:

- **Description of the benefit.** Make sure that you're describing something that's a measure of an outcome.
- **Observation.** Ensure that you can see some difference in the state of the world. If you use highly abstract terms for a benefit, the observation of the benefit just becomes a matter of judgement and may not be very useful.
- **Attribution.** Examine where the benefit will arise and, more importantly, whether the programme can claim its realization. Quite often several initiatives are running in the same part of the business. When the benefit arises in that part of the business, how much of that benefit can you claim? Knowing where the benefit will arise makes deciding on ownership and the associated change that much easier.
- **Measurement.** Consider whether the way you're going to measure the benefit is cost-effective and realistic. You don't want benefit measurement that costs more than the benefit is worth! Also some forms of measurement involve asking people questions they're unwilling to answer. If the measurement is too expensive or too intrusive, the benefit isn't achievable.

Categorising benefits

Categories for benefits are useful for two primary reasons:

- To help you identify benefits
- To give an indication of where (or by whom) a particular benefit needs to be managed

Categorisation can help you to:

- Balance benefits and risks
- Enable a portfolio-level view (if all the change initiatives in a portfolio are categorising benefits in the same way then the people up at portfolio level can look at benefits consistently)
- Enable tracking by category
- Identify overlaps where you're using two different ways of describing the same benefit
- Increase understanding through common terminology
- Manage changes of priority
- Track relationships
- Understand impact

Here are several examples of categorisation approaches, in the order in which I discuss them in the following three sections:

- Categorising by measurement mechanism
- Categorising by stakeholder
- Categorising by corporate objectives
- Categorising by value
- Categorising by financial impact

Categorising by measurement mechanism

TIP

Here's my personal favourite method of categorising benefits: by the way you measure the benefits. Working from the bottom upwards in Figure 15-6, you can measure directly benefits that can be stated in financial terms (some people call these *tangible* benefits. I use the nice neutral term *direct (financial)* benefits. Although other benefits may also be tangible (can be directly measured), putting a financial value on them may be a little harder. These are *direct (non-financial)* benefits.

The trickiest benefits, but the ones that may have the greatest impact on your programme, are those that you can't measure directly: called *intangible* or indirect benefits.

You can also categorise benefits by stakeholder, as I show in Figure 15-7.

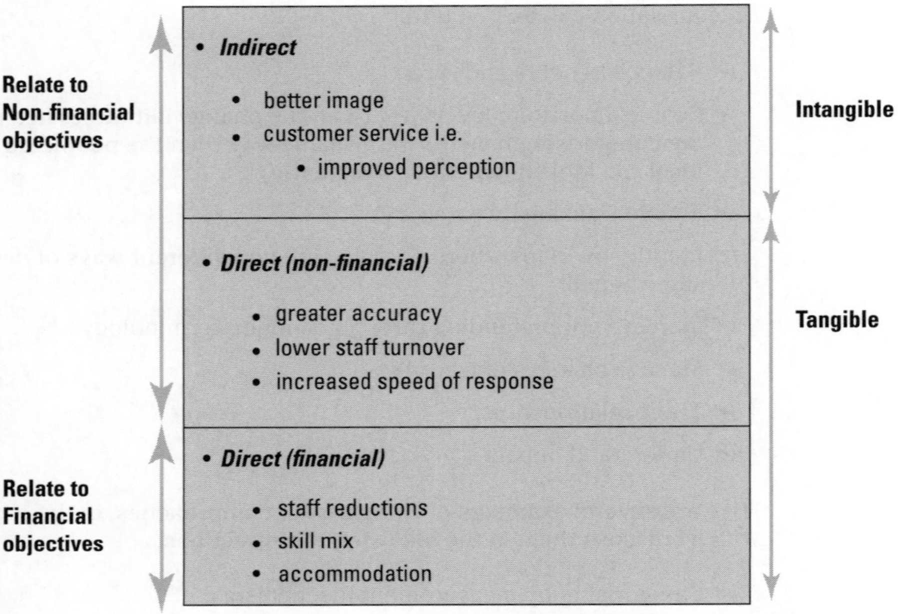

Figure 15-6: Categorising benefits by measurement mechanism.

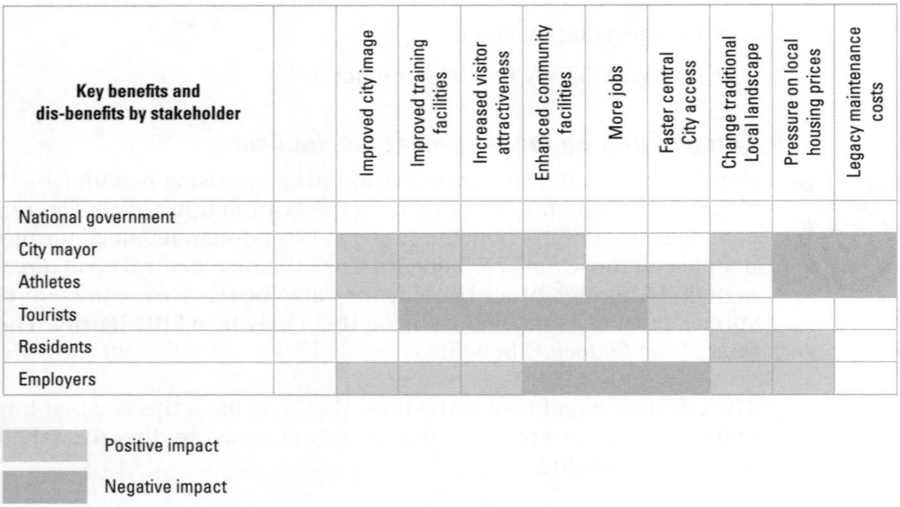
Key benefits and
dis-benefits by stakeholder
Improved city image
Improved training facilities
Increased visitor attractiveness
Enhanced community facilities
More jobs
Faster central City access
Change traditional Local landscape
Pressure on local housing prices
Legacy maintenance costs
National government
City mayor
Athletes
Tourists
Residents
Employers
Positive impact
Negative impact

Figure 15-7: Benefits distribution matrix of stakeholders.

Tying benefits to corporate objectives

Here are some typical corporate objectives to which you can link types of change you may be triggering from your programme:

- **Increased flexibility.** Delivering outcomes that allow an organization to respond to strategic demands without incurring additional expenditure.
- **Internal performance improvement.** Changes that are internal to the organization, such as improved decision-making or more efficient management processes.
- **Enhanced personnel or human resources management.** A better-motivated workforce may lead to a number of other benefits, such as more flexibility or increased productivity.
- **Policy or legal compliance.** These changes enable an organization to fulfil policy objectives or to satisfy legal requirements where the organization has no choice but to comply,
- **Process improvements.** These are 'more for the same' or 'the same with less' changes that allow an organization to do the same job with less resource, leading to reduction in costs, or to do more with the same resource.
- **Enhanced quality of service.** Improvements to services – such as a quicker response to queries or providing information in a way customers prefer – give rise to fewer customer complaints and less costly service failures.
- **Reduced costs.** Improvements in control and reduction of operating costs.
- **Improved revenue generation.** Changes that enable increased revenue or the same revenue level in a shorter timeframe, or both.
- **Reduced environmental impact.** Changes that reduce your carbon footprint or mitigate the environment impact of the organization.
- **Risk reduction.** Changes that enable an organization to be better prepared for the future, for example, hedging currency risks. They may also relate to public safety or the safety of vulnerable groups.
- **Strategic fit.** Benefits that contribute to strategic fit or enable the strategic direction through long-term investments or market positioning.

Check out Chapter 16 for more on linking programme benefits to corporate objectives.

Categorising benefits by value

I like to talk of effectiveness as being 'more for the same' and efficiency as 'the same for less'. The UK government went a little bit further and expanded on these two nice simple little terms. It created a value-for-money approach known as FABRIC, the framework for performance information where it defined three types of benefit:

- **Economic benefit:** Financial improvement, releasing cash, increased income or better use of funds. The precise definition is: an economic measure looks at the cost of acquiring the inputs to the programme.
- **Effectiveness:** Doing things better or to a higher standard. An effectiveness measure looks at whether the outputs of the programme lead to the desired outcome.
- **Efficiency:** 'More for the same or the same with less'. An efficiency measure looks at whether you're getting the maximum output from the inputs that go into the process. For example, how many patients are being treated for a given set of hospital facilities.

Consider how useful these definitions are in your organization. If you do want to use these three terms in your organization, you may have to be quite clear as to what, for you, the differences are between 'better' and 'to a higher standard'.

Categorising benefits by financial impact

You may find that categorising your benefits by financial impact is helpful. The terms I give you here are much used by the Cabinet Office Efficiency and Reform Group and similar bodies and are particularly relevant in the UK public sector.

Here are the two categories with examples:

- **Cashable (benefit can be turned into cash):**
  - Lower supply chain costs
  - Staff savings
  - Lower running costs
- **Non-cashable (benefit can't be turned into cash):**
  - Staff time savings

Staff time savings are only non-cashable if you assume that staff can't be made redundant or doing so is unacceptable, and instead they need to be redeployed. This issue relates to your organization's culture.

Using risk to classify benefits

Categorising benefits by the risk of them being achieved is an elegant and pretty sophisticated benefits management approach, one that I like to use when I'm consulting on benefits.

Some people go further and interpret the lack of certainty around benefits as being risks and then move into managing the risks associated with the benefits. For me, however, this is a step too far. I advise leaving these ideas of benefits and risk until you have a bit more experience on the subject.

Documenting the Benefits

After you identify your benefits, apply the critical tests and categorise them in a straightforward way, you need to sort out the documentation.

Linking benefits: The Benefits Map

MSP SPEAK

You need to model benefits onto a *Benefits Map*. This document shows the relationships between corporate objectives, short and long-term benefits, outcomes, processes, capabilities and outputs.

Figure 15-8 shows a Benefits Map with different types of artefact: outputs, capabilities, outcomes, benefits and corporate objectives. You have to decide how many different types of artefact you want to show on your Map. As so often, the aim is to put on as many things as help you and your colleagues in understanding your programme:

- **Project output:** A straightforward output from a project.
- **Capability:** One or more outputs in business as usual, but not yet used, are a capability.
- **Outcome:** The capability is exploited and triggers change. The effect of that change is an outcome – something you can observe. You can rephrase this as, for example, 'patients not being delayed'.
- **Corporate objective:** The benefits contribute to a corporate objective.

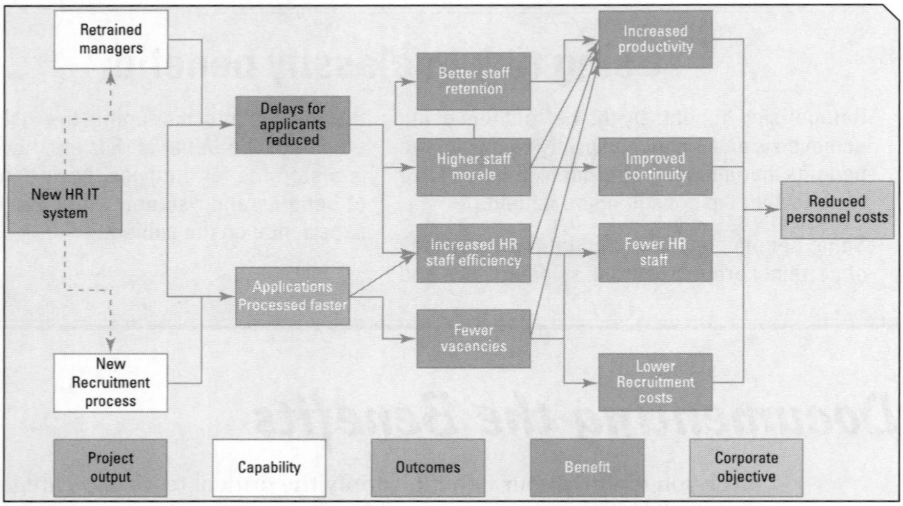

Figure 15-8: Benefits Map for a new human resource system.

The world already contains enough confusion, so don't put on so many different artefacts that you cause even more!

As well as a Benefits Map you can also have a *Benefits Register,* which summarises the information in the Benefits Profiles (see the later section 'Building a Benefits Profile'), thus providing an overview of the programme's benefits.

Assembling a Benefits Realization Plan

The *Benefits Realization Plan* is a complete view of all the benefits and dis-benefits, including dependencies and timescales. You use it to track realization of benefits and put in place the appropriate controls within benefits management. It's developed alongside the Programme Plan.

Remember the very close relationship with stakeholder engagement: benefits are improvements that stakeholders see as advantages.

Figure 15-9 illustrates a Benefits Realization Plan. A real plan is a more complex document, but I hope this one shows how the benefits need to come together into a single co-ordinated plan that includes dates.

You to need to take all the Benefit Profiles, integrate them, remove the anomalies and double counting, and plot the benefits on one or more schedules.

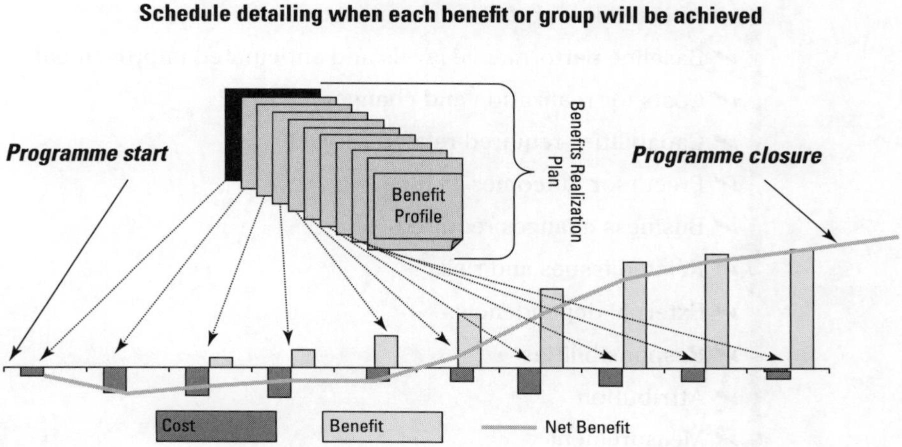

Figure 15-9: A Benefits Realization Plan.

Building a Benefits Profile

MSP SPEAK

A *Benefits Profile* describes a benefit and nothing more complicated than that. Clearly it's part of the Benefits Realization Plan, and so it supports building the Benefits Realization Plan. You create it when the benefit is identified, and again a link exists with stakeholder engagement. If you've done your stakeholder engagement properly, when you identify the benefit you can see which stakeholder is the benefit owner.

You need a benefit profile for each key benefit, that is, for each benefit that you have to describe in order to justify the Business Case. The minimum contents of a Benefits Profile are along the following lines:

- A description of the benefit
- The owner of the benefit
- How the benefit will be tested

But you can add many other headings, too. Quite often the Profile contains a great deal of detail if the benefit is large:

- Identifier
- Benefit description
- Supported objectives
- Category

- Affected key performance indicators
- Baseline performance levels and anticipated improvement
- Costs for realization and change
- Capabilities-required related project
- Precursor outcomes
- Business changes required
- Related issues and risks
- External dependencies
- Responsibilities
- Attribution
- Measurement

Deciding on your strategy for managing benefits

MSP SPEAK

The *Benefits Management Strategy* is one of the set of strategies you create during the Defining a Programme stage. It documents your approach to realizing benefits and is the framework within which benefits are realized.

Here are the sorts of things you can cover, in very broad terms:

- Do you want benefits as early as possible – no matter what sort of disruption it causes? Or do you want to minimise organizational disturbance even though that delays the realization of benefits?
- Does some overriding necessity to maintain services while you're putting in place the new world exist?
- What's the situation regarding existing projects? If yours is an emergent programme, you can cover this fact in the Benefits Management Strategy.
- What's your approach to early wins? Or to be more precise, to early benefits possibly being delivered even before you have capabilities?

Here's the composition of your Benefits Management Strategy:

- Acceptable measures
- Capabilities and benefits
- Measurement methods
- Priorities
- Responsibilities
- Scope
- Stopping double counting

Working on modelling your benefits

Try modelling your programme's benefits, based on this chapter's information. I suggest doing so in a workshop with others, though you may initially like to do it with a smaller group of close colleagues.

Consider reviewing or creating some of the benefits documentation I describe in this chapter.

Chapter 16

Reaping the Benefits: Measuring Your Outcomes

In This Chapter

- Following a cycle for realizing benefits
- Reviewing your benefits
- Getting an all-round picture of benefits

Benefits management is about a lot more than modelling benefits, which I cover in Chapter 15. After you create the benefits model and associated documentation in Defining a Programme, you need to realize them and manage that realization.

In this chapter I cover the benefits life-cycle: the simple process for making benefits happen and measuring them. This aspect includes a look at the relationship between benefits and corporate objectives, which is another way of giving you an insight into the cycle you're following. I also discuss the nature of the benefit reviews that you need to commission at various points throughout your programme. Also, benefits management is such a large subject that you can pick up useful knowledge by considering them from different viewpoints, including the areas of responsibilities and the focuses of key roles.

Turning to the Benefits Cycle

When MSP was refreshed in 2011, I was keen to make benefits management as accessible as possible. One thing I pressed hard for, and was glad to see included in the MSP method, was a simple, understandable benefits cycle. This cycle is shown in Figure 16-1.

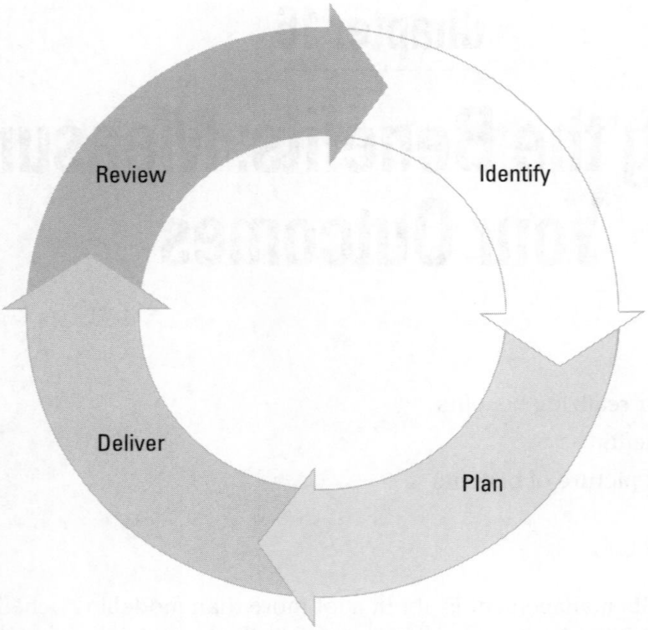

Figure 16-1: The steps in the benefits management cycle.

Pedalling through the benefits cycle process

This cycle is how you get things done in a measured way. Here are the steps of the benefits management process:

1. **Identify the benefits.** This step is another name for modelling the benefits and includes identifying, categorising and validating the benefits. It finishes around the time you have a Benefits Map that everyone is happy with (flip to Chapter 15 for more on Benefits Maps).

2. **Plan the benefits.** You're planning benefits management as you complete the benefits documentation. But that planning continues as you link the benefits plans to the other plans that you're creating.

   TIP

   First time round this step is in Defining a Programme, but you probably repeat it at each tranche boundary.

3. **Deliver the benefits.** You won't be surprised to hear that delivering benefits happens during the Realizing the Benefits process, which I cover in Chapter 20.

4. **Review the benefits.** The final step is to carry out benefits reviews, mostly as part of managing your tranches. You can find more about that in Chapter 18 and in the later section in this chapter, 'Carrying Out Benefits Reviews'.

Relating the programme and corporate objectives

A useful way of understanding the benefits cycle is to look at the relationship between benefits and other elements of programme management, such as corporate objectives. I show these relationships in Figure 16-2.

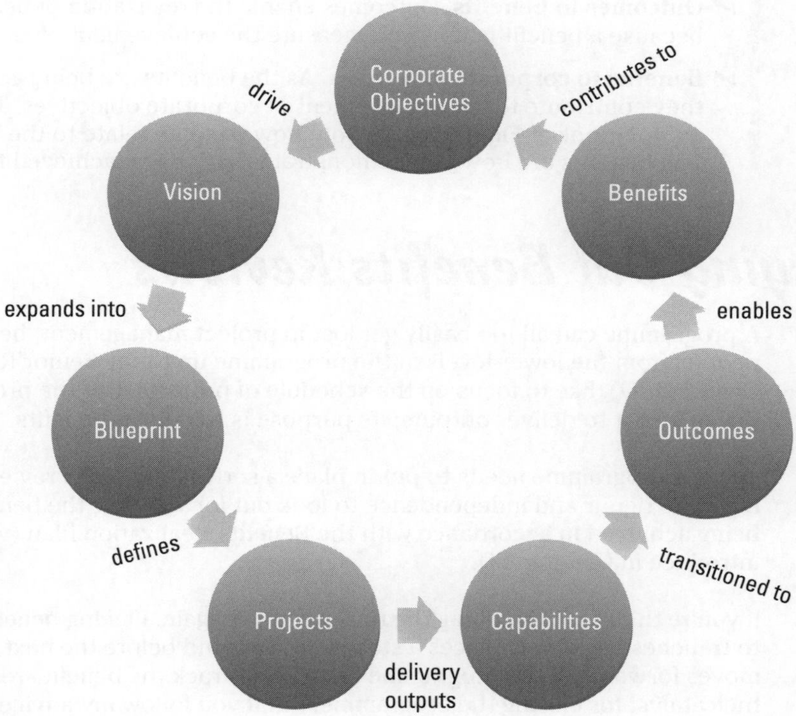

Figure 16-2: Programmes and corporate objectives.

Here are the details of Figure 16-2:

- **Corporate objectives to Vision.** Corporate objectives drive the development of the programme Vision.
- **Vision to Blueprint:** The Vision is expanded into a Blueprint (a model of the future organization, sometimes called the 'to-be' state, which I describe in Chapter 6).
- TIP **Blueprint to outputs.** The Blueprint helps you to define what projects you need to create the outputs. You do so by identifying gaps in the Blueprint between the 'as is' and 'to be' states, and analysing which outputs are needed to help fill that gap.

- **Outputs to capabilities.** Projects deliver outputs that create capabilities; or to be more precise, projects deliver outputs that are a project-orientated view of the deliverables from a project. Although in business as usual these outputs are regarded as capabilities, in most cases several outputs come together to create a single capability.
- **Capabilities to outcomes.** Capabilities are transformed into outcomes; or to put it another way, the capabilities are exploited in order to achieve outcomes.
- **Outcomes to benefits.** Outcomes enable the realization of benefits, because a benefit is how you measure the achievement of an outcome.
- **Benefits to corporate objectives.** As the benefits are being achieved, they contribute to the achievement of corporate objectives. Take another look at Figure 16-2 to note how benefits relate to the Vision. The benefits are how you demonstrate that you've achieved the Vision.

Carrying Out Benefits Reviews

A programme can all too easily get lost in project management, because people, from the lower levels in the programme up to the Senior Responsible Owner (SRO), like to focus on the schedule of projects. But the programme doesn't exist to deliver outputs; its purpose is to deliver benefits.

So your programme needs to put in place a series of benefits reviews that have the rigour and independence to look out for whether the benefits are being achieved in accordance with the Benefits Realization Plan (which I introduce in Chapter 15).

If you're thinking of skipping the reviews, think again. Linking benefits reviews to tranches effectively places a stake in the ground before the next tranche moves forwards. If the programme is badly off-track the benefits review can be the catalyst for closing the programme. But if you follow my advice in this book, your programme is sure to be much more successful than that.

Staying on track: Programme benefit reviews

A programme benefit review helps ensure that the benefits realization remains on track. You typically hold it at the end of each tranche, although it can be time- or event-driven. The review covers historic benefits, but it also needs to look forward to see whether the expectation of future benefits delivery is realistic. The reviewers take soundings from all relevant stakeholders. They check the validity of benefits and the value that they've achieved against the perception of stakeholders that the benefits are being achieved and against the environment, which of course can change significantly since the programme was first planned.

REMEMBER

The programme benefits reviews may well trigger a review of the Project Dossier. For if the benefits aren't being achieved, a different set of projects may be needed to deliver a rescheduled set of outputs or possibly even different outputs.

Setting objectives for the review

Here's a set of objectives for a benefits review. I use these frequently when I'm carrying out audits on behalf of programmes: they're a really helpful starting point for a review. You can see that these objectives focus on benefits and pay hardly any attention to projects:

- Assess and update Benefit Profiles and the Benefits Realization Plan:
  - Ensure that benefits remain achievable.
- Check the benefits still align with the programme and organizational objectives.
- Inform stakeholders of progress:
  - Identify any further potential for benefits.
- Assess performance of changed business operations against original performance.
- Assess benefits achieved against Profiles.
- Review effectiveness of benefits management:
  - Develop improved methods.
  - Improve definition of benefits.
  - Improve understanding of capability to deliver.

Scheduling programme benefit reviews

Although a benefit review can happen at any time, common practice is to carry them out at the end of tranches and to link project reviews, benefit reviews and programme (tranche) reviews together in an integrated set of reviews that inform planning for the next tranche.

REMEMBER

The Benefits Management Strategy needs to inform the frequency and timing and may set a maximum allowable interval.

Viewing Benefits From Different Angles

As you may have gathered from the fact that I take two chapters to do justice to benefits, it's a huge subject. Therefore, I think that you may appreciate the opportunity to consider benefits from different viewpoints. Think of it as like walking around a large sculpture and pausing here and there to consider it. I provide a few ideas in this section, including through the lens of the duties of the people and groups crucial to benefits management.

Quantifying benefits

You may find looking at benefits management from the point of view of quantifying benefits helpful. Ideally, you want to quantify and measure benefits in monetary terms, which certainly makes the process more straightforward. But if you can't quantify benefits in monetary terms, you need to do so numerically.

If benefits are indirect (that is, intangible, something I cover in Chapter 15), you have to measure them via indicators.

For example, if you want to measure customer satisfaction, you can carry out a customer survey. But a customer survey doesn't measure customer satisfaction; it measures responses to the survey. The responses to that survey may be an *indicator* of customer satisfaction.

You do, however, need to expend additional effort on the assessment of the indirect benefits, as does the organization on agreeing to the model that links the indicators to those indirect benefits.

Whatever the benefits, you have to baseline them before the capabilities are delivered. (See Chapter 12 for more on configuration management).

Identifying benefits

Here's a chance to look at the fundamental set of links from the viewpoint of the identification of benefits:

- Outcomes (the quantification of improvements) are first identified as early as possible, possibly in the Programme Mandate and certainly by the time of the Programme Brief.
- You then expand benefits into the Vision, which you turn subsequently into the Blueprint.
- You almost certainly need to use a Benefits Map to show the relationship between benefits.

Keeping it all in perspective

Here's a handy reminder to help you get your head around all the benefits stuff:

- Outcomes are in the Mandate:
  - Expanded into the Vision
  - Then into the Blueprint
- Benefits are quantifications of improvements described by outcomes
- A Benefits Map is crucial.

Stepping up to the plate: Ownership, responsibilities and accountabilities

You're trying to make sure that the ownership of benefits is spread out into business as usual. You don't want that ownership focused on one post at the heart of the programme. Here are some ideas on who is responsible for what, to help you get those benefits jobs shared out:

- The SRO owns the overall set of benefits.
- The SRO appoints an owner for each benefit (probably via the Business Change Managers).
- Other responsibilities are spread across the Programme Management Team.

Table 16-1 has more detail on benefits responsibilities.

Table 16-1 Responsibilities for Benefits Management

Benefits Management Process	***Accountabilities and Responsibilities***
Identifying and defining	Business Change Manager(s) Business Area Managers Agreed with SRO
Planning, monitoring and tracking	Programme Office Programme Manager's responsibility
Realization	Specific Business Area Managers working with Business Change Manager(s)
Assessment	Individuals with good knowledge of target business areas, but not directly involved in the programme

Paying attention to areas of focus for benefits

I cover the programme roles in general in Chapter 9, but here I run quickly through the areas of responsibilities as they relate to benefits.

Senior Responsible Owner

The SRO is the senior individual accountable for the success of the programme who's responsible for the following:

- Reporting to the Sponsoring Group on the delivery of the programme benefits as described in the Benefit Profiles.
- Ensuring that the programme and business areas affected maintain a focus on benefits delivery.
- Ensuring that the Benefits Management Strategy is created, adjusted, improved and enforced.
- Maintaining focus on business performance sustainability during transition. If the business performance drops off, that's a dis-benefit not being managed.
- Chairing benefit reviews involving relevant stakeholders, business managers and possibly internal auditors.
- Liaising with the Sponsoring Group on the validation of all benefits claimed by the programme.
- Authorising benefits achievements.

Programme Manager

The Programme Manager runs the programme, day-to-day, and is responsible for:

- Developing the Benefits Management Strategy on behalf of the SRO with the Business Change Managers and relevant stakeholders from the affected business areas.
- Developing the Benefits Realization Plan in conjunction with the Business Change Managers, relevant stakeholders and members of the project teams.
- Ensuring that the delivery of capability is aligned to maximise the realization of benefits.
- Initiating benefit reviews as part of the Benefits Realization Plan or in response to any other triggers.

Business Change Managers

Business Change Managers bed down the changes in their parts of the business and are responsible for:

- Identifying and quantifying the benefits with the support of relevant stakeholders, the Programme Manager and members of the project teams.
- Delivering particular benefits as profiled; this extends to ensuring that commitments and actions attributed to operational areas are delivered.
- Providing information to support the creation and delivery of the Benefits Realization Plan.
- Developing and maintaining Benefit Profiles and ensuring no double counting of benefits.
- Maintaining engagement with key individuals responsible for benefits delivery within operations.
- Setting business performance deviation levels and early warning indicators to support realizing the benefits.
- Initiating benefit reviews after the programme is closed.

Programme Office

The Programme Office looks after the administration of the programme and is responsible for:

- Monitoring the progress of benefits realization against plans.
- Gathering information for benefits reviews.
- Producing performance reports on how benefits management is going, as defined by the Programme Manager.
- Maintaining benefits information under change control and maintaining audit trails of changes.

Testing how well benefits are happening in your programme

After you've got a bit of this benefits stuff going on in your programme, look into these nice tricky questions to get a feel for how well benefits management is happening:

- Are benefit owners actively managing benefits or are they just sitting back and letting them happen?
- Are benefits being quantified and measured in monetary terms or being managed in non-monetary terms that help stakeholder engagement?
- Can you find a good solid baseline value for each benefit?
- Are benefits being routinely measured, reported and reviewed by the right people?

Chapter 17

Leading People Through Change as the Programme Delivers

In This Chapter

- Understanding the difference between leadership and management
- Designing tranches to support transition

When you start to exploit the capabilities delivered by projects, you need to do some mechanistic work, which in essence is based around controlling against a plan. For example, part of benefits management is creating a model and then managing against that plan. But a fundamental difference in tone exists in the real world of business as usual, which is less ordered and less planned than a mechanistic world and much more about people, as individuals and in teams, than about the task.

Hence my focus in this chapter is clear and effective leadership, which is essential for a successful programme. When the projects have delivered a capability, the transition really begins to take place. Leading people through change is so important that I dedicate this whole chapter to it. I look at the nature of leadership and the effect it has on how you fulfil any of the different roles. I also describe transition and give you a better appreciation of what's involved by thinking about the more people-focused aspects of programme management.

Taking a Deep Look at Leadership

Just how important leadership is in your programme depends on the programme's nature:

- If your programme is essentially a complex specification-driven set of projects, you may need little more leadership than is required in any project.
- If your programme is transformational and includes culture change (in other words, you're trying to persuade people to behave in fundamentally different ways), leadership clearly becomes more significant.

Distinguishing leadership from management

Before reading this section, have a go at noting down your ideas on the differences between leadership and management. Of course, no single set of right answers exists, but you can check your notes against my thoughts in Table 17-1. I hope you agree that leadership is distinctly different from management.

Table 17-1 Comparing Leadership and Management in Programme Management

Leadership	*Management*
Particularly required in a context of change. It clarifies the 'as is' and the vision of the future and thrives in the tension between the two.	Always required, particularly in business-as-usual contexts, and focuses more on evolutionary or continual improvement.
Inclined to clarify the 'what' and the 'why'.	Directed towards the 'how' and the 'when'.
More concerned with direction, effectiveness and purpose.	Concerned with speed, efficiency and quality.
Most effective when influencing people by communicating in face-to-face situations.	Most effective when controlling tasks against specifications or plans.
Focused on meaning, purpose and realized value.	Focused on tasks, delivery and process.

Examining the leaders' requirements

Programmes are different from business as usual (because you're using a completely different set of roles), and therefore these roles need to be clearly defined. The roles may not be familiar to the people working in the programme, so the responsibilities also need to be defined clearly.

Similarly you need to put in place a whole range of management structures and reporting arrangements to govern your programme. You need to create and communicate them, of course, but because they're new ways of working leadership is required as you introduce them.

These different characteristics of a programme place different requirements on the leaders:

- Information needs to flow in different ways to allow programme leaders to make their decisions. The flow of information needs to be more open and faster; plus the information needs to be better. It can mean more appropriate, relevant, timely, or less information, or different information, or presented in a different way. In your programme you can see if the information is presented in the right way just by looking at the faces of the people who read your reports.

  Better information isn't just more information: the danger of information overload is ever present.
- The top team in a programme changes over its life. That team needs to have a balanced set of skills for the work being done by the programme in a particular tranche, and therefore the requirement of the leaders in the programme is for them to lead that balanced team.
- More informed decision making also requires a more open culture than is common in many business-as-usual environments. The world is changing rapidly: you have to talk to different people and you have to lead in a constantly changing environment.

Looking at the three levels of governance

The rapidly changing governance landscape can be pretty confusing, and so stepping back and identifying the three levels of governance is helpful. I summarise these levels in Figure 17-1 and in the following list. I also include the relevant roles for each of these different levels of governance:

- **Direction:** Strategic guidance and championing:
  - Carried out by the Sponsoring Group and the Senior Responsible Owner (SRO).
- **Management:** Execution of capability delivery and exploitation:
  - Carried out by the Programme and Business Change Managers.
- **Co-ordination:** Of information, communication, monitoring and control:
  - Carried out by the Programme Office.

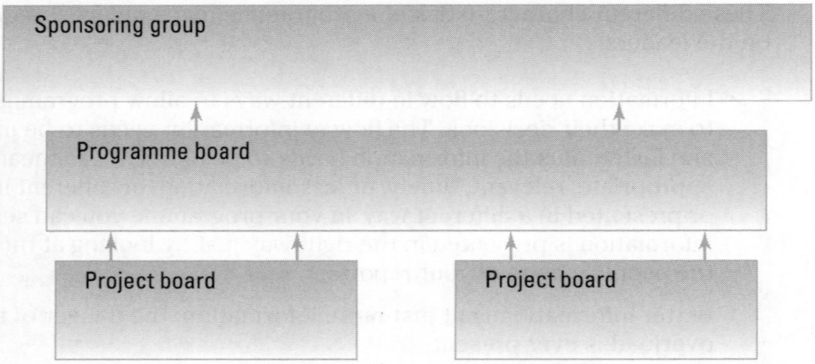

Figure 17-1: Layering of programme direction, management and co-ordination.

Be particularly careful with management and co-ordination. The Programme Office works for the Programme Manager. As the Programme Manager's role gets bigger, that person appoints specialists to carry out part of the duties. For example, a Programme Manager may appoint someone to handle risk: but is that person a Risk Manager or a Risk Co-ordinator? A co-ordination function sits in the Programme Office, but if it's a managerial function, the person in the role is managing. Managers are responsible for making it happen. But it's unlikely that a risk 'manager' manages either individual risks or executing the risk process. My advice is to have fewer managers and more co-ordinators.

I often see the Programme Office, which is designed to and works very effectively as a co-ordination function, accidentally taking on managerial responsibilities. If that's the way you design your organizational structure, that's absolutely fine; but my advice is to think carefully about these levels of governance as you design your organization structure.

Enjoying effective leadership

Helping an organization move through transformational change requires more than management: it needs leadership. But the word *leadership* is used so often that you can lose sight of what it means.

Before you read on, jot down your ideas on what effective leadership consists of in a programme environment. How can you recognise great leadership? In Chapter 13 I talked about judging the quality of the programme's leadership. That's what you're doing in this little exercise.

Here are a few of my thoughts. Those leading the programme need to:

- **Create a compelling Vision of the beneficial future as a result of carrying out the programme.** They must communicate this future in an inspirational way to a wide range of stakeholders.
- **Give individuals give the freedom and autonomy to fulfil their roles effectively.** Motivation, reward and appraisal systems can play a role in fostering the attitudes and energy to drive the programme.
- **Commit visibly with authority and enough seniority necessary to:**
  - Ensure that the correct resources are available to influence and engage with stakeholders.
  - Balance the priorities of the programme with those of on-going business operations.
  - Focus on the realization of business benefits.
- **Ensure the active management of:**
  - Cultural and people issues involved in the change.
  - Finance and the inevitable conflicting demands on resources.
  - Co-ordination of projects within the programme to see through transition to new operational services while also, crucially, maintaining business operations.
  - Risk management: that is, identification, evaluation and mitigation of risks.

Without doubt, plenty of scope exists for effective leadership in a programme!

Considering Sponsoring Group behaviour

Talking about leadership in an abstract way is all fine and dandy, but what about the crucial area where leadership needs to be displayed: the behaviour of the Sponsoring Group.

The Sponsoring Group doesn't have an onerous set of responsibilities to exercise in a programme, but its behaviour has to provide the necessary leadership for the programme.

To put it bluntly: the Sponsoring Group has to walk the talk.

HAVE A GO Try This

Jot down some of the behaviours that you feel your Sponsoring Group may be providing already or can provide in the future to help lead your programme.

REMEMBER

Here's a brief list for you to think about. The Sponsoring Group:

- Provides executive-level commitment
- Contains the senior managers responsible for investment
- Leads in establishing values and behaviours
- Works more as a group as normal reporting lines may not apply (usually each member of the Sponsoring Group runs their own bit of the business. In a programme they let their people (Business Change Managers) report to a different member of the Sponsoring Group (the SRO); this is what triggers the need for more group working)
- Forms the overarching authority
- Displays a different leadership style:
  - More team working
  - Greater empowerment
  - Encouraging initiative
  - Recognising appropriate risk taking

TIP

You can expand each of these points into a major discussion on the behaviours that reinforce these aspects of leadership. I leave you to have those conversations in your programme.

Establishing the Sponsoring Group's duties

In some business cultures the Sponsoring Group is too senior to have formal terms of reference. Nevertheless, it still needs to exercise some key responsibilities, which may have to be done quite formally. The Sponsoring Group can display leadership while doing these tasks, which include:

- Providing a context for the programme (not just initially, but on an on-going basis).
- Authorising the programme Mandate.
- Authorising programme definition.
- Participating in end-of-tranche reviews and approving progression to the next tranche for the programme.
- Authorising funding for the programme.
- Resolving strategic and directional issues between programmes that need the input of an agreement from very senior stakeholders to ensure the progress of the change.

- Authorising the organization's strategic direction against which the programme is to deliver.
- Authorising the progress of the programme against the strategic objectives and then moving from the mechanistic (where you write things down and expect people to carry out the plan) into the behavioural area (where you look at and modify what people actually do), leading by example to implement the values implied by the transformational change.
- Providing continued commitment and endorsement in support of the programme: for example, reiterating the programme objectives at executive or communications events.
- Appointing, advising and supporting the SRO.
- Authorising the Vision statement.
- Authorising delivery and sign off at the close of the programme.

Although this list seems rather long, it's mostly about authorisation, so the decisions needn't take up a lot of the Sponsoring Group's time.

TIP

You may like to compare this list of the Sponsoring Group's duties with my description of the Sponsoring Group in Chapter 9. The list in Chapter 9 is quite mechanistic, this list is more behavioural.

Tackling Transition in a Tranche

MSP SPEAK

A *tranche* is a step change in organizational capability with an associated distinct set of benefits. Projects may run across tranche boundaries, or to put it another way, several tranches may be running in parallel. But if the tranche boundary is a reasonably significant milestone in your programme, it's an ideal opportunity to assess achievements to date and consider any necessary realignment of the programme.

The main purpose of this section is to look at some of the softer considerations during transition within a tranche. But it's also a useful opportunity to think about some of the technical aspects to consider when designing and planning a tranche. The biggest need for leadership is in tranches, as business as usual changes its way of behaving.

For loads more on planning and managing tranches, check out Chapters 10 and 18, respectively.

Handling design planning

The business has to remain viable as you roll out successive tranches into business as usual. Consequently, as part of effective leadership you need to consider the design of the business during each tranche.

REMEMBER

Although, naturally, everyone gets very excited about the new aspects of the business's 'to be' state, often the difficulty comes in maintaining existing 'as is' states.

As you introduce new elements of 'to be', you may want to decommission redundant parts of 'as is'. But often two different parts of the business rely on the same back-office function. As one part of the business migrates to a new state, you can be tempted to switch off that old back-office function. But you may have to maintain it in some form until all the other elements of the business that rely on it have migrated.

This advice sounds like common sense, but it's easily overlooked in the excitement of building the brave new world.

You may need to consider aspects such as:

- **Technical architecture:**
  - Different technical environments
  - Office and homeworking environments
- **Support infrastructure:**
  - Accounting procedures
  - Human resource needs

TIP

You may also have to create more complex technical transition plans than you first imagine and to put in place more rigorous technical quality assurance to ensure that these interim states are viable. A knowledgeable and empowered design authority is a real help in getting down into this level of detail.

Managing transition

After establishing a design authority to look after the detailed technical design you're creating in a tranche, you need to engage with the Business Change Managers and think about the transition management they'll be doing. Figure 17-2 is a diagram I like to draw when explaining the complexity of transition management.

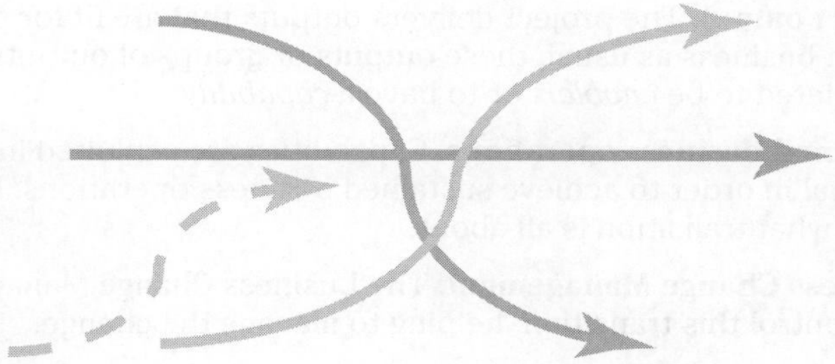

Figure 17-2: Overview of transition management.

Figure 17-2 summarises the role of the Business Change Managers while they're introducing the new state. Here's what they need to do:

- **Build up the new – the rising arrow.** Think of it simplistically as a new production line going from producing zero widgets per day to 1,000 widgets per day.
- **Run down the old – the falling arrow.** At the same time, the old production line has to run down from producing, say, 500 widgets to producing none.
- **Maintain business as usual – the level arrow.** You have to handle the balancing act, because you have to maintain business as usual. You still have to keep widgets going out to customers.
- **Prepare properly for the new before you receive any outputs – the dotted arrow.** You need to consider lots of things to do this effectively: staff training and recruitment, accommodation, procedures and the detailed plans for ramping up and ramping down.

Following the transition sequence

Here I look in detail at transition, the sequence involved and the relationships between outputs, transition management and benefits realization. This is the detail of the change occurring.

If Figure 17-2 in the preceding section looks a little simple, you may find Figure 17-3 a little too complex, which is why I take you through it in this section (I provide a fuller, step-by-step approach in Chapter 20):

1. **Baseline benefits measurement.** Pre-transition is about the Business Change Managers preparing for the receipt of outputs by producing plans. You also have to create a baseline benefits measurement. Before business as usual is disturbed, you need to measure the baseline values of benefits. Each benefit owner does this by using the measurement mechanism described in the Benefit Profile.

2. **Project output.** The project delivers outputs that are fit for purpose. Within business as usual, these outputs or groups of outputs are considered to be *enablers* or to have a *capability*.
3. **Sustained business operations.** Capabilities are exploited in business as usual in order to achieve sustained business operations. If you like, that's what transition is all about.
4. **Business Change Management.** The Business Change Managers monitor and control this transition, helping to manage the change.
5. **Outcomes.** Over time the effect of change becomes noticeable, and you see the outcomes.
6. **Benefits realization.** All the while benefits are accumulating that you measure. The cost of production decreases, for example, and you use those measures or benefits to monitor transition.
7. **Post-transition activities.** You embed the change into business as usual, remove old facilities, equipment and ways of working, and get everyone settled into the new way of working – the 'to be' state.

Use this description of transition as a prompt list and see whether you've planned for enough transition work in a tranche. Ideally, work with a forthcoming tranche in your programme. If you aren't working in a programme at the moment, use a change in business as usual that could have been a tranche in a programme. Choose one that you're familiar with.

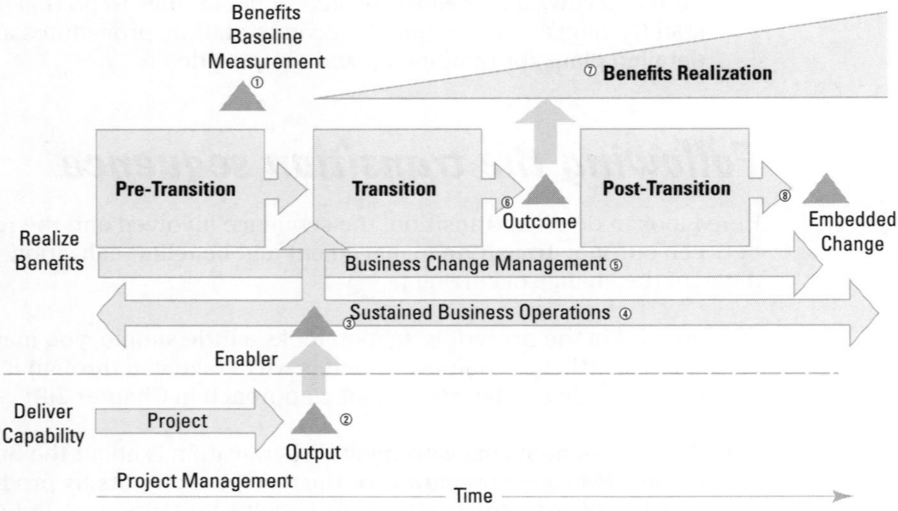

Figure 17-3: Outputs, transition management and benefits realization.

Part V

Step by Step in Your Programme

Go to `www.dummies.com/extras/msp` for free online bonus content about managing successful programmes.

In this part. . .

- Take a high-level view of each of your tranches.
- Oversee projects so that they deliver the right capabilities.
- Exploit capabilities out in business as usual so that the benefits flow.
- Close your programme.

Chapter 18

Managing a Tranche

In This Chapter

- Understanding the purpose of tranches
- Linking managing a tranche and the other processes that are going on within a tranche
- Setting up a tranche
- Taking care of a tranche
- Crossing tranche boundaries

As I describe in Chapter 10, *tranches* are sections of the programme that deliver new capability to business as usual. You need to set up and manage each tranche at a high level. Now, I'm a bit of a Star Trek fan, so I make no apologies for describing this arrangement as you being Captain James T. Kirk on the bridge of the starship *USS Enterprise:*

- The captain is Managing the Tranche from an imposing leather chair.
- The bridge officers are Delivering the Capability.
- The away team is Realizing Benefits on the planet – in other words, in business as usual (with those in red shirts looking around nervously as they suspect their time may soon be up).
- The crew members are working together on the same mission and to be successful, they have to maintain communications with each other.

In this chapter I look at what the captain (sorry, the Programme Manager) does while Managing a Tranche and break it into three simple sections: setting up a tranche; running a tranche; and handling a tranche boundary. I examine the activities that this person is responsible for in each section.

REMEMBER

Thinking that the end of each tranche is a great opportunity to review the status of the programme is great, but you can also face *unplanned* tranche boundaries that make life a little more exciting. You have to be able to review really quickly sometimes.

Discovering Why You Manage the Tranches

When the wider authoring team of MSP changed it from a process model to a transformational flow one (check out Figure 1-3 in Chapter 1), we were very keen to get across that things don't happen in separate places (silos) or even in strict sequence in a programme. Instead, I like to think of a programme as being more like a stream bubbling across rocks: the different flows of water mix and separate and little eddies form where the water goes round and round in circles.

If that model lacks a little discipline for you, we also include distinct processes in the transformational flow. At the beginning and end of the programme the processes are sequential, but in the middle is an iteration (I explain iteration in Chapter 7. It just means you're going around in circles) of three processes during each tranche, as follows:

- **Managing the Tranches:** Which I describe in this section.
- **Delivering the Capability:** Which I cover in Chapter 19.
- **Realizing the Benefits:** Which I look at in Chapter 20.

Figure 18-1 illustrates the model for the Managing a Tranche process. (I know that a programme consists of a number of tranches, but I feel that you manage them one tranche at a time. So from now on I talk about managing *a* tranche.) You're working with the agreed documentation for the programme and the controls are related to governing rather than managing. The outputs are capabilities, outcomes and benefits, as well as updated documents. I look at the activities and who's involved in more detail in this chapter.

REMEMBER

You're Managing a Tranche for the following three purposes:

- **To implement programme governance.** Reflecting on what you've learnt about governance is about more than just management. It concerns systems of direction and control and is about putting in place appropriate checks and balances.
- **To ensure that the capability being delivered is aligned to strategic objectives.** You can think of this purpose at a strategic level or at a more detailed one. What you're doing is aligning capability delivery with everything that's going on in business as usual.
- **To realize benefits.** In other words, to enable their release.

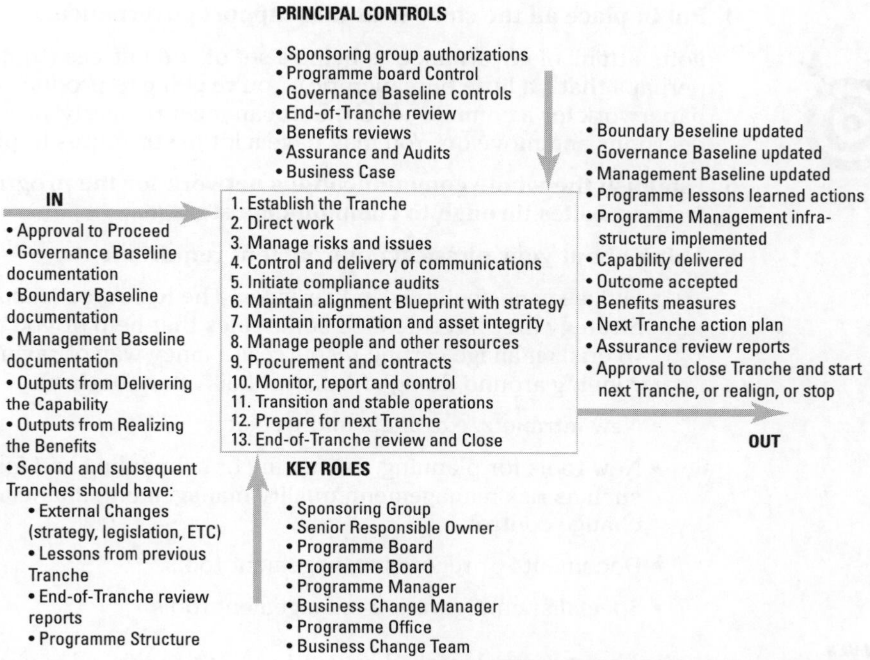

PRINCIPAL CONTROLS
• Sponsoring group authorizations
• Programme board Control
• Governance Baseline controls
• End-of-Tranche review
• Benefits reviews
• Assurance and Audits
• Business Case
IN
• Approval to Proceed
• Governance Baseline documentation
• Boundary Baseline documentation
• Management Baseline documentation
• Outputs from Delivering the Capability
• Outputs from Realizing the Benefits
• Second and subsequent Tranches should have:
• External Changes (strategy, legislation, ETC)
• Lessons from previous Tranche
• End-of-Tranche review reports
• Programme Structure
1. Establish the Tranche
2. Direct work
3. Manage risks and issues
4. Control and delivery of communications
5. Initiate compliance audits
6. Maintain alignment Blueprint with strategy
7. Maintain information and asset integrity
8. Manage people and other resources
9. Procurement and contracts
10. Monitor, report and control
11. Transition and stable operations
12. Prepare for next Tranche
13. End-of-Tranche review and Close
• Boundary Beseline updated
• Governance Baseline updated
• Management Baseline updated
• Programme lessons learned actions
• Programme Management infra-structure implemented
• Capability delivered
• Outcome accepted
• Benefits measures
• Next Tranche action plan
• Assurance review reports
• Approval to close Tranche and start next Tranche, or realign, or stop
OUT
KEY ROLES
• Sponsoring Group
• Senior Responsible Owner
• Programme Board
• Programme Board
• Programme Manager
• Business Change Manager
• Programme Office
• Business Change Team

Figure 18-1: Modelling the Managing a Tranche process.

Establishing a Tranche

Setting up the tranche is the first activity in the Managing a Tranche process. This activity is very scalable (you can apply it to a big or a little programme). If you have a modestly sized programme or one that's been running for some time and is settled, establishing the tranche may be straightforward; indeed you may have almost nothing to do.

But if you have a very large programme (and in particular if you're at the beginning of it), establishing the tranche can be highly significant. You need to carry out the following tasks, roughly in this order:

1. **Set up the organization that runs the tranche.**
2. **Appoint the Business Change Team in business as usual.**
3. **Create the Programme Office and get them up and running effectively.**

4. **Put in place all the structures that support governance.**

   I often think of governance as being a set of committees (though perhaps that's a little bureaucratic). You're going to produce the paperwork for a committee so that it can meet regularly, process the decisions and move on. You may have a lot of structures to put in place.

5. **Establish the whole communications network for the programme, from websites through to common data storage.**

6. **Think about your physical environment requirements:**

   - Office space, facilities and services. The Resource Management Strategy may have defined some rules that help or you may have to crisis manage getting resources (a fancy way of saying you're running around doing one urgent task after another).
   - New intranets, extranets and websites.
   - New tools for planning, estimating or scheduling and for functions such as risk management, quality management, financial control or change control.
   - Documents or records management tools.
   - Specialist configuration management tools.

In one giant programme I worked on, setting up this physical environment was so large that it was itself treated as a programme. In your programme you need to plan how much effort goes into establishing the tranche.

Running a Tranche

This portion of Managing a Tranche covers several activities such as managing the programme. You need to repeat each of these activities frequently, so a lot of your effort inevitably goes into them.

Managing the programme

Be in no doubt; you have plenty to do when Managing a Tranche:

- **Direct work.** You're going to put in place the governance.
  - The detail is done in Delivering the Capability process, but you need to keep an eye on it here.
- **Managing risks and issues.** You need systems at the programme level.

- **Delivering Communications.** You're going to have a communications function at the programme level.
  - How are you going to control and deliver communications?
- **Initiating audits and assurance reviews.** You need to trigger lots of checks.

  You can think of these as being Captain Kirk asking various people to check *downwards* on what the rest of the crew (not to mention the bug-eyed aliens) are doing. The Programme Office commissions audits and reviews of projects and of transition in business as usual.

  But you also need to think of audits as operating *sideways* and *upwards*. Captain Kirk (no Captain Picard; Captain Kirk isn't smart enough to think of this sort of thing) may ask another starship captain to look over his plans or suggest to the Admiral the need to ask the Klingons to take an independent view of what's going on. Okay! Enough of the starship analogy. You have to commission audits and reviews of your performance on behalf of external stakeholders, the Sponsoring Group or other external agencies.
- **Maintaining the Blueprint and a governance structure.** You need to ensure that the Blueprint remains aligned with strategic objectives, so you have to set up communication channels. If the strategic objectives change, you may have to alter the Blueprint and that can have quite significant effects on the projects that you're in the middle of delivering.
- **Ensuring information and asset integrity.** This can be a very significant piece of work on a large programme.

You also have to manage people and resources and think about procurement and contracts functions as well.

Maintaining the flow of information

You need to get your information management system up and running.

REMEMBER

Reporting must match the needs of the programme and show progress against the Programme Plan (which I discuss in Chapter 10). Information has to be flowing on subjects such as the following:

- The schedule, with particular emphasis on inter-project dependencies
- Financial reporting
- Resource use
- A benefits summary

Projects and business-as-usual activities have to provide the information and the Programme Office has to filter that information up to the Programme Manager and then out to the broader stakeholders.

Monitoring, reporting and controlling

The activity of monitoring, reporting and controlling can be a major job. You can sometimes feel as though most of your life in a programme is dominated by these tasks.

Don't let this activity take over your life. Just because you can report certain information doesn't mean that you should do so. Important stakeholders may not know what information they need and with the best possible intentions can enquire about all sorts of irrelevant detail. In particular, everyone thinks that delving down into what's happening in projects is a good thing.

TIP Try and streamline reporting so that you can focus on answering questions such as:

- Are the Blueprint and the capabilities being delivered still coherent and consistent?
- Have the Senior Responsible Owner and the Programme Board the right amount of information for them to consider:
  - Major exceptions from projects
  - Outcome achievements
  - Benefits achievements
  - Benefits realization exceptions
  - Capability delivery escalations
  - Reviews

Transitioning and maintaining stable operations

This process is what the Star Trek away team are doing down on the planet. In other words, what the Business Change Managers are doing in business as usual, when running the Delivering the Capability process.

But you need a link back to the *Enterprise*'s bridge, and that's why this activity is included in Managing a Tranche. Indeed, this activity is so important that probably the SRO authorises the beginning of transition. (I guess if the Programme Manager is the captain, the SRO must be an admiral visiting the ship.)

Transition, which ends up being a stable operation within business as usual, is absolutely vital to the programme. (A colleague of mine argues that this single topic is worthy of a whole course.) You may know examples of when transition stabilisation has gone well or gone badly.

Although from the bridge people keep an eye on these types of tasks, the Business Change Managers are responsible for this work:

- To implement those transition plans on which you've worked so carefully.
- To measure performance through transition using the new benefits measures that you've already tested and baselined.
- To continue measuring in a consistent way as operations stabilise.

You need reporting lines throughout the programme, but it's also very important for the benefits to be reported through the business as usual management structure.

You must also manage a whole series of downsides of these benefits:

- Disruption to operations because existing staff are moved to new ways of working, and because of a learning dip as people adjust to those new methods. (If somebody gives you a new tool to help you do your work, your performance drops as you learn how to use it. Eventually your performance improves.)
- Things don't settle as quickly as imagined, so the improvements don't flow as quickly as anticipated and benefits ramp-up is delayed.
- The natural tendency for people to revert to old ways of working. You need to put in place specific activities that help reinforce in the minds of staff that the new ways of working are the way things are now done round here.

The Business Change Managers also sustain existing business operations during the programme, looking at the following:

- Technical integrity of systems
- Transferring or replacing superseded ways of working
- Maintenance of continuous service
- Maintenance of morale

Take a look at Chapter 10 for more on transition and at Chapter 20 for details of realizing benefits through transition.

Dealing with a Tranche Boundary

When you grab a moment to drag yourself away from the endless cycle of monitoring and reporting and glance into the future, what do you see? The next tranche bearing down on you!

Many programmes simply don't have the capacity to organize the next tranche effectively: they're just too focused on the day-to-day effort of running the current tranche. I see this as another symptom of information overload.

Therefore, make sure to ask yourself whether you and your team have enough spare capacity to close down the current tranche properly and get ready for the next one.

When you get your head round the idea of a *planned* tranche boundary, which typically happens about once every six months in your programme, I predict that just over the horizon (say six to twelve months in the future) a dramatic and completely unexpected event will occur that fundamentally changes the nature of your programme.

Of course I don't know what that event is going to be for your particular programme, but it's in the nature of transformational change programmes: unexpected changes in direction happen surprisingly frequently. In other contexts these events are called *black swans* (explained in Chapter 6. The later sidebar 'Calling all bird-spotters: The black swan' relates an example).

The lesson for you in programme management is that as well as being ready for a planned tranche boundary, you need to expect the unexpected: you have to be prepared for an unexpected tranche boundary. Bear in mind these two ideas – the planned and the unplanned tranche boundary – as you read the next few sections.

Preparing for the next tranche

At the end of the current tranche you need to prepare for the next one. I describe the end-of-tranche review and closure activity in the next two sections, but for the moment I cover preparing for the next tranche. I want to raise two significant points that you need to consider:

- If you have a Programme Plan that's based on tranches, you need to have some resources available towards the end of each tranche to prepare for the next tranche.
- But if all your resources are devoted to managing the current tranche, where are you going to get the resources to prepare for the next tranche? And do you have a contingency plan for closing the current tranche if an unplanned tranche boundary arises?

TIP

Here are some things to do as you prepare for the next tranche:

- Learn from experience. Gather up the lessons you've acquired during this and previous tranches. Pull out what you can, study it and apply it as you go through your planning.
- Adapt your governance and organization structures, perhaps because of external factors or simply because the balance within the programme changes as it moves on.
- Consider altering your skills mix. You have to move people out of the programme and others into it. That may lead to changes to the physical environment for the next tranche.
- Review and refine the scope of the programme and of all the programme information.
- Manage and review your information baselines.
- Get approval to proceed.

As an example, if the programme moves the organization a substantial distance (say, several hundred miles), the Programme Office may need to move to the new location in the next tranche.

Moving towards tranche closure

For this stage, you need to commission an end of tranche review and arrange for the closure of the current tranche (I discuss tranche reviews in Chapter 14):

1. **Update information.**
2. **Review the viability of the programme.**
3. **Assess benefits.**
4. **Evaluate benefits if the tranche was a pilot.**

Reviewing benefits

Part of your end-of-tranche reviews is benefits reviews. You want to make sure that the reviewers are focusing on these sorts of questions:

- Were planned benefits realized or not? That is, were targets correct or too low?
  - If benefits weren't realized, why not? Can remedial action be taken?
- Does a pattern apply to the success/failure?
- Were the assumptions correct? If not, what was the effect?

- Have dis-benefits been managed and minimised?
- Did you experience any unexpected (dis-)benefits?
  - If so, can they now be maximised or minimised?
- Do any further potential benefits exist?
- Were measures correct?
  - If not, can they be refined? Was data collection effective?

Here are some typical objectives for an end-of-tranche review:

- To assess the achievements of the tranche
- To discover how far the programme is on the way to the Blueprint
- To see whether any corrective projects are needed.
- To find out whether any unexpected benefits are possible.

REMEMBER

The end-of-tranche review can ultimately result in a go or no-go decision for the programme.

TRUE STORY

Calling all bird-spotters: The black swan

I was working with a partner in a newly democratic central European country. As part of our business development I was running a small training course. A national election was being held, and as is typical in recent democracies, a number of newly formed political parties were involved and quite a bit of doubt existed about which party would win.

One evening we heard the results of the election; a new government had been elected. The next morning we got a phone call from one of the delegates on the course. She was working in a programme in central government and had been called into work in the middle of the night. The Programme Manager knew that the new government would change the direction of the programme and she had to work on preparing for the next tranche. It was a black swan!

Allocating Responsibilities Across Tranche Management

Although usually the SRO is *accountable* for all the activities in the Managing a Tranche process, the Programme Manager is *responsible* for them. The exception is the transition and stable operations activity (check out the earlier section 'Transitioning and maintaining stable operations'), for which the Business Change Managers are responsible. For activities such as communications, audits and Blueprint alignment, the Programme Manager and Business Change Managers share responsibility ('Managing the programme' earlier in this chapter has all the details on these aspects).

Thinking more closely about tranches

If you're in the middle of a tranche, I suggest that you use this chapter as a checklist. Ask yourself whether you're undertaking each of the activities properly.

If you're about to go into a new tranche, use that checklist to help you plan how you're going to manage the tranche and what resources you need.

Chapter 19

Managing Projects within a Programme: Delivering Capability

In This Chapter

- Examining the role of your programme people in projects
- Helping to start projects
- Monitoring existing projects
- Closing projects smoothly

Programme management makes project management more efficient by helping to kick-off individual or groups of projects, providing a helpful environment around projects while they're running and assisting closure.

In this chapter I continue my Star Trek analogy from Chapter 18 (hurrah!), but switch focus from the captain's chair to all those keen young people who're controlling the *Starship Enterprise.* To be more prosaic, you're leaving your cubicle (co-located with the Programme Office), where you've been chatting with the SRO and some Business Change Managers, and having a look at what your staff members in the Programme Office are doing. Some of them are helping projects to deliver capability.

I look at how you in the programme can help projects to deliver: how you can turn your programme into a project factory where project outputs slip easily off the production line. I cover what the programme can do when starting projects, running projects and closing projects

For those of you from project management, this is reasonably familiar territory. If you're the sort of project manager who likes to operate on your own, however, you may feel uncomfortable with the way the programme tries to help, even control, what you're doing.

Understanding the Purpose of Delivering the Capability

MSP SPEAK

The purpose of the *Delivering the Capability* process is to co-ordinate and manage project delivery according to the Programme Plan (which I describe in Chapter 10).

Figure 19-1 illustrates the process to help you visualise it. You're working with the agreed documentation for the programme and the principal controls are those you use to monitor and govern projects. The outputs from this process are the routine and non-routine reports coming out of the projects and of course the project outputs themselves. I look at the activities and who's involved in more detail throughout the rest of this chapter.

Delivery from projects provides outputs that enable the new capabilities to be put in place as described in the Blueprint. Also, bear in mind that Delivering the Capability is repeated for each tranche (flip to Chapters 10 and 18 for more on tranches).

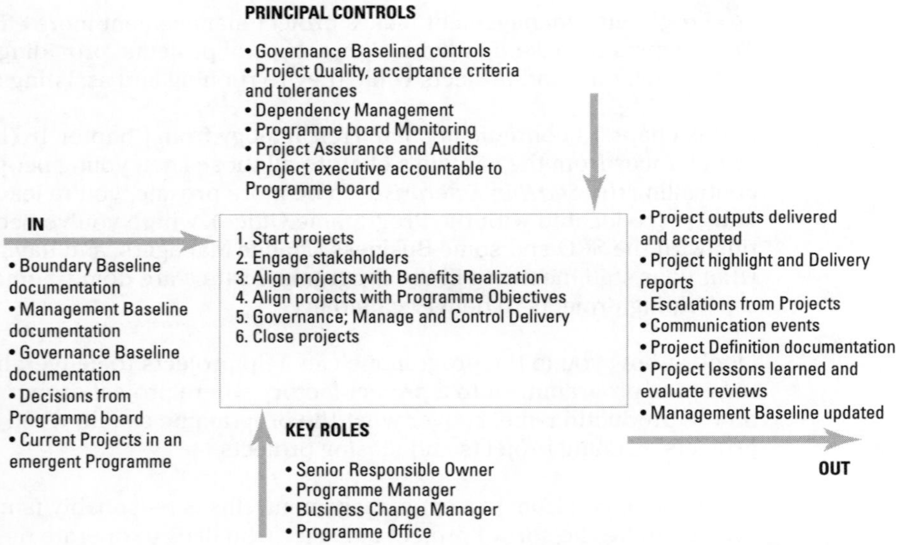

Figure 19-1: Delivering the Capability process.

Check carefully that your programme people are helping others to deliver their projects and not, accidentally, taking over, duplicating or even undermining the management of the projects. In Chapter 3, I introduce the idea of your programme being *right* not necessarily *tight* as regards control. Tightness of control may be most apparent around the relationship between the programme and its projects:

- In an extremely tightly controlled programme, the Programme Manager may well be a sort of super project manager.
- In a very loosely controlled programme, the Programme Office simply gets progress reports from projects that are otherwise being independently directed.

Neither loose nor tight control is wrong; it depends on the nature of your programme and the culture of the organizations involved. I describe a middle ground where the programme has considerable influence over projects, but they're still being run with a fair degree of delegated authority.

Starting a Group of Projects

The activities for the programme to undertake in connection with starting one or more projects are quite straightforward:

1. **Start projects.**
2. **Engage stakeholders.**
3. **Align projects with benefits realization.**
4. **Align projects with programme objectives.**
5. **Manage and control delivery using the defined governance structures.**
6. **Manage risks and resolve issues.**
7. **Close the projects.**

Clarifying the connection between projects and benefits

A good starting point is to recap the relationship between projects and benefits, as shown in Figure 19-2. This list can even be basis of the briefing you give to new project managers:

1. **Identify projects started by the programme.**
2. **Confirm how these projects fit into the big picture by referring, for example, to strategies.**
3. **Make sure that the projects are aware of and understand the interdependencies with other projects.**
4. **Explain how the project outputs are going to be used, if necessary, perhaps combined with the outputs from other projects, to enable transition, to provide capabilities that lead to outcomes and ultimately to realize benefits.**
5. **Use the information from the Defining a Programme stage, as detailed in Chapter 7, to provide projects with guidance on quality, reporting, exceptions and escalations.**

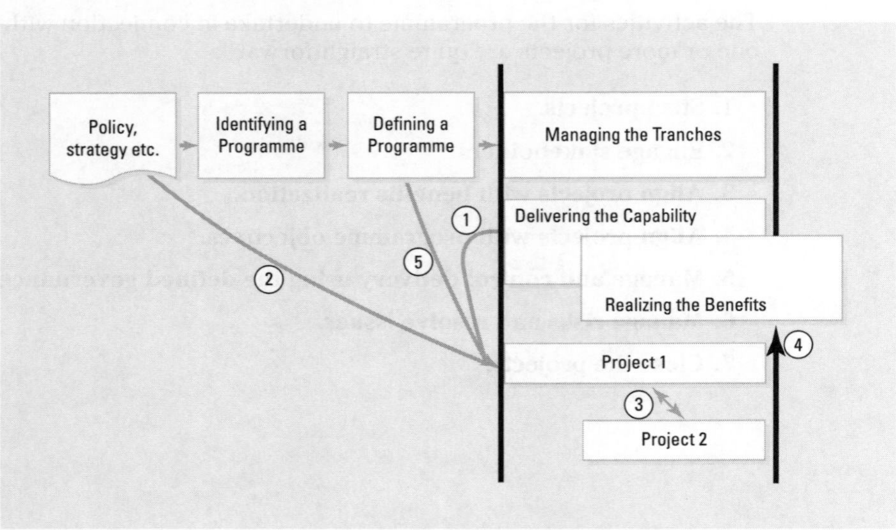

Figure 19-2: Briefing projects.

The emphasis here is on doing the things that the projects can't do themselves. They need to focus on project management – delivering capability – while you focus on the aspects of programme management that co-ordinate, focus and direct projects.

Delineating a project in a tranche

Having worked closely with the MSP reference group and authoring teams for many years, I'm a great fan of MSP: it's a pretty robust set of advice. But I do think that it's a little vague about where the detailed planning for a tranche is carried out. The high-level elements are certainly part of preparing for the next tranche, which I mention in Chapter 18, but behind the explicit activities in this process the people in the Programme Office, who are particularly focusing on projects, have some work to do as well.

The Programme Office need to carry out some detailed work to bed down a new tranche. Here's the list that I personally use:

- Scope and define projects in dossier
- Existing projects:
    - Review their status and progress
    - Re-align as necessary
    - Minimize overlapping project territories
    - Simplify inter-project dependencies
    - Consider organizational power structures
    - Develop dependency network

Another piece of preparation I suggest is to have a thorough look at the scheduling of the projects. Again, here's my personal checklist:

- Scheduling (planning) projects:
    - Look for early wins – but optimize overall benefits
    - Schedule benefit review(s)
    - Schedule the end-of-tranche review
- Refine the Programme Plan:
    - With deliverables dependencies
    - With resource dependencies
    - With tolerances
    - By updating the transition plan

Clarifying start-up responsibilities

During project start-up you want to be quite clear about who does what:

- The Programme Manager is responsible for:
  - Ensuring that Project Board appointments are appropriate.
  - Appointing the Project Executive, and maybe the Project Board, in a tighter-controlled programme.
  - Providing the project brief (including the outline business case for the project).
  - Discussing the project brief with the project management team.
  - Agreeing the project plan and tolerance in the project initiation documentation.
  - Agreeing product delivery times for products with inter-project dependencies.
- The Programme Office helps with planning.

Depending on how tightly or loosely your programme is controlled, you may want to check a brief drafted by a project manager or draft the brief and give it to the project manager. I like to make sure that the following items, from big picture stuff down into a bit of detail, go into each project brief:

- Project definition
- Business case
- Target delivery date
- Quality expectations and acceptance criteria
- Programme risks
- Project dependencies

Keeping an Eye on Existing Projects

While the projects are in flight, the programme needs to monitor progress and intervene when things go off-track: for example, if issues and risks need to be escalated.

The simplest way to make this work with the right balance between delegation and control is to ensure that everyone understands and is using tolerance and *management by exception*. These ideas are well described in PRINCE2 (get hold of *PRINCE2 For Dummies* by Nick Graham, Wiley), and they really make your life straightforward in a programme.

Management by exception means that instead of saying that a project manager must deliver the project on time, they must deliver the project within plus or minus one week of the target (the tolerance). When reporting, for example, you just want to know if the project manager is on schedule to within plus or minus a week. So management by exception simplifies reporting, while maintaining clear control.

Monitoring progress

When you're monitoring progress across a series of projects you can all too easily find yourself drowning in data. Therefore I suggest that you present only certain key information from projects to the programme and in a summary form.

Here's what I consider the minimum information:

- Outputs.
- Timely completion or progress against schedule.
- Risks, issues and assumptions that may need to be escalated.
- Changes to estimates, again within the granularity (level of detail) that needs to be escalated to the programme level. (I don't want to know all the trivia about the project; I just want to know the things that matter to me at programme level. This links very closely with the tolerance I've delegated to the project manager.)
- Costs and benefits that are relevant to the programme.
- Resources, particularly those being managed at programme level.
- Fundamental changes to the scope of the project.

Overseeing progress

Overseeing means just a little bit more than monitoring; it also includes taking actions, perhaps outside the project environment, and linking what's happening in the project to the bigger picture of what's happening in the programme. Here are some things you need to do when you oversee progress:

- **Review progress in order to make essential interventions.** This isn't second-guessing your project managers. You have project managers in order for them to manage projects. The interventions you're going to make from the programme level are those that only make sense when considered from a programme perspective.

  REMEMBER: The project reports from the project perspective; you intervene from the programme perspective.

- **Deal with escalations and exceptions.** One of the things you need to think about here is the level of management by exception you use when dealing with projects. To some extent I'm assuming that you've put in some form of management by exception, because you need to deal with escalations from projects and exceptions within projects. Again, you can't do so unless you previously defined tolerance or something similar.

  TIP: In essence you have to agree the delegated authority of the project. Beyond that tolerance, the project has to escalate to the programme.

- **Manage dependencies.** I look at three classes of dependencies in Chapter 10. You need to manage the dependencies that can't be managed within projects.
- **Check and maintain alignment with the Blueprint.** The Blueprint is an evolving document, because you put more effort into it as time goes by and because of changes in external circumstances. You need to keep an eye on projects and their alignment with the Blueprint.
- **Maintain some oversight of quality.** I look at quality in Chapters 13 and 14. Remember that the quality environment within a project may be unique to that project and focused on project outputs. You need a quality management environment that fits the whole programme and takes a wider view of the quality of what's coming out of the projects.

Deciding when to escalate risks and issues

The systems you have in place need to ensure that risks are escalated to the programme in the right circumstances, such as when:

- Other projects or programmes are impacted.
- The project doesn't have authority to resolve the risk or issue (that is, the action may exceed the project tolerance).
- The project lacks the skills or experience.

Managing conflict

You may have to become an expert on conflict management because of conflict between the narrow project needs and the wider programme needs.

The SRO has the ultimate responsibility to resolve the conflicts, but you don't want these things escalating to the SRO very often. Sometimes all that you need is to communicate effectively the effect on the programme of project issues. But sometimes the differences in viewpoint between project and programme level are more deep-seated. You may find that your soft skills, such as communication, are very useful when trying to soothe your project people. In particular, you need to think about your internal communication in Delivering the Capability. Take a look at Figure 19-3 for an illustration.

Figure 19-3: Communication is the key.

You may find that focusing on topics only apparent from a programme perspective is useful, including:

- **Interdependencies between projects.** For example, one project may think it can delay delivering an output, but that output's timely delivery is essential to another project.
- **Design compliance.** The people in a project think it is a good idea to use a different logo, but the design authority wants everybody to use the same logo.
- **Resource management across shared resources.** You've only got one specialist in using the phaser (oops, I'm back to *Star Trek* again), but two projects want to use him or her at the same time.
- **Co-ordination between project implementation and business-as-usual transition.** The project intends to deliver the new accounting system just before the end of the accounting year – bad move!

I'm a pilot, and if things are going wrong when you're flying you don't want to be playing around with all the knobs and dials – you need your head up, looking out of the window. The same thing applies in a programme when you're monitoring and overseeing delivery of the capability (your people). You need to stay out of the detail and focus on what's important:

- Manage inter-project products:
  - Quality check product descriptions and designs
  - Accept completed products
  - Control changes to products
- Analyse project issues for their programme impact
- Carry out programme quality assurance
- Communicate between projects

Closing Projects

As each project approaches its end, you want to make the closure as smooth as possible by ensuring that the following tasks take place:

- Supporting the closure process.
- Confirming the transfer of outputs to the Business Change Managers and business as usual so that they can trigger transition and ultimately benefits.

- Assigning incomplete actions from the projects to someone outside the projects and making sure that the actions are accepted.
- Making sure that lessons are recorded and passed on.
- Scheduling post-project reviews.

Allocating Responsibilities across Capability Delivery

The Programme Manager is responsible for all the activities I describe in this chapter, although the Business Change Managers help to ensure that projects are linked with benefits realization.

The Programme Office supports you, and, of course, the SRO has the overall accountability.

HAVE A GO
Try This

Working on delivering capability

Think of some ways in which your programme can carry out the following:

- Make life easier for projects.
- Control them more.
- Control them less.

Think about these topics at a project's start, middle or end.

You can also look at these things from the programme point of view or the project point of view.

Chapter 20

All Change: Realizing the Benefits through Transition

In This Chapter

- Considering the purpose of Realizing the Benefits
- Understanding the process for managing transition
- Sharing responsibilities for Realizing the Benefits

In many ways this chapter is the big one, because it concerns the ultimate aim of all programmes: achieving outcomes and realizing benefits! More specifically, I show you how you can put that final work in business as usual into an orderly process. For ease of use, I split the process into pre-transition, transition and post-transition.

I address much of the information in this book at the Programme Manager (who, as I describe in Chapter 9, undertakes the day-to-day programme management), but this chapter mostly concerns the duties and responsibilities of the Business Change Managers.

Appreciating the Purpose of Realizing the Benefits

MSP SPEAK

Realizing the Benefits is a little broader than you may at first imagine. Its purpose is to manage benefits from initial identification through to successful realization. Realizing the Benefits therefore starts as soon as you finish Defining the Programme, which I discuss in Chapter 7.

MSP uses an extremely useful and straightforward description of how to make the best use of project outputs in business as usual. As the process model in Figure 20-1 shows, the Realizing the Benefits process is broken into three simple steps:

1. **Pre-transition.** Business Change Managers make their preparations before they receive the outputs from projects.
2. **Transition.** Business Change Managers help make the changes happen.
3. **Post-transition.** Business Change Managers settle everything down again in business as usual and revert to being line managers.

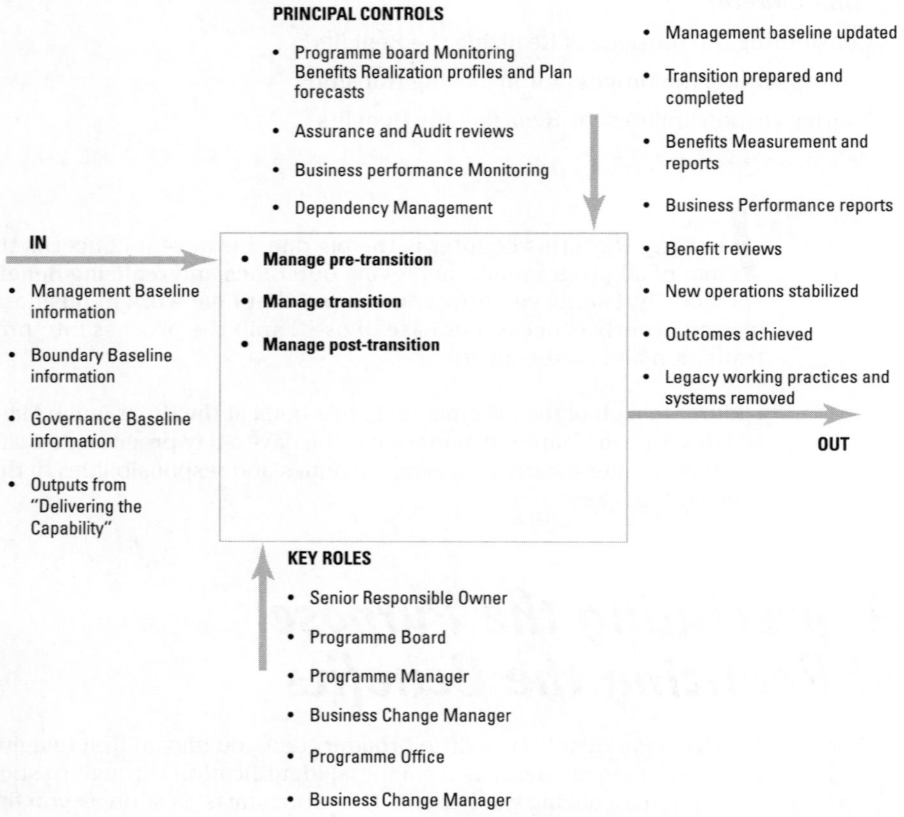

Figure 20-1: Realizing the Benefits process.

This structure means that the process model is pretty straightforward. You take the project outputs, and of course all the information you have in your documentation, run through the three-stage process model and the benefits realized from your new outcomes emerge. Furthermore, you create stability too, because old ways of working have been removed and the new operations are stable.

The controls listed in Figure 20-1 are much more focused on the performance of business as usual and the benefits being achieved: virtually nothing to do with projects is shown.

You do need to monitor the progress of projects though, to ensure that the outputs are fit for purpose (that is, fit for benefit realization) and that you can integrate those outputs into operations. You also need to plan and manage the transition from old world to new world, which is a hugely important activity for any programme. To put it another way, you need to achieve outcomes while simultaneously maintaining business as usual.

So you require a level of operational stability as you move from old to new, and you also need to maintain operational performance. You have a massive amount of work to do.

Achieving the Blueprint

You can think of Realizing the Benefits as achieving the Blueprint (Figure 20-2 sums it up nicely):

- The Blueprint expresses the Vision as follows:
  - Process
  - Organization
  - Tools and technology
  - Information

  All this material is stated in objective terms, that is, with performance indicators such as costs and service levels.
- The benefits documentation describes how you can measure achievement of the Blueprint objectively:
  - Benefits Profiles
  - Benefits Realization Plan
  - Benefits Management Strategy

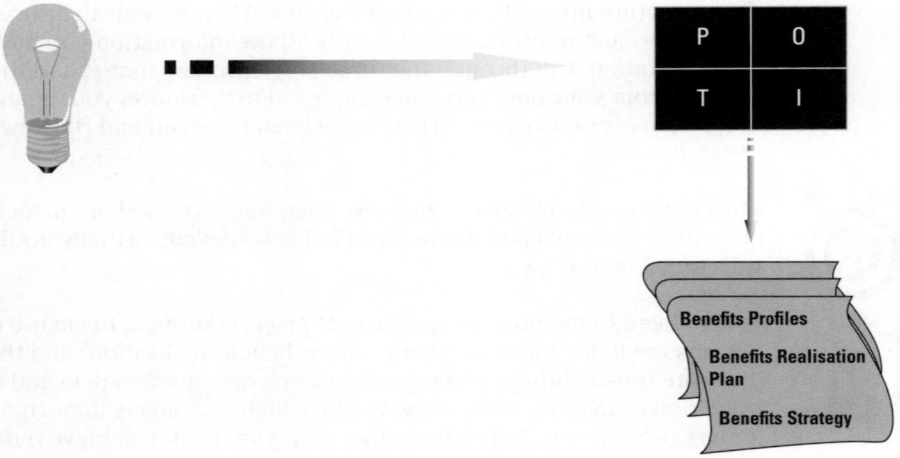

Figure 20-2: The Blueprint: P = process; O = organization; T = tools and technology; and I = information.

In Realizing the Benefits, the outcomes described in the Blueprint come to life, and you demonstrate objectively that you've achieved those outcomes by showing that you've realized the benefits.

Looking at the activities

In this section I put a little flesh on the bones of the activities in Realizing the Benefits (you may like to check out Chapter 17 and Figure 17-3, which is a diagram of transition).

You start with pre-transition, which is what you do in business as usual before you receive the capabilities that you can exploit; then comes transition and finally tidying up post-transition.

I look in detail at each of the activities in subsequent sections. But in the list below I summarise the activities in order to give you a feel for the types of things you need to do:

1. **Manage pre-transition:**
   - Analysis
   - Preparation in business as usual
   - Planning of transition
2. **Manage the transition:**
   - Deliver benefits
   - Support changes

3. **Post-transition:**
   - Review progress
   - Measure performance
   - Adapt to the change

Pre-Transition: Getting Ready

In this section, I look at each of the pre-transition activities in turn.

Establishing benefits measurement

The first pre-transition activity you look at is establishing benefits measurements:

1. Collect the data defined in each Benefits Profile using new or modified ways of measuring benefits if necessary.
2. Find that data and set up reporting. Watch out for the following series of potential pitfalls:
   - Is the data current?
   - Is it accurate?
   - Is it relevant?
3. Create a baseline of the performance when you have valid benefits measurement or, to be specific, create a baseline of the benefit using the new, modified or existing measurement mechanism.

WARNING! Don't underestimate how difficult this process can be in the real world. I've seen this work take many months to get a valid baseline using a new measurement mechanism.

Of course you need some reporting via the programme, but eventually reporting has to go via business as usual, and your best bet is to start with parallel reporting to the programme and via business as usual.

TIP If anything, make a point of ensuring that business-as-usual reporting is slightly ahead of reporting via the programme. Doing so encourages business as usual to take ownership. Business-as-usual reporting can also give you significant difficulties, so this step isn't one to underestimate.

Monitoring benefits realization

The second pre-transition activity is to monitor benefits realization and compare benefits with relevant parts of the following:

- Business Case
- Programme Plan
- Benefits Realization Plan
- Blueprint

Sometimes a debate arises as to whether to record benefits in the Programme Plan or the Benefits Realization Plan. I'm relaxed about where you record them. Just make sure that everyone who needs to know understands what you're doing in your programme.

Avoid recording the benefits in two separate places because inevitably that results in one set of data being different from the other set. If you must report benefits in two places, nominate one report as the master data and link to that data in the other report.

You're going to need to make adjustments if, for example:

- Outputs are unstable.
- The plan isn't realistic.
- External circumstances have changed.
- Programme objectives have changed.

By monitoring benefits realization you can have a benefit-focused dialogue with projects. Talking with projects isn't just about project progress; it's about whether projects are releasing outputs that ultimately allow you to realize benefits.

Planning transition: Factors to consider

The third pre-transition activity is to plan transition. Here's a brief list of factors to consider:

- Staffing levels and working practices
- Information and technology
- Creation of temporary facilities
- Cultural and infrastructural migration
- Integration with the Programme Plan

- Maintaining business operations
- *Back-out arrangements* (that is, arrangements for going back to the old-world state if moving to the new world state isn't successful.)

WARNING! Don't underestimate what's involved in planning transition. You may need to trigger some very serious discussions in the business about how to keep it going during transition.

Communicating the changes

Programmes have a tendency to communicate a great deal at the beginning (during the Defining a Programme process), and then the communication tails off as the programme proceeds.

In this fourth activity in pre-transition I suggest you do the opposite:

- While the projects are creating outputs, you may have very limited need for communication with business as usual.
- As the time for the outputs to be delivered approaches, raise the profile of the programme in business as usual:
  - Communicate the changes that are going to take place soon.
  - Communicate widely.
  - Engage and involve stakeholders and don't simply pass them bland information.

TRUE STORIES

When transition goes awry

Here are a couple of thinly disguised examples of transition going wrong:

- The project to build a new terminal at an airport was extremely successful. But transition was a PR disaster. Among reported problems, the baggage handling system was left in testing mode, so it was unable to talk to related airline systems, and staff coming into the new terminal didn't know how to get through security.
- An army was acquiring a very sophisticated new attack helicopter to replace some simple helicopters that had only unguided rockets fitted to them. The army completely underestimated the amount of training required and didn't put enough focus on getting simulators ordered. The brand-new helicopters were quietly parked in a hangar for more than a few years, while the army caught up with their transition planning and training.

If you have a Programme Communications Plan that lays out how this process is going to happen, you need to use it.

Take a realistic view of the time needed to overcome resistance. Also, raise the profile of communication early enough to be able to overcome sensibly that resistance to change.

Assessing readiness for change

The fifth pre-transition activity is to assess readiness for change. Here's a helpful little checklist of what to consider before you say 'yes, we're ready to move into transition'. The sequence enables you to consider readiness from a more distant, historical perspective then move up to transition and finally look beyond transition at how things will settle down the future:

- Business as usual's track record in successfully delivering change.
- Individuals and the organization's experience of the type of change you're going to undertake.
- Capacity and capability of the resources in business as usual to accommodate change.
- Fit of the change with the existing culture:
  - Is it merely a mechanistic change or do you also need cultural change?
- Effectiveness of the support systems that have been put in place.
- Mobility, that is the flexibility, of the workforce.
- Current performance of business as usual.
- Performance of third parties and their alignment with the old world and the changes you're putting in place.
- Capability of service management to cope with change.

This list is comprehensive. Don't be surprised if it starts some pretty serious discussions in business as usual as to whether you really are ready for transition.

Transition: Embedding Change

Compared with the effort you put into pre-transition, the transition process itself can be something of an anti-climax. Indeed, the better you prepared during pre-transition, the more straightforward transition is going to be.

I can give you only a headline list of the activities in transition. You create a much more comprehensive list as you're going through your pre-transition planning.

For transition, you need to carry out the following:

1. **Initiate transition, also considering whether the outputs are going to be ready from projects and whether you have your plans in place.**
2. **Activate support arrangements for the new ways of working.**
3. **Enact the transition.**
4. **Review whether transition is being successful.**
5. **Focus seriously on the achievement of the outcomes.**

REMEMBER

Actually do transition only when:

- Outputs are complete, ready and fit for purpose.
- Staff are trained and briefed.
- Outstanding risks and issues are owned by operations.
- Contingency arrangements are in place.
- Transition managements are in place.
- Senior Responsible Owner (with the Programme Board) has approved the start of transition.

Post-Transition: Stabilising the New Ways of Working

Here's a brief look at the post-transition activities. Although these are in sequence, they'll also overlap:

1. **Continue measuring benefits through transition and post-transition.** You made a start in pre-transition; hopefully the measurement mechanisms from the earlier section 'Establishing benefits measurement' are working.

2. **Remove access to old world working practices and systems, so that people find using new working practices and systems easier than trying to revert to old ways of working.** This can mean revoking access to old IT systems, physically removing old records or even stopping entry to old working areas!
3. **Respond to changes in requirements (because the world isn't static).**
4. **Monitor and report benefits continually to the programme and through business as usual management.**

Allocating Responsibilities Across Benefits Realization

As you may expect, the pattern of typical responsibilities for realizing benefits is pretty clear. The SRO is still accountable, and of course an interesting relationship exists between this person, colleagues on the Sponsoring Group and line managers of business as usual where these benefits are being realized.

Business Change Managers and the Business Change Teams are responsible for realizing benefits, so the Programme Manager reverts to being consulted or supporting. In the main the Programme Office is also consulted or supports: although on some occasions it's merely informed of what's happening in business as usual.

HAVE A GO — Try This

Assessing how well transition is going

I suggest that you use some of or all the checklists I provide in this chapter as follows:

- Plan a forthcoming transition.
- Assess how transition went in a change in business as usual that was formally structured as a programme.
- Assess how transition went in a change in business as usual that wasn't structured but was just the reaction to the receipt of the outputs of a stand-alone project.

Chapter 21

Closing a Programme

In This Chapter

- Recognising the right time to close your programme
- Understanding the closure process

Everything comes to an end (though *The Archers* radio show is making a good stab at immortality), and at some point your programme needs to be closed.

If you've been part of the management team of a programme for three or four years and it's reaching the end of its last tranche, you need only a little advice on how to close your programme. No doubt you're already an expert on subjects such as your stakeholders, benefits and the outcomes (if not, check out Chapters 14, 15 and 16, respectively). Therefore, this chapter comprises just a few short checklists of some of the activities you may need to do when closing your programme.

I also reflect on *when* to close a programme (it's certainly not as simple as when the last project finishes), including the different circumstances in which you need to close a programme prematurely.

Knowing When to Close the Programme

The purpose of the Closing a Programme stage is to ensure that you've maintained focus on achieving the end-goal, which means:

- Recognising formally the delivery of new capabilities as defined in the Blueprint.
- Reviewing formally the assessment of outcomes via benefit measures, and identifying the need for future assessments of benefits realization.

In essence, you can close the programme when benefits realization is embedded in business as usual.

You may not have achieved all the benefits from the programme when you close it. You (which ultimately means the SRO) can close the programme when you can demonstrate sufficient benefits realization and the Sponsoring Group is reassured that benefits will continue to be realized (benefits are likely to continue for a long time, well after the end of the programme).

Considering closure circumstances

In this section I describe the precise circumstances in which you close the programme in a planned way. You carry out closure when:

- Changes have been delivered.
- Business operations have stabilised.
- Benefit measures are underway and embedded in business as usual.

Some of the tests you can apply to decide whether closure is appropriate are as follows:

- Is the Blueprint being delivered?
- Have the outcomes been achieved?
- Is the Business Case satisfied?
- Are benefits self-sustaining?
- Has the last tranche been completed?
- Have outstanding risks and issues been transferred to business as usual?

Managing benefits after the end of your programme

You need to continue benefits management after the end of the programme. Benefits take quite a time to materialise and may not have reached the target levels mentioned in documents such as the Benefits

Realization Plan as the programme nears its close. New benefits continue to appear. Recording those unexpected benefits may be useful, particularly if the organization is going to run other programmes. Recording them means creating new Benefit Profiles so that other programmes can look at how those benefits accumulated.

The Business Change Managers are responsible for realizing these benefits, but they stop calling themselves Business Change Managers when the programme ends: they just have their business-as-usual roles and job titles.

Here are some guidelines on when the programme finishes officially:

- Certainly some time after the delivery of the last capability.
- After the benefits settle down.
- When the benefits reach previously agreed levels.

No doubt in your programme the circumstances in which your programme closes is something you need to discuss at length.

Closing a programme prematurely

In all the following circumstances you need to carry out a premature closure of your programme:

- Evidence indicates that the programme no longer has a viable Business Case.
- The organization can no longer secure funding or resources for the programme.
- External circumstances have changed so significantly that the programme is no longer valid.

Closing Down a Programme: The Process

In this section I look in detail at the programme closure process (check out Figure 21-1 for an overview).

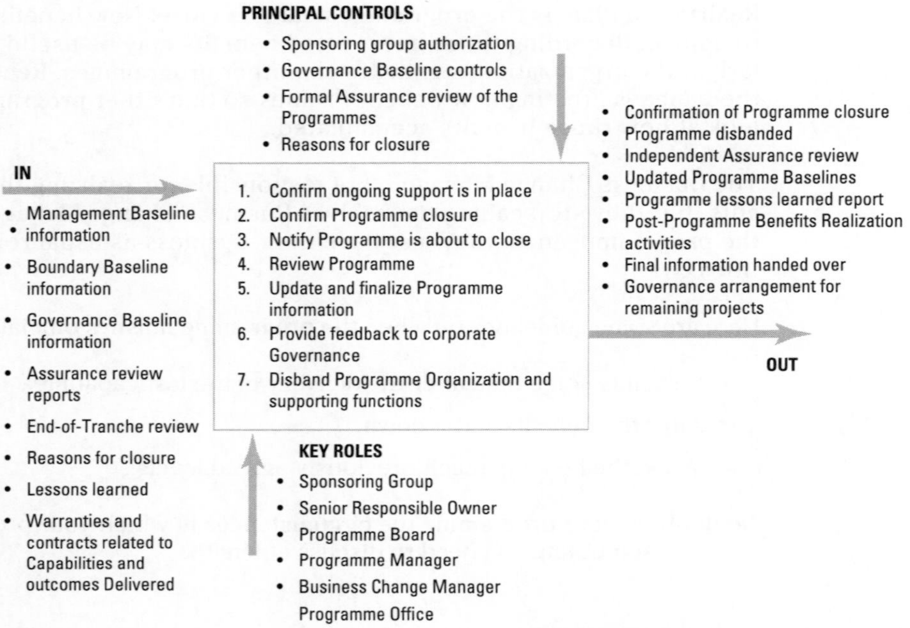

Figure 21-1: Closing a Programme.

Inputs

You need to consider some fairly straightforward inputs, illustrated in Figure 21-1, as follows:

- The management, boundary and governance document baselines.
- An assurance review is necessary at the end of the programme, so you need an assurance review report and an end-of-tranche review.
- If the programme has been closed prematurely, you may need to input the reasons for closure.
- Ensure that lessons are learnt.
- Consider any warranties, as necessary.

WARNING!

Be careful in a programme not to create contracts that are with the programme, because when it finishes those contracts are no longer valid. So, you need to carry out a little bit of contract management as well.

Principal controls

Again looking at Figure 21-1, the principal controls are pretty straightforward. The Sponsoring Group has to authorise closure. Any other controls that were specified in the governance document baselines also have to be carried out. Probably this includes a formal assurance review of the programme; the reasons for closure may in themselves be a type of control as well.

Key roles and responsibilities

The focus of the roles and responsibilities in this process is back up at the senior level that initially identified the programme and that's reflected in the key roles.

The activities themselves are a pretty straightforward checklist:

- Confirm on-going support.
- Confirm programme closure.
- Notify stakeholders that the programme is about to close.
- Review programme.
- Update and finalise information.
- Feedback to policy and strategy.
- Disband programme organization and support functions.

Responsibilities are spread around rather more than in many processes:

- The SRO is naturally accountable for all the activities.
- The Programme Manager is responsible for all the activities in Closing a Programme with the following exceptions:
  - The SRO only consults with others before confirming closure.
  - The Business Change Managers are responsible for reviewing the programme.

Outputs

The outputs shown In Figure 21-1 are the sorts of closure disbandment items that you'd expect:

- Confirmations
- Handovers
- Notifications

Thinking more about programme closure

If you're at the end of a programme, you can of course use some of the activities in this chapter as a checklist for your closure. But I suspect that you've already developed a more comprehensive checklist, in which case having a go is simply a matter of closing your programme.

If you're part way through a programme, I suggest identifying and reviewing the broader and more detailed circumstances in which you can close the programme. The really interesting thing is then to share these ideas with your colleagues and see whether they have the same conclusions on when the programme is able to close.

Part VI

The Part of Tens

Go to www.dummies.com/extras/msp for free online bonus content about managing successful programmes.

In this part. . .

- Recognize why a project might go wrong and how programme management can help.
- Understand when you might want to adopt just some parts of programme management.
- Learn how to make your benefits management even more relevant to your stakeholders.

Chapter 22

Ten Reasons Why Change Initiatives Go Wrong

In This Chapter

- Getting the nature of your change initiative clear
- Using programme management effectively

I find that *change initiative* is an extremely helpful term that's beautifully neutral and non-aligned. To me it simply means a programme or a stand-alone project. I use it when the organization I'm working with hasn't yet decided whether the initiative is to be run as a project or a programme, or when talking about a mix of programmes and stand-alone projects.

Before reading on, ask yourself why you think that organizations fail to deliver change initiatives (usually just known as projects). After you've had an opportunity to list some reasons, read through this chapter to see the ten problems that I identify.

Each of these problems is also a reason to use programme management.

Failing to Clarify whether a Change Initiative is a Programme or a Project

One crucial error to avoid, and a key element in change initiatives failing, is mistakenly labelling them as projects when they're better treated as programmes; that's really what this chapter is all about. Of course, you may also come across the opposite of this situation, where people want to call a simple project a programme. That just makes life complicated.

TIP

The following three tests are a logical way of taking an overall view of a change initiative and deciding whether to run it as a project or a programme:

- Does it affect a lot of people deeply?
- Can it be broken down into discrete projects?
- Will the senior managers sponsoring the change initiative be held accountable for realizing the benefits?

If you answer yes to all these questions, the organization is really better off running the change initiatives as a programme. If the answer to two out of three of the questions is yes, using programme management is still worth thinking about.

Gaining Insufficient Board-Level Support

People within an organization seem to want board-level sponsors for everything these days, but board members are busy and can't sponsor everything. After all, lots of important change initiatives are just projects delivering outputs that are required in the business, and so don't require board-level support.

But if a change initiative is sufficiently large and important to affect the achievement of strategic objectives, treating it as a programme is an ideal way to ensure that you have support and visibility at board level. As I describe in Chapter 9, the Senior Responsible Owner is a member of the Sponsoring Group, and the latter is just another name for the organization's board. That means that all programmes, if properly organized, have board-level support.

Suffering from Weak Leadership

If someone is reluctantly put in charge of a change initiative, that person can end up regarding it as a minor additional management task on top of business-as-usual work. Also, becoming overly involved in *managing* the change at the expense of *leading* the change is all too easy for those directing a change initiative.

By focusing on transition in business as usual, programme management makes clear the need for strong leadership (which I discuss in Chapter 17).

Forming Unrealistic Expectations of Organizational Capacity and Capability

After an organization recognises the need to change, it can sometimes press on with the change even though it doesn't have the *capability* – the necessary skills – and the *capacity* – enough people with those skills – to deliver the change successfully.

REMEMBER

Programme management helps by describing a whole range of roles from Project Manager and member of the Business Change Team up to the Senior Responsible Owner, as well as describing the skills needed for each of these roles. In addition, a useful section of the Blueprint describes the capacity and capability needed in business as usual – the organization section. I look at the Blueprint in Chapter 6 and programme organization in Chapter 9.

Focusing Insufficiently on Benefits

When directing one or more projects, you may be tempted to focus down into the detail of project planning and control. I frequently see senior managers delving into the activity list of the project and ticking those activities off one by one.

REMEMBER

Strategic change initiatives don't succeed because the projects are executed on time and on budget. They succeed when benefits flow. Programme management puts benefits first, which allows the programme to implement benefits-driven planning and benefit-led reporting. I cover these subjects in Chapter 15.

Working Without a Real Picture of Future Capability

Project management is about getting things done, placing the activities in the right sequence and then knocking them off, one by one. I think that project managers are born not made. But if you ask a number of project managers to work together in a complex change initiative they can all be happily executing activities that aren't pointing in the same direction. As a result, they can run conflicting projects in the absence of an overarching Blueprint.

In contrast, programme management brings the importance of the Blueprint to the fore and helps make sure that projects and business as usual are delivering a coherent future capability. Check out Chapter 6 for more details.

Muddling through with a Poor Vision

When you ask anyone involved to describe a change initiative's destination, they can all too easily descend into mind-numbing detail about the future or talk about what they're going to do to get to that destination. But neither overly detailed descriptions of the future nor activity lists engage and motivate stakeholders.

Programme management emphasises that the Vision needs to be a succinct and compelling description of the future. Flip to Chapter 5 for more details on the Vision.

Neglecting to Change the Culture

Projects are good at delivering outputs, whether they're tangible, such as a building, or intangible, such as computer software. But these elements are still just things that have been constructed and tested. Projects are less good at encouraging, stimulating and catalysing changes in the culture. Culture change is too subtle to be shown in graphs and charts: it happens in the hearts and minds of people bit by bit, one person a time, until a tipping point is reached and the changed attitudes become the norm.

Programme management doesn't try and squeeze culture change into the shape of a project. Instead it lets culture change happen in business as usual as part of transition. Check out Chapter 17 for how to lead people through change.

Allowing Stakeholders to be Unengaged

Treating people who use the output from a project as a single stakeholder group is beguilingly simple, as is giving them a bland, even meaningless, name such as 'the users'. But in the real world you're going to have a whole mess of overlapping stakeholder groups with a variety of interests in what's being delivered. They have emotions ranging from enthusiasm or fear to ignorance or apathy.

Programme management encourages you to engage sympathetically with this diverse range of stakeholders and understand what they're interested in. You can only engage with those stakeholders effectively and talk to them in their own language when your programme understands their real interests, concerns and priorities. I discuss this subject in Chapter 14.

Drowning in Data

If your change initiative is just plain big, running it as a project is difficult even without considering all those above-the-line topics such as stakeholder engagement, benefits management, the Vision, the Blueprint and transition. The centre of a huge project, quite naturally, tries to keep a grip on everything down to the lowest level of detail. This type of project can easily drown in data.

For the most part, programmes are big and can also suffer from information overload if the programme core – the Programme Manager and the Programme Office – try to keep a grip on everything that's going on. Fortunately, programme management is a flexible beast. Experience shows that you can set up programme structures that have strong governance, without necessarily having detailed control of everything. As a result, those directing the programme can step out of the detail and see the wood and not the trees. Chapter 10 is a good place to start when you're considering how to summarise information in your programme.

Chapter 23

Ten Reasons to Run an Initiative as a Programme

In This Chapter

- Employing parts of programme management
- Recognising when to start an emergent programme
- Using programme management to deal with risk and uncertainty

In Chapter 22, I provide three tests to help you decide whether to treat a change initiative as a project or a programme. But sometimes the world isn't that clear; you may not have a sufficiently broad perspective on your change initiative to make an easy and absolute one-thing-or-the-other decision.

So in this chapter, I provide ten symptoms that, if you spot them in your change initiative, suggest you need to think seriously about running it as a programme. I also include a number of illustrative examples from the real world to help clarify the situations. Frequently, the result is an *emergent programme* (one that evolves from concurrent projects; see Chapter 2 for details).

REMEMBER

You can use these indicators to consider employing certain elements of programme management to help you run a change initiative. You don't have to use all programme management to add value to your initiative (I discuss the principle of adding value in Chapter 4).

Co-ordinating Complex Activities

Although the basic programme management organizational structure looks simple, it gives plenty of scope for setting up additional governance structures and for creating posts, particularly in the Programme Office, to carry out extra work on behalf of the programme. None of this gets in the way of projects building their outputs.

So if you're running a change initiative as a project and you find that the project team is being distracted from creating outputs because of the number of related and important activities they end up co-ordinating, use some of the programme organizational structure to help you out.

TIP

For example, if you're running a project that includes training some users and you discover project team members setting up committees to talk to the various users and understand their training needs, take a lesson from programme management and create a design authority or create a post called *training co-ordinator* in your Project/Programme Office. I describe such additional roles in Chapter 9.

Organizing Scarce Resources

Resources are always finite – and that's a fact. When several projects are competing for the same resource, you probably need to use some programme management.

TRUE STORY

I recall a time when I was working in an IT area that delivered lots of projects. I was one of the line managers overseeing a dozen or so projects in different parts of the business. It wasn't really a programme due to very little overlap among the projects, except in one particular area. We were very short of one resource: database administrators. My project managers were always fighting for the resource and complaining that their projects were being delayed because they couldn't get those staff.

So I set up a resource co-ordinator to work for me and allocate scarce resources among my projects.

Harmonising Design Interfaces Among Projects

It's pretty normal for one project to negotiate with other projects about some design details. You don't need programme management to allow a couple of project managers to get together and come to an agreement.

But if a project needs a large number of other projects to agree on a design interface, the situation is different. (A *design interface* is just how something is passed from one place to another. When you send enclosures with emails you're using a common design interface for the format of the enclosure. It works most of the time, but occasionally you can't open a document.)

Some organizations print a lot of documents, often for legal reasons, and doing this centrally can still make sense. I had a project running to upgrade the central print function. The print jobs came from lots of different business lines and, if those lines had been stable, the upgrade would've been straightforward. But many of those business lines were changing what they wanted printing (each of those changes was run as a project). My guys in the print project were unable to find out what they needed to print.

The solution was to use programme management to co-ordinate the design interfaces among all these projects. In effect, I was putting in place a Blueprint similar to the ones I describe in Chapter 6.

Dealing with Economies of Scale Among Projects

Sometimes you face a situation where a series of projects are running that aren't very closely linked. Perhaps they all need to use similar functions but in different ways. In that case, giving the building of that function to a separate project may be more efficient. The project team's task is then to create a generic module to be reused across multiple projects. (If you're from an IT background, this idea is similar to object orientation.)

A simple example I recall, again involving IT, was when several projects wanted to put in place an online security function. I preferred using a separate project to build the security module. That meant I had to put in place the sort of communication among projects normally called programme management.

Creating a Framework in an Uncertain Environment

Of course, business rarely runs smoothly; you always face challenges. But sometimes the going is particularly rough, and seeing into the future becomes difficult. For example, perhaps external regulators are about to introduce a whole series of new rules, or technological innovation may disrupt the market. In such uncertain times, creating a programme can be helpful.

When describing most programmes, you think about creating a Vision that's stable from very early on in the programme. When creating a programme to help steer you through uncertainty, however, you may find that you set up the programme structure and co-ordinate the change initiatives some time before the situation is clear enough to describe a well-defined Vision. In this situation, the programme structures can provide reassurance for stakeholders in uncertain times.

Handling High Risk across Multi-Projects

Spotting a risk not in your area but in someone else's is fairly common. I talk about stakeholders being good at identifying risks in Chapter 11. If project people from a group of projects keep spotting risks that can only be handled elsewhere, in other projects or centrally, then that's another clue that you may need a bit of programme management.

I was working with the risk co-ordinator in a business while his workload increased. Projects were identifying risks that only other apparently unrelated projects could mitigate. These risks being bounced among projects made us think about creating a programme to cover all those projects. After we formed the programme, unsurprisingly one of the key posts in the Programme Office was a risk co-ordinator dedicated to the programme. In Chapter 11, I examine more closely how this arrangement can work.

Coping with a Contracting Universe

Finding yourself in a situation where your business universe is shrinking can mean that you need to use programme management.

I was working with a retail business that was contracting rapidly. The situation wasn't pretty, but the reality was that our market was shrinking and we had to do something about it. After operating for several years in different national markets, we now focused on the UK. So, for example, we combined separate German and French divisions into an international division. As our business universe shrank, projects or different parts of business as usual that had experienced little interaction now became increasingly connected. This spurred us into creating an emergent programme to co-ordinate all these connections.

When a business is contracting, for whatever reason, projects and pieces of business as usual that were distinct and separate often move closer together. As a result, you may need to bundle its change initiatives into programmes.

Ordering Change in Business as Usual

Sometimes the trigger for creating a programme sits within business as usual, where a particular part can develop lots of ideas for new change initiatives that may take place in the same part of the business. But if they all happen in an unco-ordinated way, business as usual faces change overload.

You can avoid this danger by creating a programme structure that focuses on sequencing the change in business as usual at a more manageable pace.

Managing Multiple Stakeholder Groups

Project management works well when you can identify a single stakeholder group that will be the users. But sometimes even a modest change initiative may affect lots of different stakeholder groups with competing interests. In these circumstances you may need to pick up on some programme management ideas around stakeholder engagement, the programme organization, the Vision and Blueprint.

For example, if different organizations are providing medical services and social care to a community, bed blocking can result. People with chronic illnesses, usually older people, aren't released into social care smoothly. Consequently they remain in hospitals, blocking valuable beds, when they really need a much less intensive level of medical support.

On a number of occasions, even when working in quite small communities, I've used an element of programme management to help deal with this situation. Where a large number of stakeholder groups from different professions and charities existed, I needed more sophisticated stakeholder engagement to bring them all on message, even though the size of the initiative was small. Chapter 14 is particularly relevant in this situation.

Funding a Busy Business Case

Thinking of a Business Case being funded by a single body sounds great, but often the world isn't that simple. If you have a change initiative where funding originates from multiple sources, managing the Business Case can become complex.

TIP

Use programme management ideas around the Business Case and the relationship to benefits to help build an alliance that funds the initiative. Chapters 8 and 15 are useful in this context.

Chapter 24

Ten Great Ways to Manage Benefits

In This Chapter

- Linking benefits and stakeholders
- Ensuring benefits ownership
- Measuring the right aspects

Benefits management is my favourite part of programme management for the following reasons:

- It's the only new idea I've come across in change delivery for a very long time.
- It helps me stay engaged with my stakeholders.
- It allows me to demonstrate to my sponsors how I've helped the business.

That's enough good reasons to be going on with I think.

WARNING!

Beware, however, of benefits management being hijacked by:

- Specialists who want to turn it into an arcane art form and build an empire.
- Finance people who want all benefits to be converted into monetary values to allow them to compare like with like.

But enough of the negatives; in this chapter I give you ten positive ways to manage your programme benefits effectively.

Doing it in Public

The fact is that you do some things in public and other in private (steady!). Modelling benefits is something to do in public (phew!).

Understand who your stakeholders are before you send out the agenda for your benefits workshop. Do everything you can to empower and engage representatives of your main stakeholder groups at the workshop. Don't be frightened of stakeholder groups you may think have a different agenda to yours. You often find that by including them you can identify points of common interest. In those areas without a common interest, you can often agree to differ.

Finding an Owner

Benefits belong to business as usual. If they're going to be used as a tool for optimising the outcome, they need to be owned in business as usual. To encourage ownership, you need to get potential owners involved early on.

As soon as somebody identifies a benefit, look round for the right owner and get that person or department involved in defining the benefit in detail. You want the benefit owner to feel that they've helped define the benefit so that they're committed to realizing the benefit.

Keeping Benefits Real

Measuring the measurable is tempting, but it can lead to some appallingly bad measures that create perverse incentives. As you refine any benefits measure, you may get involved with experts on the subject who're already measuring something around that outcome.

The classic example in the UK is waiting times in hospital Accident and Emergency (A&E) departments (the ER in the US). You can measure the amount of time a person spends in a room called A&E, but also talk to the stakeholder groups that are really impacted by the outcome: in this example, patients. Patients are more interested in how long it takes to be made better, not how long they sit in the department called A&E. If you create a benefit called 'shorter waits in A&E', the danger is that a room next door is simply given a different name. The time in A&E may go down, but patients still feel as if they're spending a long time being made better.

Tuning Out the Noise

As you start to work out the details of a particular benefits measure, and probably even as you do your initial trial measurements, you find that the numbers vary for no apparent reason, probably because factors other than your outcome are affecting the measure.

You need to play mathematical tricks to remove those extraneous factors. Scientists call this *controlling for a variable* and mathematicians call it *parameterising*. Put simply, you're getting rid of the distracting 'noise' so that you get a good measure of your outcome. Just divide by the variable you want to remove.

Here's a simple example. If you want to look at the cost of staff, you need to work with the number of employees. So divide the total staff costs by the number of employees to control for employees numbers. This gives you the average cost per employee.

Comparing Apples and Pears

Some benefits are financial, some can be reduced to a monetary value and others are just plain different. Don't force all your benefits to be reduced to a monetary value.

Although dependent on the culture, you need to recognise which stakeholders are content to reduce benefits to a monetary value and which ones want some benefits measured in another way. This means comparing apples (monetary measures) with pears (non-monetary measures). It's not a matter of a mathematical conversion; it's a judgement call – precisely the type of judgement senior people bring to your programme.

Getting People Hooked onto a Programme

Engaging stakeholders is like fishing: you jab a large hook in their throat and hang on for dear life (not really, they'll probably sue!). The best way to maintain engagement with benefits management and the whole programme is to hook people by delivering early benefits, for example: if the marketing people want better communication with customers and you need a year to develop a fancy new system to help with that, build in a controlled pilot using a Facebook page and start to count the benefits immediately.

TIP

You can deliver benefits before any capabilities exist, as long as you're sure that those capabilities will arrive pretty soon afterwards. If you know you're going to get a new piece of equipment, you can stop servicing the old one a few months before the new piece arrives to reduce costs. Or you can simply restate something that you're doing in business as usual as part of your preparation for transition in terms of a benefits measure. For example, if you're training staff, the benefit is better trained staff. Then start reporting on the benefits measure as soon as you begin your training.

Remembering that Benefits are Big Business

When I first brief people interested in programme management about benefits they tend to identify, say, six to twelve benefits. But the reality is that a reasonably sized programme brings lots of benefits – lots and lots and lots.

You can optimise benefits effectively only when you break them down into a manageable scale. If a big boss commits to delivering £10 million benefits, he or she is unlikely to personally grind out all of those financial savings. They're more likely to delegate the savings down through their divisions and departments. It's pretty ambitious to save more than 10 per cent of the budget, so at the bottom of this hierarchy are lots of quite junior managers with budgets of £100,000 who are each given the task of saving £10,000. These are the people we want to identify as the owners of those little benefits. Overall in that £10 million programme, you have 1,000 of those little £10,000 benefits, which means that you need 1,000 benefit owners.

REMEMBER

If you don't break benefits down enough, they don't get managed they just happen. A journey of 1,000 miles begins with a single step, and £10 million of benefits is built up from lots of £10,000 benefits.

Dealing with Bad News

Most programmes involve winners and losers, with the losers perceiving some of the benefits as *dis-benefits* (which I discuss more in Chapter 15). Think of a dis-benefit as the measure of an outcome perceived as a disadvantage by a stakeholder

Don't try and hide the dis-benefits, or ignore them, or treat them as risks. Face up to them and manage them as carefully – no, more carefully – than you manage the benefits.

Personally, I like to go further. I insist that a programme show some dis-benefits as well as some benefits. If you manage those dis-benefits you minimise their impact; but if you ignore them, they upset the whole programme. The analogy is that if some of your pears are rotten, you need to remove them before they spoil the whole basket of fruit – although you don't want to push that analogy too far.

Identifying Measures not Targets

If you want people to reduce costs, define a measure called *reduced costs* (logical really!). Don't start talking about reducing costs by 5 per cent (because 5 per cent is a target not a measure). Always talk in terms of the broader measure – reduced costs. If someone asks 'How much do you want to reduce costs by?' answer 'As much as possible!'

Declaring targets just encourages people to game the system. By this I mean, if you're going to reward me for completing each task in five minutes, I'm going to aim to take 4 minutes 59 seconds to do each task. If I can do some tasks more quickly, I may not tell you in case you change the target. That's known as gaming the system.

People are innovative and simply find ways to adjust their behaviour in order to hit that target. Also, having achieved the target, they sit back and don't try to reduce costs further. If you then set another target, they eventually become disillusioned with the targets being moved every time they achieve them.

So make the message clear: we just want to keep on reducing our costs.

Working Yourself Out of a Job

As the benefits start to flow, those looking at them in the Programme Office can be tempted to get heavily involved. Of course, benefits flowing is good news and everybody likes to be involved in good news, but if benefits are being reported via the Programme Office they aren't being reported through business as usual. The aim is to have benefits being owned, and that means reported, via the normal business-as-usual reporting structures. Therefore, the benefits people in the Programme Office need to have the goal of benefits management being independent of them.

Their aim is to build up the skills of benefits owners so that they don't need any help from the Programme Office. In other words, they have to work themselves out of a job.

Part VII
Appendixes

web extras

Go to www.dummies.com/extras/msp for free online bonus content about managing successful programmes.

In this part. . .

- Discover more about the various MSP exams and qualifications.
- Test your knowledge of MSP-speak with a useful glossary of main terms.

Appendix A

Looking into MSP Qualifications

If reading *MSP For Dummies* gives you the programme management bug (no nasty spots, I promise), you may want to take some of the MSP exams. Here I provide the basic structure of the MSP exam system as well as a few tips on the purpose of the exams and how to tackle them.

Examining the Exam Format and Sequence

You can take three MSP examinations:

- Foundation
- Practitioner
- Advanced Practitioner

REMEMBER

You need to pass the exams in sequence: that is, you have to pass the Foundation exam before you can sit the Practitioner exam and pass the Practitioner exam before you can pass the Advanced Practitioner exam. If you read that sentence carefully, and I'm sure you always do, you can see a slight difference in what I say about this sequence (I imply that you can *sit* the Advanced Practitioner before passing the Practitioner).

When you sit the Foundation exam, it's marked immediately. So you can sit the Foundation exam, take a break for an hour or so, and then sit the Practitioner exam.

The Practitioner exam may also be marked immediately, or you may have to wait a few weeks. You can sit the Practitioner exam and then immediately afterwards sit the Advanced Practitioner exam. But if later marking reveals that you failed your Practitioner, your Advanced Practitioner exam is put in abeyance until you pass the Practitioner exam at another attempt.

An increasingly diverse range of options exist for sitting the exams. Any list I give here would probably be out of date before you read this book. Suffice it to say that you can sit the exams as part of face-to-face training, as part of e-learning, at an open centre or by arrangement with an accredited training organization such as AFA, run by yours truly (www.AFAprojects.com).

Facing the Foundation Examination

The purpose of this qualification is to confirm that you have sufficient knowledge and understanding of the MSP guidance in order to carry out various roles in a programme. For example, you may want to interact with those involved in the management of a programme or act as an informed member of the team working within an MSP environment – perhaps in a Programme Office, a business change team or project delivery team.

In other words, the Foundation exam tests that you know the MSP vocabulary. If you attend a course, you receive instruction in this aspect so that you can understand the jargon sufficiently to speak fluent MSP. After you read this book thoroughly, you should be able to speak MSP well enough to pass the Foundation examination; a course may be unnecessary.

Understanding the exam

Here are some key points about the Foundation examination:

- It tests general understanding of the basics of MSP.
- It's for people who intend to work within a programme environment.
- It's the starting point for higher-level MSP qualifications.
- It contains 75 multiple-choice questions that cover all 11 areas of the MSP foundation syllabus. Each of those syllabus areas is then broken into about a dozen syllabus topics
- It lasts for 1 hour and is a closed-book examination.
- Its pass mark is 50 per cent.
- It features one question per topic. So, for example, one topic is the definition of a programme.

The questions are pretty straightforward. A typical question may be:

- Who's ultimately accountable for the programme?
  - Senior Responsible Owner
  - Programme Manager
  - Business Change Manager

(I hope you chose the Senior Responsible Owner!)

Appraising the exam's value

The questions test knowledge, or basic understanding, at quite a detailed level. If you have a grasp of the big picture of MSP, you can often deduce the answers. But quite often you can practise for the exam by just remembering some detailed MSP facts.

I think the Foundation exam is pretty straightforward, and most people do pass it, if they concentrate for a little while. Pass rates are extremely high, which means that it doesn't really reveal the level of your understanding of programme management; it just shows that you have an interest.

Preparing for the Practitioner Examination

The Practitioner exam is for people who are going to take a more substantial role within a programme. As well as being able to speak the language (which the Foundation exam tests; see the preceding section), such people need to understand how the different parts of programme management fit together.

Understanding the exam

The Practitioner exam:

- Tests for a thorough understanding of the principles and theory in the MSP manual.
- Is for people coming into programme management.

- Is a stepping stone up from concepts that are tested in the Foundation exam.
- Contains eight objectively marked questions, each 10 line items long. Oh, sorry about the educational jargon. *Objectively marked* just means there can only be one right answer to each question (no subjectivity needed). To you and me, each of those *line items* looks like a mini-question.
- It lasts for 150 minutes and is an open-book examination (you can take in an MSP manual, but not a book such as *MSP For Dummies* or anything else).
- Its pass mark is 50 per cent.

Appraising the exam's value

A typical Practitioner exam question may ask you to match characters described in a scenario to possible roles, or perhaps tie up pieces of information about a scenario to individual sections in a document.

WARNING! The MSP manual probably contains some detail that I don't cover in *MSP For Dummies*, but which you need for the Practitioner exam. I've never heard of anyone passing a Practitioner exam without having an MSP manual with them during the exam. So if you want to sit the Practitioner, I'm afraid you're going to have to buy or borrow an MSP manual. (Also, make sure you have a good supply of strong coffee to hand, because, although it's a really good reference manual, it's not the most riveting read.)

TIP Detail is the key to passing the Practitioner exam. You're being tested about precise and detailed information from the manual. Although you're applying it to a scenario, you're not applying your real-world experience, however. You're just showing that you know how the manual is put together.

Most people find the Practitioner exam pretty hard work. It's over two hours of focused cross-referencing between a scenario and different parts of the MSP manual. If you have the sort of mind that can concentrate and assimilate a fair amount of information, you should be able to get through, even without experience of programme management. But some people do find the exam a bit of a hurdle.

About two thirds of people who sit the Practitioner pass it first time, so in the real world it shows that you've got your mind round the theory of MSP. But it doesn't necessarily indicate any experience.

Considering the Advanced Practitioner Examination

The Advanced Practitioner exam is how you demonstrate that you've been working in programmes and you have opinions about how programme management works (or should work).

Understanding the exam

The Advanced Practitioner examination:

- Tests excellent understanding of the MSP manual and its practical application.
- Is for people who've worked in programme management.
- Features one compulsory, complex scenario.
- Contains up to three compulsory essay-style questions, each of two or more parts.
- Lasts for 180 minutes and is a completely open-book examination (as with the Practitioner exam, you can take in an MSP manual and also a book such as *MSP For Dummies* or anything else).
- Has a pass mark of 50 per cent.
- Also features additional material. You have a chance to look at the scenario before the exam. But then they slip in a black swan like the programme budget has been cut in half or the timescale is reduced by 50 per cent, just to keep you on your toes.

Alternatively you can write an essay of about 2,000 words, about a programme you've worked on.

Appraising the exam's value

The Advanced Practitioner is an extremely useful qualification. If I were recruiting people to take important roles within a programme, this qualification would indicate to me that someone had experience and had taken some time to pass an examination that demonstrated that experience.

The Advanced Practitioner isn't for the fainthearted. Whether you do the exam in the classroom or complete a paper in your own time, you need to understand MSP thoroughly and have your own views on how it works.

Interestingly, the markers of the Advanced Practitioner don't have a set of answers they're looking for. If you can make a persuasive argument for why, say, quality should be managed by Business Change Managers and not Programme Managers, they read and consider your reasoning. You score marks if your reasoning:

- Starts from a clear understanding of MSP.
- Shows an understanding of the exam scenario or the programme you're describing.
- Makes a persuasive argument.

You need to be highly organized and a master of MSP and the scenario. But that's what I'd expect of someone I was appointing to a programme, so it's a pretty good test.

You may be the sort of person who's sufficiently well organized that you can take an Advanced Practitioner exam, or write the paper, without any guidance. But I think that's unlikely. Most of the people I've coached through the Advanced Practitioner find that they need some help with their writing technique. Very few people write naturally with the level of precision you need for an Advanced Practitioner, against the clock.

For some reason, virtually no one sits the Advanced Practitioner exam; it's not very popular (though trainers and consultants have to sit it). Therefore very few people have the qualification and it's not widely known. That's a real pity. I encourage people to do the Advanced Practitioner exam.

Adding some Advanced Practitioner exam thoughts

Here are my top tips for succeeding at the Advanced Practitioner exam:

- Write your answer in the style of a consultant to a client:
  - Be bold and make recommendations.
  - Show you understand the scenario environment.
- Always argue and support your position.
- Support your opinions with evidence from your experience.
- Remember that your answer is never complete – so ensure that you hit the main points.

Taking the Three Exams on One Course

Theoretically you can sit all three exams on one training course, but in practice doing so is extremely difficult and very few training companies offer this option.

A much more realistic approach is to sit the Foundation and Practitioner on a course and then arrange to do your Advanced Practitioner a little later. You can do this exam on a course or with a little remote coaching. Be clear what you want when you select a training provider:

- Distance or e-learning can get you match-fit for the exams, but may not improve your understanding of MSP. You also need to be pretty disciplined to make sure that you undertake an e-learning course in the right environment. You aren't likely to get on very well if you try and do e-learning while watching TV and eating a pizza (even one packed with brain-power nutrients!).
- A face-to-face course makes sure that you're in one place for a period of time, and so allows you to concentrate on getting the knowledge and understanding you need for the exam.

  But again a word of caution: some training companies offer what's in effect an exam cram. If that's what you want, you'll find it's competitively priced.
- If you want to prepare for the exams and improve your understanding of programme management in discussion with others, the best approach is probably to pay just a little more for a training course.

As with so much in life, *caveat emptor* (buyer beware): you get what you pay for.

Appendix B

Glossary of the Main MSP Terms

This appendix contains the terms that are relevant to MSP. I draw the detail from the AXELOS Project and Programme Management (PPM) Common Glossary at `www.axelos.com/glossaries-and-acronyms/common-glossary/`. Axelos is the name of the new joint-venture set up by the UK government to hold the intellectual property rights for MSP and a number of other change-delivery practices.

The Common Glossary is much more than a simple glossary for MSP or any other change-delivery practice such as PRINCE2. The Common Glossary Reference Group tries to apply consistency to the definitions used across different manuals. But they try not to be too inflexible; if there's a good reason for a manual to use a slightly different definition because of the context in which the term is used, then that's fine.

I've been heavily involved in the Common Glossary since its inception. I drafted the first version and have been on the Common Glossary Reference Group, which continues to approve new entries. Hardly surprising therefore that I think the Common Glossary is pretty useful.

I'm not a fan of adding a lot of additional information to glossary entries. I think that makes the glossary difficult to maintain and more complex than it needs to be. In my view a glossary should just give definitions. So, in the main, I give you the exact definition from the Common Glossary here, with a couple of exceptions. Firstly, my editors have made a couple of very minor tweaks just to make the sentences flow a bit more easily. Secondly, I've added a further explanation for particularly obscure terms. I put these explanations in italics. I've also added a few definitions of my own, which are also in italics to differentiate them from terms in the Common Glossary.

Glossaries within Your Programme

Publishing a glossary within your programme is a good idea. Here's a little guidance:

- By all means change definitions if doing so is necessary in your culture:
  - Be careful not to turn creating definitions into a cottage industry.
  - Remember that you need to maintain any new definitions.
- If you find that one word is used with two meanings within your programme, include both meanings and state the circumstances in which each definition is relevant.
- If you find two words with one meaning in use in your organization, again be inclusive and include both terms. Don't force one group who use one term to drop a favourite word. This sort of glossary is sometimes also known as a *lexicon*.
- If you find that two communities have apparently different definitions and disagreement exists over which is right, try to find some common ground. Let me give you an example of how to do this. If one community talks about a Senior Responsible Owner and another one talks about the Programme Director, define a term called, say, Programme Sponsor, which could mean Programme Director or Senior Responsible Owner. You can then also include both definitions and state the circumstances when they're relevant.

In other words, use your glossary to build a consensus and to celebrate diversity rather than impose conformity.

MSP Glossary

Accountable: Describes the individual who's personally answerable for an activity. Accountability can't be delegated, unlike responsibility.

Aggregated risk: The overall level of risk to the programme when all the ***risks*** are viewed as a totality rather than individually: can include the ***outputs*** of particular scenarios or ***risk*** combinations.

As-is state: The current operating structure and performance of the parts of the business that will be impacted by a ***programme***.

Assumption: A statement that's taken as being true for the purposes of planning, but which can change later. An assumption is made where some facts aren't yet known. The risk exists that assumptions aren't correct.

Baseline: A reference level against which an entity is monitored and controlled.

Benefit(s): The measurable improvement resulting from an ***outcome*** perceived as an advantage by one or more ***stakeholders***, and which contributes towards one or more organizational objective(s).

Benefits management: The identification, definition, tracking, realization and optimization of ***benefits*** within and beyond a ***programme***.

Benefit Profile: Used to define each benefit (and dis-benefit) and provide a detailed understanding of what will be involved and how the benefit will be realized.

Benefits Realization Plan: Used to track realization of benefits across the programme and set review controls.

Benefits Register: Summary document that contains key information from the ***Benefit Profiles***.

Best practice: A defined and proven method of managing events effectively.

Blueprint: A description of the future (the 'to be' state) in some detail, used to maintain focus on delivering the required transformation and business change.

Border: The time-bound limitations of a ***tranche***, that is, when end-of-tranche reviews are held and the programme receives endorsement to move into the next tranche.

Boundary: The scope of what a programme covers; the extent of its influence and authority.

Business as usual: The way the business normally achieves its objectives.

Business Case: Used to validate the initiation of the programme and the on-going viability of the programme.

Business Case management: The manner in which a programme's rationale, objectives, ***benefits*** and ***risks*** are balanced against the financial investment, and how this balance is maintained, adjusted and assessed during the programme.

Business change authority: An individual who represents a group of ***Business Change Managers***, similar to a senior Business Change Manager or business change sponsor.

Business Change Manager: The role responsible for ***benefits*** management, from identification through to realization, and for ensuring that the implementation and embedding of the new ***capabilities*** are delivered by the ***projects***. Typically allocated to more than one individual and also known as a *change agent*.

Business Change Team: A group of specialists appointed to support a ***Business Change Manager*** in the business change management aspects of ***benefits*** realization.

Capability: The completed set of ***project outputs*** required to deliver an ***outcome***; this exists prior to transition. It's a service, function or operation that enables the organization to exploit opportunities.

Change manager: Reports to the ***Business Change Manager*** and may operate at a ***project*** level to support ***benefits*** realization, namely focus on the realization of a particular benefit.

Configuration: A generic term, used to describe a group of ***products*** or items that work together to deliver a product or service, or a recognisable part of a product or service. A configuration may be configuration item of a larger configuration.

Configuration item: An asset subject to ***configuration management***. The asset may be a component of a ***product***, a product or a set of products in a release.

Configuration management: Technical and administrative activities concerned with the creation, maintenance and controlled change of configuration throughout the life of a ***product***.

Consult: Give groups or individuals the opportunity to contribute to and make recommendations on an action or document.

Corporate governance: The on-going activity of maintaining a sound system of internal control by which the directors and officers of an organization ensure that effective management systems, including financial monitoring and control systems, have been put in place to protect assets, earning capacity and the reputation of the organization.

Corporate portfolio: The totality of the change initiatives within an organization; it may comprise a number of ***programmes***, standalone ***projects***

and other initiatives that achieve congruence of change. *In other words, all the changes that you're making fit together.*

Corporate portfolio board: One name for the body within the organization that has authority to make decisions about the composition and prioritisation of the organization's portfolio of ***programmes*** and ***projects***. This may be the corporate board, and in MoP (Management of Portfolios) it's also referred to as the *portfolio direction group* or *investment committee. MoP is another manual produced by Axelos and published by TSO.*

Cross-organizational programme: A ***programme*** requiring the committed involvement of more than one organization to achieve the desired ***outcomes***; also referred to as a *cross-cutting programme*.

Dependency: An activity, ***output*** or decision required to achieve some aspect of the ***programme***. It can be internal or external to the programme.

Design Authority: *Provides expert advice or has responsibility for some aspect of the programme that needs to be controlled; for example, a target operating model. It aims to ensure appropriate alignment and control when changes are being planned and implemented.*

Dis-benefit: A measurable decline resulting from an ***outcome*** perceived as negative by one or more ***stakeholders***, which reduces one or more organizational objective(s).

Emergent programme: A ***programme*** that subsumes one or more pre-existing ***projects*** into a coherent alignment with corporate policy and strategy.

End goal: The ultimate objective of a ***programme*** – the same as the ***to-be state*** (also called the *future state*).

Feedback log: A document used to capture, track and ensure that all ***stakeholder*** feedback is dealt with.

Gated review: A structured review of a ***project***, ***programme*** or ***portfolio*** as part of formal governance arrangements carried out at key decision points in the life-cycle to ensure that the decision to invest as per the agreed ***Business Case*** remains valid.

Governance: The functions, responsibilities, processes and procedures that define how a ***programme*** is set up, managed and controlled.

Inform: In the context of a RACI table, a group or individual that has to be advised of a change or a decision. In MSP, this term is typically used in the context of something that affects activities or document creation. *A RACI table is a table showing which role is responsible, accountable, consulted or informed for or about an activity. I haven't included RACI tables for each process in this book, but I have summarised them when I give the responsibilities around the process.*

Issue: A relevant event that happened, wasn't planned and requires management action. It can be a problem, query, concern, change request or ***risk*** that occurred.

Key performance indicator (KPI): A metric (financial or non-financial) used to set and measure progress towards an organizational objective.

Leadership: The ability to direct, influence and motivate others towards a better ***outcome***.

Programme Mandate: Used to describe the required outcomes from the programme, based on strategy or policy objectives.

Margin: The flexibility that a ***programme*** has for achieving its ***Blueprint***, ***benefits*** and ***Business Case***.

Opportunity: An uncertain event that can have a favourable impact on objectives or ***benefits***.

Outcome: The result of change, normally affecting real-world behaviour or circumstances. Outcomes are desired when a change is conceived. Outcomes are achieved as a result of the activities undertaken to effect the change; they're the manifestation of part of or all the new state conceived in the ***Blueprint***.

Output: The tangible or intangible artefact produced, constructed or created as a result of a planned activity.

P3M3: The Portfolio, Programme and Project Management Maturity Model that provides a framework with which organizations can assess their current performance and put in place improvement plans.

Plan: A detailed proposal for doing or achieving something, detailing the what, when, how and by whom.

Policy: A course of action (or principle) adopted by an organization; a business statement of intent, setting the tone for an organization's culture.

Portfolio: The totality of an organization's investment (or segment of it) in the changes required to achieve its strategic objectives.

Product: An input or ***output***, whether tangible or intangible, that can be described in advance, created and tested; also known as an output or *deliverable*.

Programme: A temporary flexible organization structure created to co-ordinate, direct and oversee the implementation of a set of related ***projects*** and activities in order to deliver ***outcomes*** and ***benefits*** related to an organization's strategic objectives; a programme is likely to have a life that spans several years.

Programme assurance: Independent assessment and confirmation that the ***programme*** as a whole or any of its aspects are on track, that it's applying relevant practices and procedures, and that the ***projects***, activities and business rationale remain aligned to the programme's objectives. See also ***gated review***.

Programme Brief: Used to assess whether the programme is viable and achievable.

Programme Board: A group established to support a ***Senior Responsible Owner*** in delivering a ***programme***.

Programme management: The co-ordinated organization, direction and implementation of a dossier of ***projects*** and transformation activities (that is, the ***programme***) to achieve ***outcomes*** and realize ***benefits*** of strategic importance.

Programme Manager: The role responsible for the set-up, management and delivery of a ***programme***; typically allocated to a single individual.

Programme Office: The function providing the information hub and standards custodian for a ***programme*** and its delivery objectives; it can provide support for more than one programme.

Programme organization: How a ***programme*** will be managed throughout its life-cycle, the roles and responsibilities of individuals involved in the programme, and personnel management or human resources arrangements (also known as *programme organization structure*).

Project: A temporary organization created for the purpose of delivering one or more business ***outputs*** according to a specified ***Business Case***.

Project register: Document that records the list of **projects**; an alternative term for ***projects dossier***.

Proximity (of risk): The time factor and how close an event is; that is, ***risks*** occur at particular times and the severity of their impact varies depending on when they occur.

Quality: The degree to which the features and inherent or assigned characteristics of a ***product***, person, process, service and/or system bear on its ability to show that it meets expectations or stated needs, requirements or specification.

Quality assurance: The planned systematic process used to provide confidence that ***outputs*** will match their defined quality criteria.

Quality control: The process of monitoring specific results to determine whether they comply with the relevant standards and identifying ways to eliminate causes of unsatisfactory performance.

Quality management system: The complete set of quality standards, procedures and responsibilities for a site or organization.

Register: A formal repository that's managed and requires agreement on its format, composition and use.

Responsible: Describes the individual who has the authority and is expected to deliver a task or activity; responsibility can be delegated.

Risk: An uncertain event or set of events that, if it occurs, has an effect on the achievement of objectives. A risk is measured by a combination of the probability of a perceived ***threat*** or ***opportunity*** occurring and the magnitude of its impact on objectives.

Risk appetite: The amount of ***risk*** the organization, or a subset of it, is willing to accept.

Risk assessment: The identification and evaluation of ***risks***.

Risk estimation: The estimation of probability and impact of an individual ***risk***, taking into account predetermined standards, target risk levels, interdependencies and other relevant factors.

Risk evaluation: The process of understanding the net effect of identified threats and opportunities on an activity when aggregated together.

Risk identification: Determination of what can pose a ***risk***; a process to describe and list sources of risk (***threats*** and ***opportunities***).

Risk management: The systematic application of principles, approaches and processes to the tasks of identifying and assessing ***risks***, and then planning and implementing risk responses.

Senior Responsible Owner (SRO): The single individual with overall responsibility for ensuring that a ***project*** or programme meets its objectives and delivers the projected ***benefits***.

Sponsor: The main driving force behind a ***programme*** or ***project***. Some organizations use the term instead of ***Senior Responsible Owner***.

Sponsoring Group: The driving force behind a programme, which provides the investment decision and top-level endorsement for the rationale and objectives of the programme.

Stakeholder: Any individual, group or organization that can affect, be affected by, or perceives itself to be affected by, a programme.

Stakeholder Map: A diagrammatic representation of the stakeholders relevant to an organizational activity and their respective interests.

Stakeholder Register: A document that contains a summary of the information in the stakeholder profiles.

Strategy: An approach or line to take, designed to achieve a long-term aim. Strategies can exist at different levels in an organization – in MSP corporate strategies achieve objectives that give rise to programmes. Programmes then develop strategies aligned with these corporate objectives against particular delivery areas.

Threat: An uncertain event that can have a negative impact on objectives or ***benefits***.

To-be state: The future planned state of an organization as described by the ***Blueprint***.

Tranche: A programme management term describing a group of ***projects*** structured around distinct step changes in ***capability*** and ***benefit*** delivery.

Transformation: A distinct change to the way an organization conducts all or part of its business.

Transition: *The changes that need to take place in business as usual, which are hopefully managed, as project outputs are exploited in order to achieve programme outcomes.*

Transition plan: The schedule of activities to cover the transition phase of the ***Benefits Realization Plan***.

Vision: A picture of a better future that will be delivered by the programme.

Workstream: The logical grouping of ***projects*** and activities that together enable effective management. Workstreams may delineate projects against a variety of criteria.

Index

• A •

• B •

• D •

• E •

• F •

• G •

• H •

• I •

• N •

• O •

• P •

• Q •

• R •

• S •

• T •

• U •

• V •

• W •

About the Author

Alan Ferguson is the Managing Director of AFA. This training and consultancy company has specialized in change delivery practices for nearly 20 years. Starting off in project management it spread to programme, portfolio, change and risk management, P3O and a host of other disciplines related to helping organizations change. It provides training and consultancy globally, both directly and through a network of partners who use AFA training material.

Alan has been in project and programme management for an awfully long time. He was certainly looking after a collection of projects (which would now be called multi-project programme management) in the 1970s. So that means he's getting to the end of his fourth decade in this game.

His first career was as an engineering officer in the Royal Air Force. His first projects were looking after airplanes; getting them back in the air after a couple of months in a hangar. Before he left the RAF, he moved across into IT and in the late 1980s and early 1990s worked on IT projects and within so-called strategy stufies. Nowadays those strategies would be called programmes. So he really was in at the beginning of programme management.

Alan also spent a few years working in an international insurance company on IT projects and programmes. Here, and in the RAF he earned his spurs as a practising project and programme manager.

With AFA, Alan has worked with a hugely diverse range of clients in the UK, Europe and around the world. His complaint at the moment is that he hasn't done much in South America, if any of you want to invite him across there. Alan is particularly proud of the work he has done with the UN in their field missions in some parts of the world that others wouldn't dream of travelling to. When he gets back from one of those assignments he always says he has had fun. He has a very strange sense of fun!

Alan's hobbies focus around aviation in all its many aspects. You can have a look at his airplane photographs on Flickr, but if you're feeling a little braver you can fly with him in one of his powered aircraft or in the gliders he regularly flies. His other hobbies range from helping St John Ambulance, to renovating the Windmill in Dereham; the East Anglian town where he lives and where AFA is based.

If you ever meet Alan, you won't forget him. Everyone describes him as enthusiastic and challenging. Alan is originally from Belfast and likes nothing better than a bit of craic.

`www.AFAprojects.com`

Dedication

This book is undoubtedly dedicated to Susan, my wife, soul mate and business partner. She has put up with me yelling at a computer for months without resigning. Don't worry, I haven't been losing my temper, I've been using voice dictation software. As Susan has walked into the room, her words have often ended up in the book. They are the real words of wisdom.

Author's Acknowledgements

First of all I'd like to thank Nick Graham, the author of *PRINCE2 For Dummies* for putting Wiley in touch with me.

Claire Ruston, as my commissioning editor, used all her charms to entice me into the *For Dummies* trap. Once I got into writing one of these books, I fear I have become addicted. Thanks Claire for breaking me in so gently.

Next I want to thank Rachael Chilvers at Wiley for holding my hand so patiently as I've dropped chapter after chapter into her mailbox.

I'd also like to thank Andy Finch, my development editor, who turned my random babblings into *For Dummies*-speak, and for adding a few really corny jokes.

I also want to thank my team at AFA who have put up with me disappearing into the office for so many hours. It is unfair to single out just one of the guys, but I have to mention Roni Holmes, my material production coordinator, who did a lot of the spadework on diagrams and lots of other stuff around this book.

Next I want to talk about the gang of MSP trainers I've worked with over several decades. I think you of all people have taught me most about programme management. I have to put John Vivian and Bill Shuttle pretty near the top of that list.

I also have to say a thank you to the delegates I've trained and the clients I've worked with for sharing their experiences with me. These are what I've funneled into the book, particularly in the examples.

Finally I want to mention the broader MSP community, and the people I've worked with to make MSP the world-leading programme management practice that it is. You know you are; thanks everyone.

Publisher's Acknowledgements

Project Editor: Rachael Chilvers

Commissioning Editor: Claire Ruston

Associate Commissioning Editor: Ben Kemble

Development Editor: Andy Finch

Proofreader: Kelly Cattermole

Technical Editor: Axelos Global Best Practice

Production Manager: Daniel Mersey

Publisher: Miles Kendall

Cover Photos: © Alex Slobodkin/iStockphoto.com

Project Coordinator: Sheree Montgomery

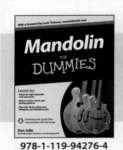

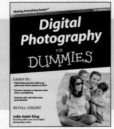

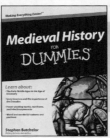